THE LITTLE BOOK OF
ECONOMICS

Penguin
Random
House

DK LONDON

Senior Art Editor Helen Spencer
Project Art Editors Anna Hall, Duncan Turner
Senior Editor Janet Mohun
Editors Rose Blackett-Ord, Lizzie Munsey
Senior Managing Art Editor Lee Griffiths
Managing Art Editor Michelle Baxter
Managing Editors Gareth Jones, Camilla Hallinan
Publisher Sarah Larter
Art Director Philip Ormerod
Associate Publishing Director Liz Wheeler
Publishing Director Jonathan Metcalf
Illustrations James Graham
Jacket Design Development Manager Sophia MTT
Picture Research Louise Thomas
Producer Rachel Ng
Pre-producer Jacqueline Street
Production Editor Ben Marcus
Production Controller Sophie Argyris

DK DELHI

Senior Art Editors Ira Sharma, Ivy Roy
Art Editors Anukriti Arora, Shipra Jain, Arijit Ganguly
Assistant Art Editors Sampda Mago,
Sanjay Chauhan, Kanika Mittal
Consultant Art Director Shefali Upadhyay
Senior Editors Janashree Singha, Anita Kakar
Editors Nandini D. Tripathy, Rupa Rao,
Priyaneet Singh
Deputy Managing Editor Alka Thakur
Managing Editors Soma B. Chowdhury, Rohan Sinha
Senior Managing Art Editor Arunesh Talapatra
Pre-production Manager Balwant Singh
Production Manager Pankaj Sharma
DTP Designers Anita Yadav, Nand Kishor Acharya,
Vishal Bhatia, Bimlesh Tiwary

produced for DK by
TALLTREE LTD
Managing Editor David John
Commissioning Editor Sarah Tomley
Senior Designer Ben Ruocco
Senior Editors Rob Colson, Deirdre Headon

original styling by
studio8 design

Content previously published in *The Economics Book*.
This abridged edition first published in Great Britain
in 2020 by Dorling Kindersley Limited, One Embassy
Gardens, 8 Viaduct Gardens, London, SW11 7AY

Copyright © 2012, 2020 Dorling Kindersley Limited
A Penguin Random House Company
2 4 6 8 10 9 7 5 3 1
001 – 317634 – May/2020

A CIP catalogue record for this book is available
from the British Library.
ISBN: 978-0-2414-2644-9

Printed in the United Kingdom

For the curious
www.dk.com

CONTRIBUTORS

NIALL KISHTAINY, CONSULTANT EDITOR

Niall Kishtainy teaches at the London School of
Economics, and specializes in economic history
and development. He has worked for the World
Bank and the United Nations Economic
Commission for Africa.

GEORGE ABBOT

George Abbot is a UK economist who worked in
2012 on Barack Obama's presidential re-election
campaign. He previously worked with Compass,
the influential UK think-tank, on strategic
documents such as *Plan B: A New Economy
for a New Society*.

JOHN FARNDON

John Farndon is the London-based author of
many books on contemporary issues and the
history of ideas, including overviews of the
booming economies of China and India.

FRANK KENNEDY

Frank Kennedy worked for over 25 years in
investment banking in the City of London,
as a top-ranked investment analyst and as a
managing director in capital markets, where
he led a European team advising financial
institutions. He studied economic history at
the London School of Economics.

JAMES MEADWAY

UK economist James Meadway works at the
New Economics Foundation, an independent
British think-tank. He has also worked as a
policy adviser for the UK Treasury.

CHRISTOPHER WALLACE

Christopher Wallace is Head of Economics at
the UK's prestigious Colchester Royal Grammar
School. He has been teaching economics for
more than 25 years.

MARCUS WEEKS

Marcus Weeks studied philosophy and worked
as a teacher before embarking on a career as an
author. He has contributed to many books on
the arts and popular sciences.

CONTENTS

WAR AND DEPRESSIONS
1929–1945

POST-WAR ECONOMICS
1945–1970

CONTEMPORARY ECONOMICS
1970–PRESENT

INTRODU

F ew people would claim to know very much about economics, perhaps seeing it as a complex and esoteric subject with little relevance to their everyday lives. It has been generally felt to be the preserve of professionals in business, finance, and government. Yet most of us are becoming more aware of its influence on our wealth and well-being, and we may also have opinions – often quite strong ones – about the rising cost of living, taxes, government spending, and so on. Sometimes these opinions are based on an instant reaction to an item in the news, but they are also frequently the subject of discussions in the workplace, or over the dinner table. So to some extent, we do all take an interest in economics. The arguments we use to justify our opinions are generally the same as those used by economists, so a better knowledge of their theories can give us a better understanding of the economic principles that are at play in our lives.

Economics in the news

Today, with the world in apparent economic turmoil, it seems more important than ever to learn something about economics. Far from occupying a separate section of our newspaper or making up a small part of the television news, economic news now regularly makes the headlines. As early as 1997, the US Republican political campaign strategist Robert Teeter noted its dominance, saying, "Look at the declining television coverage [of politics]. Look at the declining voting rate. Economics and economic news is what moves the country now, not politics".

Yet how much do we really understand when we hear about rising unemployment, inflation, stock market crises, and trading deficits? When we're asked to tighten our belts, or pay more taxes, do we know why? And when we seem to be at the mercy of risk-taking banks and big corporations, do we know how they came to be so powerful, or understand the reasons for their original and continued existence? The discipline of economics is at the heart of questions such as these.

The study of management

Despite the importance and centrality of economics to many issues that affect us all, economics as a discipline is often viewed with suspicion. A popular conception is that it is dry and academic, due to its reliance on statistics, graphs, and formulas. The 19th-century Scottish historian Thomas Carlyle described economics as the "dismal science", that is "dreary, desolate and, indeed, quite abject and distressing". Another common misconception is that it is "all about money", and while this has a grain of truth, it is by no means the whole picture.

So, what is economics all about? The word is derived from the Greek word *Oikonomia*, meaning "household management", and it has come to mean the study of the way we manage our resources, and more specifically, the production and exchange of goods and services. Of course, the business of producing goods and providing services is as old as civilization, but the study of how the process works in practice is comparatively new. It evolved only gradually; philosophers and politicians have expressed their opinions on economic matters since the time of the ancient Greeks, but the first true economists to make a study of the subject did not appear until the end of the 18th century.

At that time, the study was known as "political economy", and had emerged as a branch of political philosophy. However, those studying its theories increasingly felt that it should be distinguished as a subject in its own right, and began to refer to it as "economic science". This later became popularized in the shorter form of "economics".

A softer science

Is economics a science? The 19th-century economists certainly liked to think so, and although Carlyle thought it dismal, even he dignified it with the label of science. Much economic theory was modelled on mathematics and even physics (perhaps the "-ics" ending of "economics" helped to lend it scientific respectability), and it sought to determine the laws that govern how the economy behaves, in the same way that scientists had discovered the physical laws underlying natural phenomena. Economies, however, are man-made and are dependent on the rational or irrational behaviour of the humans that act within them, so economics as a science has more

in common with the "soft sciences" of psychology, sociology, and politics.

Economics was perhaps best defined by British economist Lionel Robbins. In 1932, he described it in his *Essay on the Nature and Significance of Economic Science* as "the science which studies human behaviour as a relationship between ends and scarce means which have alternative uses". This broad definition remains the most popular one in use today.

The most important difference between economics and other sciences, however, is that the systems it examines are fluid. As well as describing and explaining economies and how they function, economists can also suggest how they ought to be constructed or can be improved.

The first economists

Modern economics emerged as a distinct discipline in the 18th century, in particular with the publication in 1776 of *The Wealth of Nations*, written by the great Scottish thinker Adam Smith. However, what prompted interest in the subject was not so much the writings of economists as the enormous changes in the economy itself with the advent of the Industrial Revolution. Previous thinkers had commented on the management of goods and services within societies, treating questions that arose as problems for moral or political philosophy. But with the arrival of factories and mass producers of goods came a new era of economic organization that looked »

at the larger picture. This was the beginning of the so-called market economy.

Smith's analysis of the new system set the standard, with a comprehensive explanation of the competitive market. Smith suggested that the market is guided by an "invisible hand", where the rational actions of self-interested individuals ultimately give the wider society exactly what it needs. Smith was a philosopher, and the subject of his book was "political economy" – it stretched beyond economics to include politics, history, philosophy, and anthropology. After Smith, a new breed of economic thinkers emerged, who chose to concentrate entirely on the economy. Each of these built upon our understanding of the economy – how it works and how it should be managed – and laid the foundations for the various branches of economics.

As the discipline evolved, economists identified specific areas to examine. One approach was to look at the economy as a whole, either at a national or international level, which became known as "macroeconomics". This area of economics takes in topics such as growth and development, measurement of a country's wealth in terms of output and income, and its policies for international trade, taxation, and controlling inflation and unemployment. In contrast, what we now call "microeconomics" looks at the interactions of individual people and firms within the economy: the business of supply and demand, buyers and sellers, markets and competition.

New schools of thought

Naturally, there were differences of opinion among economists, and various schools of thought evolved. Many welcomed the prosperity that the modern industrial economy brought, and advocated a "hands-off" or laissez-faire approach to allow the competitive market to create wealth and stimulate technological innovation. Others were more cautious in their estimation of the market's ability to benefit society, and identified failings of the system. They thought these could be overcome by state intervention, and argued for a role for governments in providing certain goods and services, and in curbing the power of the producers. In the analysis of some, notably the German philosopher Karl Marx, a capitalist economy was fatally flawed and would not survive.

The ideas of the early "classical" economists such as Smith were increasingly subjected to rigorous examination. By the late 19th century, economists educated in science were approaching the subject through the disciplines of mathematics, engineering, and physics. These "neoclassical" economists described the economy in graphs and formulae, and proposed laws that governed the workings of the markets and justified their approach.

By the end of the 19th century, economics was beginning to develop national characteristics: centres of economic thinking had grown as university departments were established, and there were distinguishable

differences between the major schools in Austria, Britain, and Switzerland, particularly on the desirability of some degree of state intervention in the economy.

These differences became even more apparent in the 20th century, when revolutions in Russia and China brought almost a third of the world under communist rule, with planned economies rather than competitive markets. The rest of the world, however, was concerned with asking whether the markets alone could be trusted to provide prosperity. While continental Europe and Britain argued about degrees of government intervention, the real battle of ideas was fought in the USA during the Great Depression after the Wall Street Crash of 1929.

In the second half of the 20th century, the centre of economic thought shifted from Europe to the USA, which had become the dominant economic superpower and was adopting ever-more laissez-faire policies. After the collapse of the Soviet Union in 1991, it seemed that the free-market economy was indeed the route to economic success, as Smith had predicted. Not everyone agreed. Although the majority of economists had faith in the stability, efficiency, and rationality of the markets, there were some who had doubts, and new approaches arose.

Alternative approaches

In the late 20th century, new areas of economics incorporated ideas from disciplines such as psychology and sociology into their theories, as well as new advances in mathematics and physics, such as game theory and chaos theory. These theorists also warned of weaknesses in the capitalist system. The increasingly severe and frequent financial crises that took place at the beginning of the 21st century reinforced the feeling that there was something fundamentally wrong in the system; at the same time, scientists concluded that our ever-increasing economic wealth came at a cost to the environment in the form of potentially disastrous climate change.

As Europe and the USA begin to deal with perhaps the most serious economic problems they have ever faced, new economies have emerged, especially in Southeast Asia and the so-called BRIC countries (Brazil, Russia, India, and China). Economic power is once again shifting, and no doubt new economic thinking will evolve to help manage our scarce resources.

One prominent casualty of the recent economic crises is Greece, where the history of economics started, and where the word "economics" comes from. In 2012, protesters in Athens pointed out that democracy also comes from the Greeks, but is in danger of being sacrificed in the search for a solution to a debt crisis.

It remains to be seen how the world economy will resolve its problems, but, armed with the principles of economics outlined in this book, you will see how we got into the present situation, and perhaps begin to see a way out. ■

LET TRADIN

400 BCE–1820 CE

As civilizations evolved in the ancient world, so too did systems for providing goods and services. These early economic systems emerged naturally as various trades and crafts produced goods that could be exchanged. People began to trade, first by bartering and later with coins of precious metal, and trade became a central part of life. The business of buying and selling goods operated for centuries before it occurred to anyone to examine how the system actually worked.

Rise of the city-states

A major change occurred in the 15th century, as city-states developed in Europe and became wealthy through international trade. A new, prosperous class of merchants replaced the feudal landowners as the important players in the economy, and they worked hand-in-hand with dynasties of bankers, who financed their trading and voyages of discovery.

New trading nations replaced small-scale feudal economies, and economic thinking began to focus on how best to manage the exchange of goods and money between countries. The dominant approach of the time, known as mercantilism, was concerned with the balance of payments – the difference between what a country spends on imports and what it earns from exports. To prevent a trade deficit and protect domestic producers against foreign competition, mercantilists advocated the taxing of imports.

As trade increased, it moved beyond the hands of individual merchants and their backers. Partnerships and companies were set up, often with government backing, to oversee large trading operations. The huge increase in trading also prompted a renewed interest in the working of the economy, and led to the beginnings of the discipline of economics.

A new science

Emerging at the beginning of the 18th century, the Age of Enlightenment, which prized rationality above all, took a scientific approach to "political economy". Economists attempted to measure economic activity, and described the working of the system, rather than looking only at moral implications. One such economist was Frenchman Jean Bodin (p.19), who noticed that the more money there is in circulation, the higher prices rise, which became a cornerstone idea of his quantity theory of money.

Also in France, a group of thinkers known as the physiocrats analysed the flow of money around the economy, and produced the first macroeconomic (whole-economy) model. They placed agriculture rather than trade or finance at the heart of the economy. Meanwhile, political philosophers in Britain shifted the emphasis away from mercantilist ideas of trade, and towards producers, consumers, and the value and utility of goods. The framework for the modern study of economics was emerging, and a Scotsman, Adam Smith (p.39), put flesh on the bones.

Rational economic man

His background in the philosophy of British Enlightenment thinkers led Smith to approach the subject initially as one of moral philosophy. However, in his book *The Wealth of Nations* (1776), he presented an analysis of the market economy at the beginning of the Industrial Revolution, and how it contributed to the economic welfare of the people. Central to his thesis was the concept of "rational economic man". Smith argued that individuals made economic decisions on the basis of reason and self-interest, not for the good of society. When they were allowed to act in this way in a free society with competitive markets, an "invisible hand" guided the economy for the benefit of all. This was the first detailed description of a free-market economy, which Smith advocated as the means of ensuring prosperity and freedom – what we now know as capitalism. However, *The Wealth of Nations* was more than a description of the economy: it also examined issues such as the division of labour, the factors involved in giving value to goods, and weaknesses in the market economy such as collusion between traders to raise prices.

Ending protectionism

The most influential of Smith's followers, David Ricardo (p.57) put the final nail in the coffin of protectionism, as he showed how all countries, even those that were less productive, could benefit from free trade. He also cast a critical eye over the ways that government spending and borrowing affect the economy. Many of Smith's ideas were also taken up by the French physiocrat school, most notably Anne-Robert-Jacques Turgot (p.41) and François Quesnay (p.29), who argued for a fair system of taxation, and Jean-Baptiste Say (p.51), who first described the relationship between supply and demand in a market economy. ■

YOU DON'T NEED TO BARTER WHEN YOU HAVE COINS
THE FUNCTION OF MONEY

IN CONTEXT

FOCUS
Banking and finance

KEY EVENT
Kublai Khan adopts fiat money in the Mongol Empire during the 13th century.

BEFORE
3000 BCE In Mesopotamia, the shekel is used as a unit of currency: a unit of barley of a certain weight equals a certain value of gold or silver.

700 BCE The oldest known coins are made on the Greek island of Aegina.

AFTER
13th century Marco Polo brings promissory notes from China to Europe, where they are used by Italian bankers.

1696 The Bank of Scotland is the first commercial operation to issue bank notes.

1971 US President Nixon cancels the convertibility of the US dollar to gold.

The Tiwa tribal people of Assam, India, exchange goods through barter during the Jonbeel Mela, an age-old festival to preserve harmony and brotherhood between tribes.

I n many parts of the world, people are increasingly moving towards a cashless society in which goods are bought with credit cards, electronic transfers, and mobile-phone chips. But dispensing with cash does not mean that money is not used. Money remains at the heart of all our transactions. The disturbing effects of money are well known, inciting everything from miserliness to crime and warfare. Money has been used as a tribute (sign of respect), in religious rites, and for ornamentation. "Blood money" is paid as recompense for murder; brides are bought with "bride money" or given away with dowries to enrich their husbands. Money lends status and power to individuals, families, and nations.

A barter economy

Without money, people could only barter. Many of us barter to a small extent, when we return favours. A man might offer to mend his neighbour's broken door in return for a few hours' babysitting, for instance. Yet it is hard to imagine these personal exchanges working on a larger scale. What would happen if you wanted a loaf of bread and all you had to trade was your new car? Barter depends on the double coincidence of wants, where not only does the other person happen to have what I want, but I also have what he wants.

Money solves all these problems. There is no need to find someone who wants what you have to trade; you simply pay for your goods with money. The seller can then take the money and buy from someone else. Money is transferable and deferrable – the seller can hold on to it and buy when the time is right. Many argue that complex civilizations could never have arisen without the flexibility of exchange that money allows. Money also gives a yardstick for deciding the value of things. If all goods have a monetary value, we can know and compare every cost.

Different kinds of money

There are two kinds of money: commodity and fiat. Commodity money has intrinsic value besides its specified worth, for example when gold coins are used as currency. Fiat money, first used in China in the 10th century, is money that is simply a token of exchange with no value other than that assigned to it by the government. A paper bank note is fiat money.

Many paper currencies were initially "promises to pay" against gold held in reserve. In theory, dollars issued by the US Federal Reserve could be exchanged for their gold value. Since 1971, the value of a dollar has no longer been convertible to gold, and is set entirely as the US Treasury wishes, without reference to its gold reserves. Such fiat currencies rely on people's confidence in a country's economic stability, which is not always assured. ∎

Shelling out

Wampum were strings of white and black shell beads treasured by the indigenous North Americans of the Eastern Woodland tribes. Before the European settlers arrived in the 15th century, wampum was used mainly for ceremonial purposes. People might exchange wampum to record an agreement, or to pay tribute. Its value came from the immense skill involved in making it, and in its ceremonial associations.

When Europeans arrived, their tools revolutionized wampum making, and Dutch colonizers mass-produced the beads by the million. Soon, they were using wampum to trade and buy things from the native peoples, who had no interest in coins, but valued wampum. Wampum soon became a currency with an accepted exchange rate. In New York, eight white or four black wampum equalled one stuiver (a Dutch coin of the time). The use and value of wampum diminished from the 1670s.

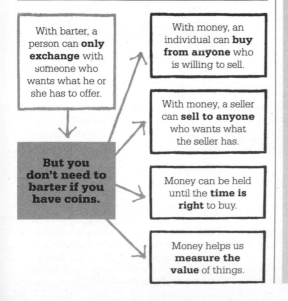

With barter, a person can **only exchange** with someone who wants what he or she has to offer.

But you don't need to barter if you have coins.

With money, an individual can **buy from anyone** who is willing to sell.

With money, a seller can **sell to anyone** who wants what the seller has.

Money can be held until the **time is right** to buy.

Money helps us **measure the value** of things.

This Shawnee shoulder bag is decorated with wampum beads, which developed into a currency for some North American tribes.

MAKE MONEY FROM MONEY
FINANCIAL SERVICES

Merchant bankers of the late 14th century arranged deposits and loans but also converted foreign currencies and watched over the circulation for signs of forged or forbidden coins.

Humans have long engaged in borrowing and lending. There is evidence that these activities took place 5,000 years ago, in Mesopotamia (present-day Iraq) at the very dawn of civilization. But modern banking systems did not emerge until the 14th century, in northern Italy.

The word "bank" comes from the Italian word for "bench", on which the bankers sat to conduct business. In the 14th century, the Italian peninsula was a land of city-states that benefited from the influence and revenue of the papacy in Rome. The peninsula was ideally located for trade between Asia, Africa, and the emerging nations of Europe. Wealth began to accumulate, especially in Venice and Florence. Venice relied on sea-power: institutions were created there to finance and insure voyages. Florence focused on manufacturing and trade with northern Europe, and here merchants and financiers came together at the Medici Bank.

Florence was already home to other banking families, such as the Peruzzi and the Bardi, and to different types of financial bodies – from pawnbrokers who lent money secured by personal belongings, to local banks that dealt in foreign currencies, accepted deposits, and lent to local businesses. The bank founded by Giovanni di Bicci de' Medici in 1397 was different.

The Medici Bank financed long-distance trade in commodities such as wool. It differed from existing banks in three ways. First, it grew to a great size. In its heyday, under the founder's son, Cosimo, it ran branches in 11 cities, including London, Bruges, and Geneva. Second, its network was decentralized. Branches were managed not by an employee but by a local junior partner, who shared in the profits. The Medici family in Florence were the senior partners, watching over the network, earning most of the profit, and retaining the family trademark, which symbolized the bank's sound reputation. Third, branches took in large deposits from wealthy savers, multiplying the lending that could be given out for a modest amount of initial capital, and so multiplying the bank's profits.

Economics of banking

These elements of the Medici success story correspond to three economic concepts highly relevant to banking today. The first is "economies of scale". It is expensive for an individual to draw up a single legal loan contract, but a bank can draw up 1,000 such contracts at a fraction of the "per-contract" cost. Dealings in money (cash investments) are suitable for economies of scale. The second is "diversification of risk". The Medicis lowered the risk of bad lending by spreading their lending geographically. Moreover, because the junior partners shared in profits and losses, they needed to lend wisely – in effect, they took on some of the Medici risks. The third concept is "asset transformation". Merchants might want to deposit earnings or borrow money. One merchant might want a safe place to store his gold, from where he can withdraw it quickly if necessary. Another might want a loan – which is riskier for the bank, and may tie

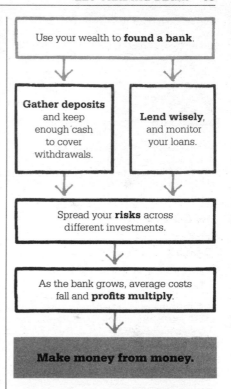

Use your wealth to **found a bank**.

Gather deposits and keep enough cash to cover withdrawals.

Lend wisely, and monitor your loans.

Spread your **risks** across different investments.

As the bank grows, average costs fall and **profits multiply**.

Make money from money.

up money for a longer time. So the bank came to stand between the two needs: "borrowing short, and lending long". This suited everybody – the depositor, the borrower, and of course the bank, which used customer deposits as borrowed money ("leverage"), to multiply profits and make a high return on its owners' invested capital.

However, this practice also makes the bank vulnerable – if a large number of depositors demand their money back at the same time (in "a run on the bank"), the bank may be unable to provide it because it will have used the depositors' money to make long-term loans, and it retains only a small fraction of depositors' money in ready cash. This risk is a calculated one, and the advantage of the system is that it usefully connects savers and borrowers.

Financing long-distance trade was a high-risk business in 14th-century Europe. It involved time and distance, so it » suffered from what has been called the "fundamental problem of exchange" – the danger that someone will run off with the goods or the money after a deal has been struck. To solve this problem, the "bill of exchange" was developed. This was a piece of paper witnessing a buyer's promise to pay for goods in a specific currency when the goods arrived. The seller of the goods could also sell the bill immediately to raise money. Italian merchant banks became particularly skilled at dealing in these bills, creating an international market for money.

By buying the bill of exchange, a bank was taking on the risk that the buyer of the goods would not pay up. It was therefore essential for the bank to know who was likely to pay up, and who was not. Lending – indeed finance generally – requires skilled, specialized knowledge, as a lack of information (known as "information asymmetry") can result in serious problems. The borrowers least likely to repay are the ones most likely to ask for loans; and once they have received a loan, there are temptations not to repay. A bank's most important function is its ability to lend wisely, and then to monitor borrowers to deter "moral hazard" – when people succumb to the temptation not to repay, and default on the loan.

Bills of exchange, such as this one from 1713, later developed into the common bank cheque. All types promise to pay the bearer a specific amount of money on a certain date.

Geographical clusters

Banks often cluster together in the same place to maximize information and skill. This explains the development of financial districts in large cities. Economists call this phenomenon "network externalities", which refers to the fact that, as a cluster starts to form, all the banks benefit from the network of deepening skills and information. Florence was one such cluster. The City of London, with its goldsmiths and shipping experts, became another. In the early 1800s, the remote northern inland province of Shanxi became China's leading financial centre. Today, the internet creates new ways of clustering online.

The benefit of specialization explains why there are so many different types of banks – covering savings, mortgages, car

---

A 21st-century banking crisis

Granting mortgages to "subprime" borrowers (people unable to repay) led to a wave of house repossessions and the financial crisis of 2007–08.

The global financial crisis, which began in 2007, has led to a rethink about the nature of banking. Leverage, or borrowed money, lay at the heart of the crisis. In 1900, about three-quarters of the assets of a bank might be financed by borrowed money. In 2007, the proportion was often 95–99 per cent. The banks' enthusiasm for placing financial bets on future movements in the market, known as derivatives, magnified this leverage and the risks it carried.

Significantly, the crisis followed a period of banking deregulation. A variety of financial innovations seemed lucrative in a rising market. However, they led to poor lending standards by two groups: those providing housing loans to poor US families, and bond investors over-reliant on the advice of credit rating agencies. These are the issues faced by all banks since the Medicis: poor information, financial incentives, and risk.

A banker is a fellow who lends you his umbrella when the sun is shining, but wants it back the minute it begins to rain.
Mark Twain
US author (1835–1910)

loans, and so on. The form a bank takes can also address information problems. Mutual societies and cooperative banks, for instance, which are effectively owned by their customers, first arose in the 19th century to increase trust between the bank and its customers at a time of social change. Because the members of these organizations checked up on each other, and the managers had good local knowledge, they could provide the long-term loans that their customers needed. In some countries, such as Germany, they thrived. The Dutch bank Rabobank is an example of a cooperative model, as is Bangladesh's "micro-finance" Grameen Bank, which makes many loans of small amounts.

However, clustering can also lead to risky competition and crowd-like behaviour. It is especially important for banks to have a good reputation because they have an asset transformation role – they transform deposits into loans – and their loan-assets are riskier, longer, and less easy to turn into cash (less "liquid") than their deposit-liabilities.

Bad news can lead to panics. Bank failures can have severe knock-on consequences for other banks, and for government and society, as witnessed in the failure of

Creditanstalt Bank in Austria in 1931, which led to a run on the German mark, UK sterling, and then the US dollar, triggering further bank runs in the USA and contributing to the Great Depression.

Consequently, banks need to be regulated, and most countries have strict rules about who can form a bank, the information they must disclose, and the scope of their business activities.

Finance broadly

Banking is just the largest part of finance, but all finance is about connecting people who have more money than they need with people who need more money than they have – and will use it productively. Stock exchanges connect these needs directly, through equities (shares conferring ownership of a company), bonds (lending that can be traded), or other instruments.

These exchanges are either physical places, such as the New York Stock Exchange, or regulated markets where trading takes place through phone calls and computers, like the international bond market. The clustering created by exchanges makes these long-term investments more liquid: they can easily be sold and turned into money. Savings can also be pooled to lower transaction costs and diversify risks. Mutual funds, pension funds, and insurance companies all perform this role. ∎

The City of London is home to a dense cluster of banks built over medieval streets. Today it is the world's largest centre for foreign-exchange trading and cross-border bank lending.

MONEY CAUSES INFLATION
THE QUANTITY THEORY OF MONEY

IN CONTEXT

FOCUS
The macroeconomy

KEY THINKER
Jean Bodin (1530–96)

BEFORE
1492 Christopher Columbus arrives in the Americas. Silver and gold flow into Spain.

AFTER
1752 David Hume states that the money supply has a direct relationship to the price level.

1911 Irving Fisher develops a mathematical formula to explain the quantity theory of money.

1936 John Maynard Keynes says that the velocity of money in circulation is unstable.

1956 Milton Friedman argues that a change in the amount of money in the economy can have a predictable effect on people's incomes.

In 16th-century Europe, prices were rising inexplicably. Some said that rulers were using an old practice of "debasing" currencies by minting coins with ever-smaller amounts of gold or silver in them. This was true. However, Jean Bodin, a French lawyer, argued that something much more significant was also happening.

In 1568, Bodin published his *Response to the Paradoxes of Malestroit*. The French economist Jean de Malestroit (?–1578) had blamed the price inflation solely on currency debasement, but Bodin showed that prices were rising sharply even when measured in pure silver. He argued that an abundance of silver and gold was to blame. These precious metals were entering Spain from its new colonies in the Americas, and then spreading throughout Europe.

Bodin's calculations of the increase in coinage were remarkably accurate. Later economists concluded that prices in Europe quadrupled during the 16th century, at the same time as the amount of physical silver and gold circulating in the system trebled; Bodin had estimated the increase in precious metals at more than 2.5 times. He also highlighted other factors behind the inflation: a demand for luxuries; a scarcity of goods for sale due to exports and waste; greedy merchants able to restrict the supply of goods through monopolies; and, of course, the rulers adulterating the coins.

The money supply
Bodin was not the first to point to the new influence of American treasure and the effect of the abundance or scarcity of money on price levels. In 1556, a Spanish theologian named Martín de Azpilcueta (better known as Navarrus) had come to the same conclusion. However, Bodin's essay also discussed the demand for and the supply of money, the operation of these two sides of an economy, and how disturbances to the supply of money

led to inflation. His thorough study is considered the first important statement of the quantity theory of money.

The reasoning behind this theory is partly based on common sense. Why is the price of a cup of coffee in a rich part of town so much higher than in a poor part? The answer is that customers in the rich part have more money to spend. If we consider the population of a whole country, and double the money in people's pockets, it is natural that they will want to use their increased spending power to buy more goods and services. But goods and services are always in limited supply, so there will be too much money chasing too few goods, and prices will rise.

This chain of events shows the important relationship between the quantity of money in an economy and the general price level. The quantity »

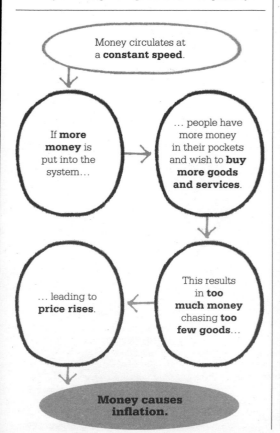

Money circulates at a **constant speed**.

If **more money** is put into the system…

… people have more money in their pockets and wish to **buy more goods and services**.

… leading to **price rises**.

This results in **too much money** chasing **too few goods**…

Money causes inflation.

Jean Bodin

The son of a master tailor, Jean Bodin was born in 1530 in Angers, France. He was educated in Paris, and went on to study at the University of Toulouse. In 1560, he became a king's advocate in Paris. Bodin's scholarship (he read law, history, politics, philosophy, economics, and religion) attracted royal favour, and between 1571 and 1584 he served as aide to the powerful Duke of Alençon.

In 1576, he married Françoise Trouilliart and succeeded his brother-in-law as the king's procurator in Laon, northern France. In 1589, King Henry III was assassinated, and religious civil war broke out. Bodin believed in tolerance, but in Laon was forced to declare for the Catholic cause, until the victorious Protestant King, Henry IV, took control of the city. Bodin died of the plague, aged 66, in 1596.

Key works

1566 *Method for the Easy Comprehension of History*
1568 *Response to the Paradoxes of Malestroit*
1576 *Six Books of a Commonwealth*

theory of money states that a doubling of the supply of money will result in a doubling in the value of transactions (or income or expenditure). In the theory's more extreme form, a doubling of money will lead to a doubling of prices, but not real value. Money will be neutral in its effect on the real, relative value of goods and services – for example, on how many jackets can be bought for the price of a computer.

Real price, nominal price

After Bodin, many economists developed his idea further. They came to recognize that there is a distinct separation between the real side of the economy and the nominal, or money, side. Nominal prices are simply money prices, which can change with inflation. This is why economists focus on real prices – on what quantity of a thing (jackets, computers, or time spent working) has to be given up in return for another kind of thing, no matter what the nominal price is. In the extreme quantity theory, changes in the money supply may influence prices, but it has no effect on the real economic variables, such as output and unemployment. What is more, economists realized that money is itself a "good" that people want to own for

> The abundance of gold and silver... is greater in this kingdom today than it has been in the last 400 years.
> **Jean Bodin**

its spending power. However, the money they want is not nominal money, but "real money" – money that can buy more.

Fisher's equation

The fullest statement of the quantity theory of money was made by the US economist Irving Fisher (1867–1947), who used the mathematical formula $MV = PT$. Here "P" is the general level of prices, and "T" is the transactions that take place in a year, so PT (Prices × Transactions) is the total value of transactions occurring annually. "M" is the supply of money. But because PT is a total flow of goods, while M represents a stock of money that can be used over and over again, the equation needs something to represent the circulation of money. This circular flow, which causes money to rotate through

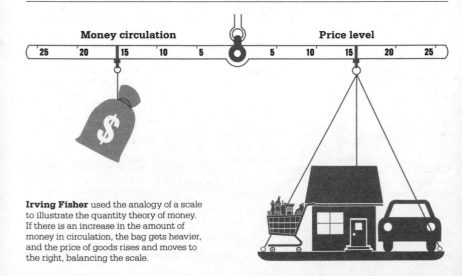

Money circulation   **Price level**

| 25 | 20 | 15 | 10 | 5 | | 5 | 10 | 15 | 20 | 25 |

Irving Fisher used the analogy of a scale to illustrate the quantity theory of money. If there is an increase in the amount of money in circulation, the bag gets heavier, and the price of goods rises and moves to the right, balancing the scale.

This painting by Dutch master Pieter Bruegel (1559) shows vagrants rubbing shoulders with the rich during Lent. Steep price rises in the 15th century led to much hardship among the poor, a rise in vagrancy, and peasant revolts.

the economy – like the spinning drum of a washing machine – is "V", the velocity of money.

This equation becomes a theory when we make assumptions about the relationships between the letters, which economists do in three ways. First, V, the velocity of money, is assumed to be constant, since the way in which we use money is part of habit and custom and does not change much from year to year (our washing machine drum spins at a steady rate). This is the key assumption behind the quantity theory of money. Second, it is assumed that T, the quantity of transactions in an economy, is driven solely by consumers' demand and producers' technology, which together determine prices. Third, we allow that there can be one-off changes to M (the supply of money), such as the flow of New World treasure into Europe. With V (velocity) and T (transactions) fixed, it follows that a doubling of money will lead to a doubling of prices.

Combined with the difference between nominal and real, the quantity theory of money has led to the notion that money is neutral in its effect on the economy.

Challenge and restatement
But is money really neutral? Few believe that it is neutral in the short run. The immediate effect of more money in the pocket is for it to be spent on real goods and services. John Maynard Keynes (p.99) said it was probably neutral in the long run, but in the

short run it would affect real variables such as output and unemployment. Evidence also suggests that money velocity (V) is not constant. It seems to rise in booms when inflation is high and falls in recessions when inflation is low.

Keynes had other ideas that challenged the quantity theory of money. He proposed that money is used, not just as a medium of exchange, but also as a "store of value" – something you can keep, either for buying goods, for security in case of hard times in the future, or for future investments.

Keynesian economists argue that these motives are affected less by income or transactions (PT in the formula) than by interest rates. A rise in the interest rate will lead to a rise in the velocity of money.

In 1956, US economist Milton Friedman (p.117) defended the quantity theory of money, arguing that an individual's demand for real money balances (where money buys more) depends on wealth. He claimed that it is people's incomes that drive this demand.

Today, central banks print money electronically and use it to buy government debt in a process known as quantitative easing. Their aim has been to prevent a feared fall in the money supply. So far, the most visible effect has been to reduce interest rates on government debt. ∎

 Inflation is always and everywhere a monetary phenomenon.
Milton Friedman

PROTECT US FROM FOREIGN GOODS

PROTECTIONISM AND TRADE

IN CONTEXT

FOCUS
Global economy

KEY THINKER
Thomas Mun (1571–1641)

BEFORE
c.1620 Gerard de Malynes argues that England should regulate foreign exchange to stop the nation's gold and silver going abroad.

AFTER
1691 English merchant Dudley North argues that the main spur to increased national wealth is consumption.

1791 US Treasury Secretary Alexander Hamilton argues for protection of young industries.

1817 British economist David Ricardo argues that foreign trade can benefit all nations.

1970s US economist Milton Friedman insists that free trade helps developing countries.

For the last half century, many economists have championed free trade. They argue that only by removing restrictions on trade (such as tariffs) can goods and money flow freely around the world and global markets develop without inhibition. Some disagree, arguing that where there is a huge imbalance of trade between two countries, it can impact jobs and wealth.

A mercantilist view

The argument over free trade dates back to the mercantilist era, which began in Europe in the 16th century and continued until the late 18th century. With the rise of Dutch and English seaborne trade, wealth began to shift from southern Europe towards the north.

This was also the age when nation-states began to emerge, along with the idea of the wealth of the nation, which was measured by the amount of "treasure" (gold and silver) it possessed. Mercantilists believed that the world drew from a "limited pot", so the wealth of each nation depended on ensuring a favourable "balance of trade", in which more gold flows into the nation than out. If an excess of gold flows out, the nation's prosperity declines, wages fall, and jobs are lost. England sought to cut the outflow of gold by imposing sumptuary laws, which aimed to limit the consumption of foreign goods. For instance, laws were passed restricting the types of fabric that could be used for clothes, reducing the demand for fine foreign cotton and silk.

Malynes and Mun

Gerard de Malynes (1586–1641), an English expert on foreign exchange, believed that the outflow of gold should be restricted. If too much flowed out, he argued, the value of English currency would fall.

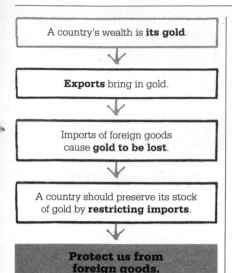

A country's wealth is **its gold**.

↓

Exports bring in gold.

↓

Imports of foreign goods cause **gold to be lost**.

↓

A country should preserve its stock of gold by **restricting imports**.

↓

Protect us from foreign goods.

However, the century's greatest mercantilist theorist, Englishman Thomas Mun, insisted that what matters is not the fact that payments are made abroad, but how trade and payments finally balance out. Mun wanted to boost exports and cut imports through more frugal consumption of domestic produce. However, he saw no problem in spending gold abroad if it was used to acquire goods that were then re-exported for a larger sum, ultimately returning more gold to the country than had initially been spent. This would boost trade, provide work for the shipping industry, and increase England's treasure.

Free trade agreements

In the 18th century, Adam Smith (p.39) was to disagree with this view. What matters, he insisted in *The Wealth of Nations*, is not the wealth of individual nations but the wealth of all nations. Nor is the pot fixed; it can grow over time – but only if trade between nations is unrestricted. If left free, Smith insisted, the market would always grow to enrich all countries eventually.

For the last half century, Smith's view has dominated, as most Western economists argue that restrictions on trade between nations hobble their economies. Today, free trade areas such as the EU (European Union), ASEAN (Association of Southeast Asian Nations), and NAFTA (North American Free Trade Agreement) are the norm, while global organizations such as the World Trade Organization (WTO) and the International Monetary Fund (IMF) urge countries to reduce tariffs and other trade barriers to allow foreign firms to enter their domestic markets. Today, the creation of barriers to foreign trade is criticized as protectionism.

However, some economists are concerned that exposure to mighty global businesses has the potential to damage developing countries, who are unable to nurture infant industries behind protective barriers, as Britain, the USA, Japan, and South Korea did before they became economically powerful. China, meanwhile, pursues a trade policy that in many ways echoes Mun's thinking, by running large trade surpluses and building up a huge reserve of foreign exchange. ∎

Thomas Mun

Born in 1571, Thomas Mun grew up in a family of wealthy London merchants. His father died when he was three, and his mother married Thomas Cordell, who became a director of the East India Company, Britain's largest trading company. Mun began trading as a merchant in the Mediterranean. In 1615, he became a director of the East India Company. His ideas were developed originally to defend the company's export of large amounts of silver, on the grounds that this generated re-export trade. In 1628, the company appealed to the British government to protect their trade against Dutch competition. Mun represented their case to Parliament. He had amassed a considerable fortune by the time he died in 1641.

Key works

1621 *A Discourse of Trade*
c.1630 *England's Treasure by Foreign Trade*

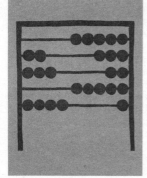

THE ECONOMY CAN BE COUNTED

MEASURING WEALTH

IN CONTEXT

FOCUS
Economic methods

KEY THINKER
William Petty (1623–87)

BEFORE
1620 English scientist Francis Bacon argues for a new approach to science, based on the collection of facts.

AFTER
1696 English statistician Gregory King writes his great statistical survey of England's population.

1930s Australian economist Colin Clark invents the idea of gross national product (GNP).

1934 Russian-US economist Simon Kuznets develops modern national income accounting methods.

1950s British economist Richard Stone introduces balanced, double-entry national accounting.

Wealth includes people as well as property.

↓

Both population and a typical person's average expenditure **can be estimated**.

↓

Multiplying average expenditure by the population gives the **national income**.

↓

Deducting an estimated amount for rents and profits leaves a sum for the **total worth** of labour.

↓

The economy can be counted.

Today we take it for granted that the economy can be measured, and its expansions and contractions accurately quantified. But this was not always the case. The idea of measuring the economy dates back to the 1670s and the pioneering work of English scientist William Petty. His insight was to apply the new empirical methods of science to financial and political affairs – to use real world data, rather than relying on logical reasoning. He decided to express himself only "in terms of number, weight, or measure". This approach helped form the basis of the discipline that would become known as economics.

In his 1671–2 book *Political Arithmetick*, Petty used real data to show that, contrary to popular belief, England was wealthier than ever. One of his ground-breaking decisions was to include the value of labour, as well as land and capital. Although Petty's figures are open to dispute, there is no doubting the effectiveness of his basic idea. His calculations included population size, personal spending, wages per person, the value of rents, and others. He then multiplied these figures to give a total figure for the nation's total wealth, creating accounts for an entire nation.

Similar methods were developed in France by Pierre de Boisguilbert (1646–1714) and Sébastien le Prestre (1633–1707). In England, Gregory King (1648–1712) analysed the economies and populations of England, Holland, and France. He calculated that none had the finances to continue the war they were then engaged in – the Nine Years' War – beyond 1698. His figures might have been correct, as the war ended in 1697.

Measures of progress

Statistics are now at the heart of economics. Today, economists generally measure gross domestic product (GDP) – the total value of all the goods and services exchanged for money within a country in a particular period (usually a year). However, there is still no definitive way of calculating national accounts, although efforts have been made to standardize methods.

Economists have now begun to broaden the measurement of prosperity. They have formulated new measures such as the genuine progress indicator (GPI), which includes adjustments for income distribution, crime, pollution, and the happy planet index (HPI), a measure of human well-being and environmental impact. ∎

The Battle of La Hogue was fought in 1692 during the Nine Years' War. English statistician Gregory King calculated how long each country involved could afford to fight.

William Petty

Born in 1623 to a humble family in Hampshire, England, William Petty lived through the English Civil War and rose to high positions in both the Commonwealth government and then the restored monarchy. As a young man, he worked for the English political philosopher Thomas Hobbes in Holland. After returning to England, he taught anatomy at Oxford University. A great believer in the new science, he found universities uninspiring, so left for Ireland, where he made a monumental land survey of the entire country.

In the 1660s, he returned to England and began the work on economics for which he is now known. For the remainder of his life he moved between Ireland and England, both physically and in the focus of his work. Petty is regarded as one of the first great political economists. He died in 1687, aged 64.

Key works

1662 *Treatise of Taxes and Contributions*
1671–2 *Political Arithmetick*
1682 *Quantulumcunque Concerning Money*

MONEY AND GOODS FLOW BETWEEN PRODUCERS AND CONSUMERS
THE CIRCULAR FLOW OF THE ECONOMY

IN CONTEXT

FOCUS
The macroeconomy

KEY THINKER
François Quesnay (1694–1774)

BEFORE
1664–76 English economist William Petty introduces the concepts of national income and expenditure.

1755 Irish merchant banker Richard Cantillon's *Essay*, first published in France, discusses the circulation of money from city to countryside.

AFTER
1885 Karl Marx's *Capital* describes the circulation of capital using a model inspired by Quesnay.

1930s Russian-American economist Simon Kuznets develops modern national income accounting.

I n economics, one can think small – microeconomics – or one can think as large as the entire system: this is the study of macroeconomics. In 18th-century France, a group known as the physiocrats tried to think big – they wanted to understand and explain the whole economy as a system. Their ideas form the foundation of modern macroeconomics.

The physiocrats

Physiocracy is an ancient Greek word meaning "power over nature". The physiocrats believed that nations gained their economic wealth from nature, through their agricultural sector. Their leader, François Quesnay, was surgeon and physician to King Louis XV's mistress, Madame de Pompadour. His complicated model of the economy was thought by some to reflect the circulation of blood in a human body.

The mercantilist approach (pp.22–23) dominated economic thinking at the time. Mercantilists thought the state should behave like a merchant, growing business, acquiring gold, and actively interfering with the economy through taxes, subsidies, controls, and monopoly privileges. The physiocrats took the opposite view: they argued that the economy was naturally self-regulating, and needed only to be protected from bad influences. They favoured free trade, low taxes, secure property rights, and low government debt. Where the mercantilists said that wealth came from treasure, Quesnay and his

Madame de Pompadour (the mistress of Louis XV) installed Quesnay at Versailles as her physician. To him, her lifestyle must have epitomized the lavish surplus of landowners' wealth.

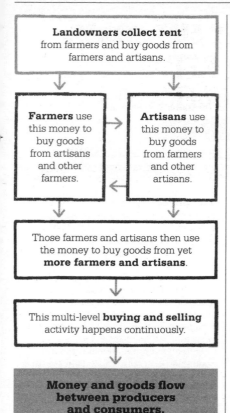

Landowners collect rent from farmers and buy goods from farmers and artisans.

Farmers use this money to buy goods from artisans and other farmers.

Artisans use this money to buy goods from farmers and other artisans.

Those farmers and artisans then use the money to buy goods from yet **more farmers and artisans**.

This multi-level **buying and selling** activity happens continuously.

Money and goods flow between producers and consumers.

followers viewed it as being rooted in what modern economists call the "real" economy – those sectors that create real goods and services. They believed that agriculture was the most productive of these sectors.

The physiocrats were influenced by the thinking of an earlier French landowner, Pierre de Boisguilbert. He said that agriculture is superior to manufacture, and consumables are more valuable than gold. The more goods consumed, he said, the more money moves in the system, making consumption the driving force in the economy. He also said that a little money in the hands of the poor (who spend it) is worth far more to the economy than in the hands of the rich (who hoard it). The movement, or circulation, of money is all-important.

The Economic Table

The physiocratic system of circulation was set out in Quesnay's *Economic Table*, which was published and revised several times between 1758 and 1767. This is a diagram that illustrates, through a series of crossing and connecting lines, the flow of money and goods between three groups in society: landowners, farmers, and artisans. The goods are agricultural and manufactured products (produced by the farmers and artisans). Although Quesnay used corn as his example of an agricultural product, he said that this category could include anything produced from the land, including mining products.

Quesnay's model is best understood through an example. Imagine each of the three groups starts with £2 million. The landowners produce nothing. They spend their £2 million equally between farming and artisan products, and consume all of them. They receive £2 million in rent from the farmers – which the farmers can just afford, since they are the only group to produce a surplus – and so the landowners end up back where they started. The farmers are the productive group. From a starting point of £2 million, they produce £5 million-worth of agricultural products, over and above what they consume themselves. Of this, £1 million-worth is sold to landowners for their consumption. They sell £2 million-worth to artisans, half for consumption and half as raw materials for the goods the artisans will produce. This leaves £2 million-worth to be used towards next year's growing season. In terms of production, they are back where they started. However, they also have £3 million from sales, of which they spend £2 million on rent, and £1 million on artisan goods (tools, agricultural implements, and so on). »

 Let the sum total of the revenues be annually returned into and along the entire course of circulation.
François Quesnay

Quesnay referred to any group outside the land-based farmers and landowners as "sterile", because he believed that they could not produce a net surplus. The artisans, in this instance, use their starting amount of £2 million to produce £2 million-worth of manufactured goods over and above what they consume themselves. These are sold equally to landowners and farmers. But they spend their entire revenue on agricultural products: £1 million for their own consumption, and £1 million on raw materials. They have consumed everything they have.

Quesnay's model does more than present end-of-year results – it also shows how money and goods circulate through the year, and demonstrates why this is so important. The sale of products between the various groups continues to generate revenue, which is then used to buy more products, which produces yet more revenue. A "multiplier effect" occurs (in Quesnay's scheme it appeared as a zig-zag series of lines), similar to that presented by John Maynard Keynes (p.99) in the 1930s, when he pointed out the beneficial knock-on effects of government spending in a depressed economy.

Analysing the economy

The kinds of questions Quesnay asked, and the way he went about answering them, anticipated modern economics. He was one of the first to attempt to uncover general abstract laws that govern economies, which he did by breaking economies down into their constituent parts and then rigorously analysing the relationships between the parts. His model included inputs, outputs, and the interdependencies of different

According to the physiocrats, investment in agriculture was key to ensuring the national wealth of France. Free export was a way of sustaining demand and restricting merchant power.

sectors. Quesnay suggested that these might exist in a state of equilibrium, an idea that was later developed by Léon Walras (p.77), becoming one of the foundations of economic theorizing.

Quesnay's approach to quantifying economic laws makes his *Economic Table* possibly the first empirical macroeconomic model. The numbers in his Table were the result of a close study of the French economic system, giving them a firm empirical basis. This study indicated that farming technology was sufficient for farmers to generate a net surplus of at least 100 per cent. In our example, this is what they achieve – starting with £2 million of corn, they receive this back plus a net surplus of £2 million, which is then paid in rent. Modern economists use these kinds of empirical results to think about the impact of policy changes, and Quesnay used his Table for a similar purpose. He argued that if farmers had to pay too much tax, either directly or indirectly, they would cut back their capital investment in farming technology, and production would fall below the level needed for the economy to thrive. This led the physiocrats to argue that there should be only one tax: on the rental value of land.

Based on his empirical findings, Quesnay made a host of other policy recommendations, including investment in agriculture, the spending of all revenue, no hoarding, low taxes, and free trade. He thought capital was especially important, because his entrepreneur-farmers needed to borrow cheaply in order to pay for land improvements.

Classical ideas

Quesnay's idea of sectors being productive or unproductive has reappeared throughout the history of economic thought, as economists consider industry versus services, and the private sector versus the government. His sole focus on agriculture may look narrow to modern eyes, as it is now understood that wealth generation from industry and services is vital to an economy's growth. However, his emphasis on the "real" side of the economy was an important step towards modern economic

The interdependence of consumers and producers was first
illustrated by Quesnay. Consumers rely on producers for goods and
services, who in turn rely on the consumers for sales and labour.

thinking. He most obviously anticipated
modern national income accounting, which
is used to assess nations' macroeconomic
performance. This income accounting is
based on the circular flow of income and
expenditure around the economy. The
value of the total product of an economy is
equal to the total income earned – a notion
that was an important part of Quesnay's
theory. In the 20th century, much of the
analysis of macroeconomies has revolved
around the Keynesian multiplier (pp.100–101).
Keynes showed how government spending
could stimulate further spending in a
"multiplier effect". This idea has obvious
links to Quesnay's circular flow, with its
susceptibility to expansion and stagnation.

Perhaps most importantly, Quesnay's
concepts of surplus and capital became key
to the way that the classical economists
analysed economic growth. A typical
classical model focuses on three factors
of production: land, labour, and capital.
Landowners receive rent and spend
wastefully on luxuries; labourers accept
a low wage, and if it rises they produce
more children. However, entrepreneurs
earn profit and re-invest it productively
in industry. So profit drives growth and
economic performance depends on sectors
of the economy generating surpluses.
Thus, Quesnay anticipated later ideas
about the growth of economies and
inspired Karl Marx (p.68), who produced
his own version of the *Economic Table*.
Marx said of Quesnay that "never before
had thinking in political economy reached
such heights of genius". ∎

François Quesnay

Born near Paris,
France, in 1694, François
Quesnay was the son of a
ploughman and the eighth
of 13 children. At the age
of 17 he began an
apprenticeship in
engraving, but then
transferred to university,
graduating from the college
of surgeons in 1717.

He made his name as
a surgeon and specialized
in treating the nobility; in
1749 he moved to the royal
palace at Versailles, near
Paris, as physician to
Madame de Pompadour. In
1752, he saved the king's
son from smallpox and was
awarded a title and enough
money to buy an estate for
his own son.

His interest in economics
began in the early 1750s,
and in 1757 he met the
Marquis de Mirabeau,
with whom he formed
les Economistes – the
physiocrats. He died
in 1774.

Key works

1758 *Economic Table*
1763 *Rural Philosophy*
(with Marquis de
Mirabeau)
1766 *Analysis of the
Arithmetic Formula for
the Economic Table*

PRIVATE INDIVIDUALS NEVER PAY FOR STREET LIGHTS
PROVISION OF PUBLIC GOODS AND SERVICES

IN CONTEXT

FOCUS
Decision-making

KEY THINKER
David Hume (1711–76)

BEFORE
c.500 BCE In Athens, indirect taxes are used to finance city festivals, temples, and walls. Occasional direct taxes are levied at times of war.

1421 The first patent is granted to Italian engineer Filippo Brunelleschi, to protect his invention of hoisting gear for barges.

AFTER
1848 *The Communist Manifesto* advocates collective ownership of the means of production by the workers.

19th century Public street lighting is introduced in Europe and America.

1954 US economist Paul Samuelson develops a modern theory of public goods.

Street lights are an example of a **public good** because…

⬇   ⬇

… it is difficult to stop people **benefitting** from street lighting.

… one person's **use of street lighting** does not diminish another's enjoyment of it.

⬇

Private firms do not provide street lights as they can't **stop non-payers** from using them.

⬇

Essential public goods are usually provided by the government, because…

⬇

… private individuals never pay for street lights.

Even within a well-functioning market economy, there are areas in which markets fail. One important example of market failure is in the provision of public goods – goods that are to become freely available to all, or where it would be difficult to prevent their use by non-payers. These goods, which include things such as

national defence, are difficult for a private firm or individual to supply profitably. This problem, known as "free-riding" (where consumers enjoy the goods without paying for them) means that there is no profit incentive. However, there is a demand for these goods, and because private markets may not be able to satisfy this demand, public goods are usually provided by governments and funded through taxation.

A failure of the market to provide these goods was recognized by the philosopher David Hume in the 18th century. Influenced by Hume, Adam Smith (p.39), an ardent advocate of the free market, conceded that a government's role was to provide those public goods that it would not be profitable for individuals or firms to produce.

There are two distinguishing characteristics of public goods that cause them to be undersupplied by the markets: non-excludability, meaning that it is difficult to prevent people who don't pay for the goods from using them; and non-rivalry, meaning that one person's consumption of the good does not diminish the ability of others to consume it. A classic example is street lighting; it would be almost impossible to exclude non-payers from enjoying its benefits, and no individual's use of it detracts from that benefit to other users.

As industrial economies developed in the 19th century, countries had to overcome the problem of free-riding in areas such as intellectual property. Intangible goods, such as new knowledge and discoveries, have the attributes of non-excludability and non-rivalry, and so are at risk of being undersupplied by the market. This could discourage the development of new technologies, unless they can be protected in some way. To do this, countries developed laws granting patents, copyright, and trademarks to protect the returns from new knowledge and inventions. Most economists acknowledge that government has a responsibility to provide public goods, but debate continues about the extent of that responsibility. ∎

Lighthouses are a public good from which it is hard to exclude non-payers, and which many people can use at the same time. They are invariably provided collectively.

David Hume

The epitome of the "Scottish Enlightenment", David Hume was one of the most influential British philosophers of the 18th century. He was born in Edinburgh in 1711, and from an early age showed signs of a brilliant mind: he entered Edinburgh University at the age of 12, studying first law, and then philosophy.

In 1734, Hume moved to France, where he set out his major philosophical ideas in *A Treatise of Human Nature*. He then devoted much of his time to writing essays on literary and political subjects, and struck up a friendship with the young Adam Smith, who had been inspired by his writings. In 1763, Hume was given a diplomatic role in Paris, where he befriended the revolutionary French philosopher Jean-Jacques Rousseau. He settled in Edinburgh again in 1768, where he lived until his death in 1776, aged 65 years.

Key works

1739 *A Treatise of Human Nature*
1748 *An Enquiry Concerning Human Understanding*
1752 *Political Discourses*

MAN IS A COLD, RATIONAL CALCULATOR

ECONOMIC MAN

IN CONTEXT

FOCUS
Decision-making

KEY THINKER
Adam Smith (1723–90)

BEFORE
c.350 BCE Greek philosopher Aristotle claims that innate self-interest is the primary economic motivator.

1750s French economist François Quesnay claims that self-interest is the motivation behind all economic activity.

AFTER
1957 US economist Herbert Simon argues that people cannot acquire and digest all available information about every topic, so their rationality is "bounded" (limited).

1992 US economist Gary Becker receives the Nobel Prize for his work on rational choice in the fields of discrimination, crime, and human capital.

As individuals, we are **self-interested**.

↓

We aim to improve our **personal well-being** by consuming goods and services, and achieving goals.

↓

We make decisions by **collecting information and calculating** which actions will help us achieve our aims without being too costly.

↓

Man is a cold, rational calculator.

Most economic models are underpinned by the assumption that humans are essentially rational, self-interested beings. This is *Homo Economicus*, or "economic man". The idea – which applies equally to men and women – assumes that every individual makes decisions designed to maximize their personal well-being, based on a level-headed evaluation of all the facts. They choose the option that offers the greatest utility (satisfaction) with the least effort. This idea was first expounded by Adam Smith (p.39) in his 1776 work, *The Wealth of Nations*.

Smith's central belief was that human economic interaction is governed mainly by self-interest. He argued that "it is not from the benevolence of the butcher, the

Family economics

Parents' investments in children, especially through education, are an important source of an economy's capital stock, according to Becker.

US economist Gary Becker (1930–2014) was one of the first to apply economics to areas usually thought of as sociology. He argues that decisions relating to family life are made by weighing costs and benefits. For example, he views marriage as a market, and has analysed how economic characteristics influence the matching of partners. Becker also concluded that family members will help each other, not out of love, but out of self-interest in the hope of a financial reward. He believed that investment in a child is motivated by the fact that it often produces a better rate of return than traditional retirement savings. However, children cannot be legally forced to sustain their parents, so they are brought up with a sense of guilt, obligation, duty, and love, which effectively commits them to helping their parents. For this reason it can be argued that the welfare state damages families, by reducing their need for interdependence.

brewer, or the baker, that we can expect our dinner, but from their regard to their own interest". In making rational decisions, suppliers seek to maximize their own profit; the fact that this supplies us with our dinner matters little to them.

Smith's ideas were developed in the 19th century by the British philosopher John Stuart Mill (p.63). Mill believed people were beings that desire to possess wealth, by which he meant not just money, but a wealth of all things good. He saw individuals as motivated by the will to achieve the greatest well-being possible, while at the same time expending the least possible effort to achieve these goals.

Costs and benefits

Today, the idea of *Homo Economicus* is referred to as rational choice theory. This says that people make all kinds of economic and social decisions based on costs and benefits. For example, a criminal thinking of robbing a bank will weigh up the benefits (increased wealth, greater respect from other criminals) against the costs (the chances of getting caught and the effort involved in planning the raid), before deciding whether to commit the crime.

Economists consider actions to be rational when they are taken as a result of a sober calculation of costs and benefits in relation to reaching a goal. Economics

may have little to say about the goal itself, and some goals may appear to be quite irrational to most people. For example, while to most of us it may seem a dangerous decision to inject the human body with unverified performance-enhancing drugs, for numerous athletes – in the context of the desire to be the best – the decision may be a rational one.

Some people have questioned whether the idea of *Homo Economicus* is realistic. They argue that it does not allow for the fact that we cannot weigh up every relevant factor in a decision – the world is too complex to collate and evaluate all the relevant facts needed to calculate costs and benefits for every action. In practice we often take quick decisions based on past experience, habit, and rules of thumb.

The theory also falters when there are conflicting long- and short-term goals. For instance, someone might buy an unhealthy burger to stave off immediate hunger, despite knowing that this is an unhealthy choice. Behavioural economists have begun to explore the ways in which humans act differently to *Homo Economicus* when making choices. The idea of "economic man" may not be entirely accurate for explaining individual behaviour, but many economists argue that it remains useful in analysing the actions of profit-maximizing firms. ∎

THE INVISIBLE HAND OF THE MARKET BRINGS ORDER
FREE-MARKET ECONOMICS

Covent Garden Market in London is pictured here in 1774. Smith thought markets were key to making society fair. With the freedom to buy and sell, people could enjoy "natural liberty".

According to the Scottish thinker Adam Smith, the West had embarked on a great revolution before the 18th century, with nations changing from agrarian, or agricultural, societies to commercial ones. During the Middle Ages, towns had developed, and they were slowly joined up by roads. People brought goods and fresh produce to the towns, and the markets – with their buying and selling – became a part of life. Scientific innovation produced reliable, agreed units of measurement, along with new ways of doing things, and centralized nation-states formed from the mix of principalities that had dotted Europe. People enjoyed a new freedom, and had begun to exchange goods for their own personal gain, not merely for that of their overlord.

Smith asked how the actions of free individuals could result in an ordered, stable market – where people could make, buy, and sell what they wanted without enormous waste or want. How was this possible without some kind of guiding hand? In his great work of 1776, *The Wealth of Nations*, he provided the answer. Man, in his freedom, rivalry, and desire for gain, is "led by an invisible hand to promote an end, which was no part of his intention" – he inadvertently acts on behalf of the wider interest of society.

Laissez-faire economics

The idea of "spontaneous order" was not new. It was proposed in 1714 by the Dutch writer Bernard Mandeville, in his poem *The Fable of the Bees*. This told the story of a beehive that was thriving on the "vices" (self-interested behaviour) of its bees. When the bees became virtuous (no longer acting in their own self-interest but trying to act for the good of the hive), the beehive collapsed. Smith's notion of self-interest was not a vicious one. He saw humans as having an inclination to "truck and barter" (bargain and exchange) and to better themselves. Humans, in his view, were social creatures who act with moral restraint, using "fair play" in competition.

Smith believed that governments should not interfere with commerce, a view that was also held by other Scottish thinkers around him, including the philosopher David Hume (p.31). An earlier French writer, Pierre de Boisguilbert, used the phrase *laisse faire la nature* ("leave nature alone"), by which he meant "leave business alone". The term "laissez-faire" is used in economics to advocate minimal government. In Smith's view, government did have an important role, supplying defence, justice, and certain "public goods" (pp.30–31) that private markets were unlikely to provide, such as roads.

Smith's vision was essentially optimistic. The English philosopher Thomas Hobbes had earlier argued that without strong »

Mandeville's *Fable of the Bees* explored the idea that when people act out of self-interest, they benefit the whole of society, as the self-interested behaviour of bees benefits the hive.

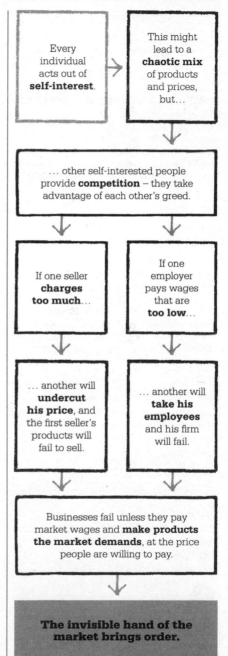

Every individual acts out of **self-interest**.

This might lead to a **chaotic mix** of products and prices, but…

… other self-interested people provide **competition** – they take advantage of each other's greed.

If one seller **charges too much**…

If one employer pays wages that are **too low**…

… another will **undercut his price**, and the first seller's products will fail to sell.

… another will **take his employees** and his firm will fail.

Businesses fail unless they pay market wages and **make products the market demands**, at the price people are willing to pay.

The invisible hand of the market brings order.

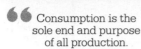

Consumption is the sole end and purpose of all production.
Adam Smith

authority, human life would be "nasty, brutish, and short". British economist Thomas Malthus (p.45) looked at the market and predicted mass starvation as a direct result of increased wealth. After Smith, Karl Marx (p.68) would predict that the market leads to revolution. Smith, however, saw society as perfectly functional, and the entire economy as a successful system, an imaginary machine that worked. He mentioned the "invisible hand" only once in his five-volume work, but its presence is often felt. Smith described how his system of "perfect liberty" could have positive outcomes. First, it provides the goods that people want. If demand for a product exceeds its supply, consumers compete with each other to bid the price up. This creates a profit opportunity for producers, who compete with each other to supply more of the product.

This argument has stood the test of time. In an essay in 1945, titled *The Use of Knowledge in Society*, the Austrian economist Friedrich Hayek (p.105) showed how prices respond to individuals' localized knowledge and desires, leading to changes in the amounts demanded and supplied in the market. A central planner, Hayek said,

could not hope to gather up so much dispersed information. It is widely believed that communism collapsed in Eastern Europe because central planning failed to deliver the goods that people wanted. Some criticisms of Smith's first point have been raised, such as the fact that the market might only provide the goods that are wanted by the rich; it ignores the desires of the poor. It also responds to harmful desires – the market can feed drug addiction and promote obesity.

Fair prices

Second, Smith said that the market system generates prices that are "fair". He believed that all goods have a natural price that reflects only the efforts that went into making them. The land used in making a product should earn its natural rent. The capital used in its manufacture should earn its natural profit. The labour used should earn its natural wage. Market prices and rates of return can differ from their natural levels for periods of time, as might happen in times of scarcity. In that case, opportunities for gain will arise and prices will increase, but only until competition brings new firms into the market and prices fall back to their natural level. If one industry begins to suffer a slump in demand, prices will drop and wages will fall, but as a different industry rises, it will offer higher wages to attract workers. In the long run, Smith says, "market" and "natural" rates will be the same: modern economists call this equilibrium.

Competition is essential if prices are to be fair. Smith attacked the monopolies occurring under the mercantilist system, which demanded that governments should control foreign trade. When there is only one supplier of a good, the

Smith described the ways in which labour, landowners, and capital (here invested in the horses and plough) work together to keep the economic system moving and growing.

Demand in a market can change for many reasons. As it does so, the market responds by altering supply. This happens spontaneously – there is no need for a guiding hand or plan in a market that encourages competition among self-interested people.

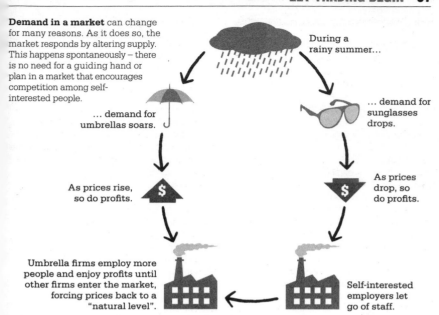

During a rainy summer...

... demand for umbrellas soars.

... demand for sunglasses drops.

As prices rise, so do profits.

As prices drop, so do profits.

Umbrella firms employ more people and enjoy profits until other firms enter the market, forcing prices back to a "natural level".

Self-interested employers let go of staff.

Staff go to work in the booming umbrella business.

firm that supplies it can permanently hold the price above its natural level. Smith said that if there are 20 grocers selling a product, the market is more competitive than if there are just two. With effective competition and low barriers to entry into a market – which Smith also said was essential – prices tend to be lower. Much of this underlies mainstream economists' views about competition, although dissenters, such as Austrian-American economist Joseph Schumpeter (p.91), would later say that innovation can also lower prices, even where there appears to be little competition. As inventors come forward to provide higher quality products at lower prices, they blow away existing firms in a storm of creative destruction.

Fair incomes

Smith also argued that market economies provide incomes that are fair and can be spent on goods in a sustainable "circular flow", in which money paid in wages circulates back into the economy when the worker pays for goods, only to be paid back out in wages to repeat the process. Capital invested in production facilities helps to increase labour productivity, which means that employers can afford to pay higher wages. And if employers can afford to pay more, they will, because they have to compete with each other for workers.

Turning to capital, Smith said that the amount of profit that capital can expect to earn through investments is roughly equal to the rate of interest. This is because employers compete with each other to borrow funds to invest in profitable opportunities. Over time, the rate of profit in any particular field falls, as capital accumulates and opportunities for profit are exhausted. Rents gradually rise as incomes rise and more land is used.

Smith's realization of the interdependence of land, labour, and capital was a real breakthrough. He noted that workers and landowners tend to consume their incomes, while »

> There is no art which one government sooner learns of another than that of draining money from the pockets of the people.
> **Adam Smith**

employers are more frugal, investing their savings in capital stock. He saw that wage rates vary, depending on different levels of "skill, dexterity, and judgement", and that there are two forms of labour: productive (engaged in agriculture or manufacturing) and what he called "unproductive" (supplying services needed to back up the main work). The highly unequal outcomes of today's market system are some way from what Smith envisaged.

Economic growth

Smith claimed that the invisible hand itself stimulates economic growth. The source of growth is two-fold. One is the efficiencies gained through the division of labour (pp.42–43). Economists call this "Smithian growth". As more products are produced and consumed, the economy grows, and markets also grow. As markets grow, there are more opportunities for specialization of work.

The second engine of growth is the accumulation of capital, driven by saving and the opportunity for profit. Smith said that growth can be reduced by commercial failures, a lack of resources required to maintain the fixed capital stock, an inadequate money system (there is more growth with paper money than with gold), and a high proportion of unproductive workers. He claimed that capital is more productive in agriculture than in manufacturing, which is higher than in trade or transport. Ultimately, the economy will grow until it reaches a wealthy, stationary state. In this, Smith underestimated the role of technology and innovation – the Schumpeterian growth described earlier (p.37).

Classical legacy

Smith's system was comprehensive. It considered small (microeconomic) details and the large (macroeconomic) picture. It looked at situations in both the short and long run, and its analysis was both static (the state of trade) and dynamic (the economy in motion). It looked in detail at the class known as workers, distinguishing entrepreneurs such as farmers and factory owners from suppliers of labour. In essence, it established the parameters for "classical" economics, which focuses on the factors of production – capital, labour, and land – and their returns. Later, free-market theory took a different, "neoclassical" form with general equilibrium theory, which sought to show how a whole economy's prices could reach a state of stable equilibrium. Using mathematics, economists such as Léon Walras (p.77) and Vilfredo Pareto (p.81) reframed Smith's claim that the invisible hand would be socially beneficial. Kenneth Arrow and Gérard Debreu (pp.122–25) showed how free markets do this, but they also showed that the conditions needed were stringent and did not bear much relation to reality.

This was not the end of the story. After World War II, the idea of laissez-faire was in hibernation. However, from the 1970s, Keynesian policies, which advocated state intervention in economies, seemed to break down, and laissez-faire enjoyed a strong resurgence. The seeds of this flowering can be found in works on the

Localized markets such as this one in Kerala, India, exhibit all the hallmarks of Smith's free market, and demonstrate the natural way in which supply and price adjust to demand.

Smith didn't foresee the kinds of inequalities that can arise from free markets in their present form. In stock exchanges and money markets, notions of "fairness" become almost irrelevant.

market economy by Milton Friedman (p.117) and the Austrian School, notably Friedrich Hayek (p.105), who were sceptical about the good that interfering governments can do and argued that social progress would be attained through unfettered markets. Keynesians, too, recognized the power of markets – but for them, markets needed to be nudged to work best.

The free-market approach enjoyed an important boost from theories in the 1960s and 70s based on the role of rationality and rational expectations. Public choice theory, for example, depicts government as a group of self-seeking individuals, who maximize their own interests and extract money without regard to the social good ("rent-seeking"). New classical macroeconomics uses Smith's assumption that markets always sort themselves out, and adds the point that people can see the future implications of any government actions and understand the workings of the economic system, so state intervention will not work. Even so, most economists today believe that the market can fail. They focus on disparities in information, held by various participants in a market. George Akerlof referred to this in his *The Market for Lemons*. Behavioural economists have questioned the whole notion of rationality, and see the non-rationality of humans as a reason for markets to fail.

The issue of laissez-faire economics divides economists along political lines. Those on the political Right embrace laissez-faire; those from the Left align themselves with Keynesian intervention. This remains a central debate in economics today.

The financial crisis of 2007–08 has added fuel to this dispute. The free-marketeers felt vindicated in their theories about the business cycle, while Keynesians pointed to market failure. US economist Nouriel Roubini (1959–), who predicted the crash, was speaking of those who had distorted Smith's ideas when he said that "decades of free-market fundamentalism laid the foundation for the meltdown". ∎

Adam Smith

The founder of modern economics, Adam Smith was born in Kirkcaldy, Scotland, in 1723, six months after his father's death. An absent-minded, reclusive scholar, he went to Glasgow University at the age of 14, then studied at Oxford University for six years before returning to Scotland to take up a professorship in logic at Glasgow University. In 1750, he met and became close friends with the philosopher David Hume.

In 1764, Smith resigned his post at Glasgow to travel to France as tutor to the Duke of Buccleuch, a Scottish aristocrat. In France, he met the physiocrat group of economists (pp.26–29) and the philosopher Voltaire, and he began writing *The Wealth of Nations*. He devoted 10 years to the book before accepting a position as Commissioner of Customs. He died in 1790.

Key works

1759 *The Theory of Moral Sentiments*
1762 *Lectures on Jurisprudence*
1776 *An Inquiry into the Nature and Causes of the Wealth of Nations*

MAKE TAXES FAIR AND EFFICIENT

THE TAX BURDEN

IN CONTEXT

FOCUS
Economic policy

KEY THINKER
Anne-Robert-Jacques Turgot
(1727–81)

BEFORE
1689–1763 Expensive wars, together with an inefficient tax system that exempted landowners and guilds, lays the ground for French financial crisis and the Revolution.

AFTER
1817 In his *Principles of Political Economy and Taxation*, British economist David Ricardo argues that taxes should fall on luxuries.

1927 British mathematician Frank Ramsay emphasizes the importance of price-elasticity.

1976 Economists Anthony Atkinson and Joseph Stiglitz suggest uniform commodity taxes are optimal in *The Design of Tax Structure*.

Who bears the burden of tax? The key question of "tax incidence" intrigued the gifted economist Anne-Robert-Jacques Turgot, who was the French Minister of Finance from 1774–76. The question is not as simple as "who should pay tax?" because taxes affect many things, from prices and profits to amounts of goods consumed and incomes received. Changes in these can ripple through the economy in surprising ways. The "burden" of a tax – which is taken to mean a decrease in happiness, welfare, or money – can be shifted from one person or group to another. If you are planning a holiday, and a new fuel tax puts the airfare above the level you are prepared to pay, the tax has made you unhappy. The new fuel tax has reduced your welfare, but not necessarily the airline company's profits.

Who should pay taxes?

Turgot argued that taxes interfere with the free market and should be simplified. Powerful groups should not be exempt from taxation, and the details of its implementation matter. His recommendation was for a single tax on a country's net product – the value of its total goods and services minus depreciation.

His thinking was influenced by an early school of economists known as the physiocrats, who believed that only agriculture (land) produces a surplus. Other industries do not produce a surplus, and so cannot afford to pay tax – they will always try to pass it on by increasing prices and charges until finally it reaches the landowners. As farmers pay much of their surplus in rent to landowners, who produce nothing, Turgot argued that the landowners should be taxed on the rent they charged.

Later economists refined the principles of fairness and efficiency that go into an optimal tax system. Fairness includes the idea that those most able to pay should pay the most; that similar people should face

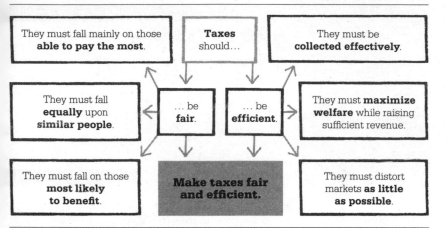

| They must fall mainly on those **able to pay the most**. | **Taxes** should… | They must be **collected effectively**. |

They must fall **equally** upon **similar people**. ← … be **fair**. … be **efficient**. → They must **maximize welfare** while raising sufficient revenue.

They must fall on those **most likely to benefit**. **Make taxes fair and efficient.** They must distort markets **as little as possible**.

similar taxes; and that those who benefit from government spending, such as users of a new bridge, should contribute to it. Efficiency means both effectiveness in collection, and maximizing society's welfare while raising the required revenue. Economists argue that efficiency means disturbing the market as little as possible, particularly to avoid blunting incentives for work and investment.

Perfect tax design
The last few decades have seen huge strides in the sophistication of tax design, integrating both fairness and efficiency.

"Perfect markets" theory, for example, suggests commodity taxes should be uniform and apply only to "final" goods (for sale to final users); income taxes should be linked to ability rather than income; and taxes on company profits and income from capital should be minimal. "Market failure" analysis, on the other hand, suggests that taxes on undesirables such as pollution increase people's welfare.

In general, tax policies have moved in the directions shown by such theories, while paying attention to revenue and political acceptability. ∎

Anne-Robert-Jacques Turgot

Born in Paris, France, in 1727, Turgot was destined for the priesthood until an

inheritance in 1751 allowed him to pursue a career in administration. By the late 1760s, he had become friendly with the physiocrats, and later met Adam Smith. From 1761 to 1774 he was the *Intendant* of Limoges, a regional administrator. On the accession of Louis XVI in 1774, Turgot became Minister of Finance, and set about making reforms that encouraged free trade. In 1776, he abolished the guilds and ended a government policy that used unpaid, forced

labour to build roads by instituting a road-building tax instead. Louis XVI did not approve and dismissed Turgot from office. His reforms – which some felt might have averted the French Revolution of 1789 – were overturned. He died aged 54 in 1781.

Key works

1763 *Taxation in General*
1766 *Reflections on the Production and Distribution of Wealth*
1776 *The Six Edicts*

DIVIDE UP PIN PRODUCTION, AND YOU GET MORE PINS
THE DIVISION OF LABOUR

IN CONTEXT

FOCUS
Markets and firms

KEY THINKER
Adam Smith (1723–90)

BEFORE
380 BCE In *The Republic*, the Greek philosopher Plato explains how a city emerges, then grows by exploiting the gains made by dividing labour.

1705 Dutch philosopher Bernard Mandeville coins the term "division of labour" in his *The Fable of the Bees*.

AFTER
1867 Karl Marx argues that division of labour alienates workers and is a necessary evil that will eventually be superseded.

1922 Austrian economist Ludwig von Mises argues that division of labour is not alienating but brings huge benefits, including greater leisure time.

In a busy stockroom, labour may be divided between porters, inventory keepers, a manager, accountants, distribution specialists, IT workers, and truck drivers.

Whenever people work in a group, they invariably start by deciding who is going to do what. It was the great Adam Smith (p.39) who turned this division of labour into a central economic idea. At the very start of his influential book *The Wealth of Nations*, Smith explains the differences between production when one person carries out the full sequence required to make something,

and when several people each do just one task each. Writing in 1776, Smith noted that if one man set about making a pin, going through the many steps involved, he might make "perhaps not one pin in a day". But by dividing the process among several men, with each specializing in a single step, many pins could be made in a day. Smith concluded that the division of labour causes "in every art, a proportionable increase of the productive powers of labour".

The engine of growth
Smith was not the first to appreciate the value of the division of labour. About 2,200 years earlier, Plato had argued that a state needs specialists, such as farmers and builders, to supply its needs. The Islamic philosopher Al-Ghazali (1058–1111) noted that if we take into account every step involved in making bread, from clearing

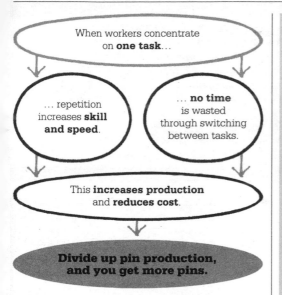

When workers concentrate on **one task**...

... repetition increases **skill and speed**.

... **no time** is wasted through switching between tasks.

This **increases production** and **reduces cost**.

Divide up pin production, and you get more pins.

the weeds in the fields, to harvesting the wheat, we would find that the loaf takes its final form with the help of over a thousand workers.

Many early thinkers linked division of labour to the growth of cities and markets. Some thought that the division of labour caused the growth, while others proposed that the growing cities allowed the division of labour.

What was ground-breaking about Smith's idea was that he put division of labour at the heart of the economic system, insisting that it is the engine that drives growth. The more specialized the workers and businesses, the greater the market growth and the higher the returns on investments.

A necessary evil

Karl Marx (p.68) saw the power of this idea but believed that the division of labour was a temporary, necessary evil. Specialization alienates, condemning workers to the dispiriting condition of a machine performing repetitive tasks. He distinguished between the technical division of labour, such as each specialized task in house building, and social division, which is enforced by hierarchies of power and status.

Labour division is the norm within most companies today. Many large corporations now outsource tasks formerly carried out by their own staff to cheaper overseas workers, giving the division of labour a new, international dimension. ∎

All-American jobs?

When people working in industry worry about the strength of their home economy and rates of employment, they sometimes urge consumers to buy home-produced goods. However, it can be hard to know what is home-produced, as division of labour has now become global in scope. For example, Apple is a US company, so consumers might suppose that by buying an iPhone they are contributing to US jobs. In fact, of all the processes involved in making an iPhone, only the product and software design and marketing occur primarily in the USA.

Each iPhone is assembled by workers in China, using parts – such as the case, screen, and processor – made by workers in South Korea, Japan, Germany, and six other countries. In addition, each of these parts has been assembled by a range of specialists around the world. The iPhone is a truly global product, made by perhaps tens of thousands of people.

Assembly-line workers in China build computer processors with components made in up to nine different countries.

POPULATION GROWTH KEEPS US POOR
DEMOGRAPHICS AND ECONOMICS

IN CONTEXT

FOCUS
Growth and development

KEY THINKER
Thomas Malthus (1766–1834)

BEFORE
17th century Mercantilist thought argues that a large populace benefits the economy.

1785 French philosopher Marquis de Condorcet argues for social reform to raise living standards.

1793 English philosopher William Godwin advocates the redistribution of national resources to help the poor.

AFTER
1870s Karl Marx attacks Malthus's ideas, characterizing him as a reactionary defender of the status quo.

1968 US ecologist Garrett Hardin warns of the dangers of over-population in his essay *The Tragedy of the Commons*.

D uring the 18th century, enlightened thinkers began to consider the possibility of improving society's lot through wise social and economic reforms. The British economist Thomas Malthus was a pessimistic voice in this optimistic era, claiming that the growth of populations dooms societies to poverty. Malthus argued that the human sex drive causes faster and faster expansion of the populace. Food production would not keep up because of the law of diminishing returns: as more people work on a fixed amount of land, less and less output is added. The result is an ever-widening imbalance between the number of people and the supply of food.

However, there is a counteracting force. Malthus saw that malnutrition and disease caused by a more limited food supply would lead to increased mortality and stop the imbalance from getting out of control. Less food to go around would also mean fewer children could be supported, and the birth rate would fall. This would lessen the pressure on land, restoring living standards.

The Malthusian trap

As well as preventing total starvation, changes in birth and death rates stop the population from benefitting from higher living standards for very long. Suppose that the economy has a windfall through the discovery of land. Extra land gives a one-off boost to food production, and allows more food per person. People become healthier and the death rate falls. Higher living standards allow for more children. Together, these forces add to population growth. Food production cannot keep up, and the economy reverts to the original, lower level of living standards. This is called the Malthusian trap: higher living standards are always choked off by population growth. So whatever

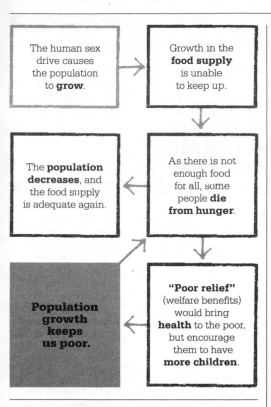

The human sex drive causes the population to **grow**.

Growth in the **food supply** is unable to keep up.

As there is not enough food for all, some people **die from hunger**.

The **population decreases**, and the food supply is adequate again.

"Poor relief" (welfare benefits) would bring **health** to the poor, but encourage them to have **more children**.

Population growth keeps us poor.

Thomas Malthus

Thomas Robert Malthus was born in Surrey, England, in 1766, and was given a liberal education by his father, a country squire. His godfathers were the philosophers David Hume and Jean-Jacques Rousseau. He was born with a hare lip and cleft palate and suffered a speech defect.

At Cambridge University, Malthus was tutuored by a religious dissenter, William Frend, before being ordained into the Church of England in 1788. Like his teacher, he never shied away from controversy. In 1798, he published his *Essay on the Principle of Population*, the work that would bring him notoriety. In 1805, the new East India College appointed him Professor of Political Economy, a subject not yet taught at universities, which perhaps makes him the first academic economist. Malthus died of heart disease in 1834, aged 68.

Key works

1798 *An Essay on the Principle of Population*
1815 *The Nature of Rent*
1820 *Principles of Political Economy*

happens, the economy always reverts to the level of food output that is just enough to support a stable population.

Malthus's vision was one of economic stagnation, with the population eking out a living and its growth being checked by hunger and disease. However, his model – an economy of farmers toiling with simple tools on a fixed amount of land – was already out of step with the times by the turn of the 18th century. New techniques allowed more food to be produced from the same amount of land and labour. New machines and factories allowed more goods to be produced per worker. Technological progress meant that growing populations enjoyed ever-higher living standards. By 2000, Britain had more than three times the population of Malthus's time, with incomes 10 times higher.

Over time, technology has overcome the constraints of land and demographics. Malthus did not foresee this. Today, his ideas are echoed in fears that population levels are pushing against the capacity of the Earth in ways that new technology cannot offset. ∎

MEETINGS OF MERCHANTS END IN CONSPIRACIES TO RAISE PRICES
CARTELS AND COLLUSION

IN CONTEXT

FOCUS
Markets and firms

KEY THINKER
Adam Smith (1723–90)

BEFORE
1290s Wenceslas II, Duke of Bohemia, introduces laws to prevent metal ore traders colluding to raise prices.

1590s Traders from the Netherlands collaborate in a cartel with a monopoly of the spice trade in the East Indies.

AFTER
1838 French economist Augustin Cournot describes competition in oligopolies.

1890 The first antitrust law is passed in the USA.

1964 US economist George Stigler publishes *A Theory of Oligopoly*, examining the problems of maintaining successful cartels.

Competition is key to the efficient working of free markets. The presence of several producers in a market drives production and keeps prices down, as each competes to attract customers. If there is only a single supplier – a monopoly – it can choose to restrict its output and charge higher prices.

Between these two extremes sits the oligopoly, where a few suppliers – sometimes only two or three – dominate the market for a particular product. Competition between producers in an oligopoly would clearly be in the interests of the consumer, but there is an alternative for the producers that may be more beneficial to their profit levels: cooperation. If they choose this route, and can agree not to undercut one another, they can act collectively like a monopoly, and dictate the terms of the market to their own benefit.

Forming cartels

This sort of cooperation between firms is known by economists as "collusion". The price fixing that results makes markets less efficient. Scottish economist Adam Smith (p.39) recognized the importance of self-interest in free markets but was suspicious enough of the motives of suppliers to warn: "People of the same trade seldom meet together, even for merriment and diversion, but the conversation ends in a conspiracy against the public, or in some contrivance to raise prices."

Collaborations between producers have existed for as long as there have been markets, and businesses in many areas of commerce have formed associations to their mutual benefit. In the USA in the 19th century, these restrictive or monopolistic practices were known as "trusts", but the word "cartel" is now used to describe such collaborations, which operate on a national or international level. The word has gained a negative connotation despite being a notable feature of the German and US economies in the 1920s and 1930s.

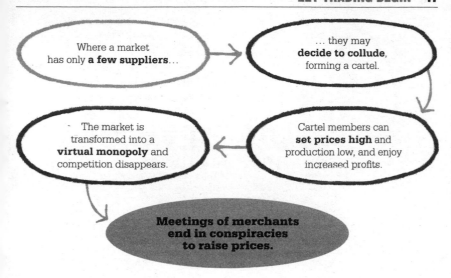

Where a market has only **a few suppliers**... → ... they may **decide to collude**, forming a cartel.

The market is transformed into a **virtual monopoly** and competition disappears. ← Cartel members can **set prices high** and production low, and enjoy increased profits.

Meetings of merchants end in conspiracies to raise prices.

In the 20th century, the USA and the European Union (EU) used legislation to discourage collusion. However, cartels among producers remain a feature of market economies. Collaborations might be a simple agreement between two firms, such as when Unilever and Procter & Gamble colluded to fix the price of washing powder in Europe in 2011, or they can take the form of an international trade association, such as the International Air Transport Association (IATA). The IATA's original function was to set prices for fares, which led to accusations of collusion, but it still exists as a representative organization for the airline industry. Cartels can even be formed through cooperation between governments of countries producing a particular commodity, as happened in the case of the Organization of Petroleum Exporting Countries (OPEC), which was founded in 1960 to coordinate petrol prices among member countries.

Challenges for cartels

However, there are problems in setting up and sustaining a cartel, which focus around prices and trust between members. Participants in a cartel cannot simply fix prices. They also have to agree on output quotas to maintain those prices and, of course, the share of the profits. The fewer the members of a cartel, the easier these negotiations are. Cartels are more robust when there are a small number of firms accounting for most of the supply.

The second problem is to ensure that members of a cartel abide by the rules. Producers are attracted to collusion by the prospect of higher prices, but this self-interest is also the weakness of the arrangement. Individual members of a »

British Airways was fined more than £300 million for collusion in 2007, after Virgin Atlantic admitted that the two companies had met six times to discuss proposed price rises.

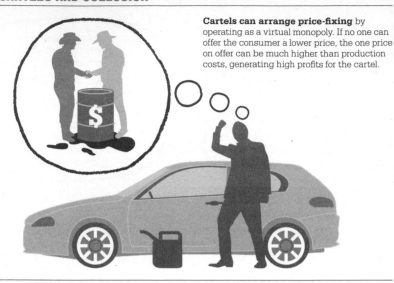

Cartels can arrange price-fixing by operating as a virtual monopoly. If no one can offer the consumer a lower price, the one price on offer can be much higher than production costs, generating high profits for the cartel.

cartel may be tempted to "cheat" by over-producing and undercutting their collaborators. In effect, this is a version of the prisoner's dilemma (p.140), in which two prisoners can each choose either to remain silent or confess. If both remain silent or both confess, they will receive light sentences; but if only one confesses, he will receive immunity while his partner in crime will get a heavy sentence. The best strategy for each of them is to remain silent (this incurs the shortest jail term), but the temptation is to opt for immunity and confess in the hope that the other does not. The strategies that apply here are equally applicable to cartels, where the rewards for all the players are greater if they collaborate than if they compete, but are greatest for any one player who breaks the agreement, while the others suffer as a consequence.

In practice, this is what tends to happen within a cartel, particularly when the quotas are unequally divided. The 12 members of OPEC, for example, meet regularly to agree on output and prices, but these are seldom adhered to. The smaller, less wealthy members see the chance of gaining some extra profit and exceed their output quota, introducing an element of competitiveness and weakening the power of the cartel as a

whole. It only takes one cheat to undermine the operation of a cartel, and the more members in the cartel, the greater the danger of the rules being broken.

Enforcing agreements

Very often, one of a cartel's members – the most powerful in terms of production – emerges as an "enforcer". When the efficacy of OPEC becomes threatened, for instance, by a country such as Angola over-producing to increase its profits, Saudi Arabia, the largest member of the cartel, can take action to stop this. As the largest producer with the lowest production costs, it can afford to increase production and lower prices to a level that will punish or may even bankrupt the smaller countries, while only lowering its own profits in the short term. However, in many cases, the temptation to cheat and the reluctance of the enforcer to reduce its profits eventually lead to the break-up of cartels.

The difficulty in forming and maintaining cartels means that these "conspiracies" are less common than Adam Smith might have expected. In the 1960s, US economist George Stigler showed that the natural suspicion of competitors acts against collusion in a cartel, and that cartels are less likely to occur as more firms enter a market. As a result, even in industries where there are only a few large producers, such as for video games consoles and mobile phones, the preference is generally for competition rather than cooperation.

Nevertheless, the few cartels that do exist pose enough of a threat to the market for governments to feel the need to intervene. Public pressure from consumers opposed to price-fixing drove the move to "antitrust" legislation (see below) during the 20th century, outlawing cartels in most countries. Because of the difficulty of proving collusion, many of these laws offer immunity to the first member of a cartel to confess – just as in the prisoner's dilemma – offering yet another incentive to break up the cartel. This tactic was notably successful in 2007, when Virgin Atlantic Airlines, worried by an investigation into price-fixing of Atlantic flights, confessed its collusion with British Airways, who were heavily fined.

Government approval

Some libertarian economists, such as Stigler, are sceptical of the need for such laws, given the instability of cartels. Governments are often ambiguous about cartels, seeing some forms of

 Economists have their glories, but I do not believe that antitrust law is one of them.
George Stigler

cooperation as potentially desirable. For example, while IATA's price-setting policy was considered collusion, OPEC has sometimes been seen in a more benign light as a trade bloc whose policies lead to stability. The same argument has been put forward in defence of public cartels in certain industries, such as oil or steel, in countries during times of depression. When regulated by governments, cooperation between producers can stabilize production and prices, protect the consumer and smaller producers, and make the industry as a whole more competitive internationally. Public cartels such as these were common in both Europe and the USA during the 1920s and 1930s, but mostly disappeared after World War II. National cartels are still a feature of the Japanese economy. ∎

Antitrust laws

Cartels, like monopolies, are generally seen as harmful to the efficiency of free markets and a threat to overall economic well-being. Most governments have attempted to prevent this kind of collusion by legislation in the form of antitrust or competition laws. The first such intervention was in the USA in 1890, when the Sherman Act outlawed every contract or conspiracy that restrained interstate or foreign trade. This was followed by further antitrust laws including the Clayton Act in 1914,

which prohibited local price cutting to "freeze out" competition. Economists have tended to be sceptical about antitrust legislation, which is, in any case, often difficult to enforce. They point out that cooperation does not always lead to collusive practices, such as price-fixing and bid-rigging, and many believe that much "trust-busting" legislation has been motivated by political pressure rather than economic analysis.

This 1906 cover of a political paper lampoons US politician Nelson Aldrich for building a "web" of tariffs to protect US goods from foreign competition and raise local prices.

SUPPLY CREATES ITS OWN DEMAND
GLUTS IN MARKETS

IN CONTEXT

FOCUS
The macroeconomy

KEY THINKER
Jean-Baptiste Say (1767–1832)

BEFORE
1820 British economist Thomas Malthus argues that under-employment and over-production can occur.

AFTER
1936 John Maynard Keynes states that supply does not create its own demand – it is possible for a lack of demand to cause production to slow, creating unemployment.

1950 Austrian economist Ludwig von Mises argues that Keynes's denial is at the basis of Keynesian fallacies about economics.

2010 Australian economist Steven Kates defends Say's law, and calls Keynesian economics a "conceptual disease".

People produce commodities and sell them **to earn money**.

↓

Nobody wants to hold on to money because it **falls in value**, so...

↓

... people swap money for the **other products** they want.

↓

Supply creates its own demand.

I n 1776, when Adam Smith wrote *The Wealth of Nations* (pp.34–39), he noted that merchants around him commonly felt there were two reasons why business failed: a scarcity of money or over-production. He debunked the first of these myths by explaining the role of money in an economy, but it was left to a later French economist, Jean-Baptiste Say, to dismiss the second. His 1803 work, *A Treatise on Political Economy*, is devoted to explaining the impossibility of over-production. Say claimed that as soon as a product is made, it creates a market for other products "to the full extent of its own value." This means, for example, that the money a tailor receives when he makes and sells a shirt is then used to buy bread from the baker and beer from the brewer. Say believed that people had no desire to hoard money, and therefore the total value of commodities supplied would equal the total value of goods demanded. The common expression of what is known as Say's law has become "supply creates its own demand". In fact, Say never used this phrase; it was probably coined in 1921 by the US economist Fred Taylor in his *Principles of Economics*.

The idea was important to Say because if supply creates an equal value of demand, there can never be over-production, or "gluts", in the economy as a whole. Of course, firms could mistake the level of demand for a commodity and over-produce, but as the Austrian-born US economist Ludwig von Mises (p.89) later said, "the bungling entrepreneur" would soon be driven from that market by losses, and the unemployed resources would be reallocated to more profitable areas of the economy. In fact, it is impossible to over-produce overall, because human wants are far greater than our ability to produce commodities.

Say's law has become a forum for conflict between the classical and the Keynesian economists. The former, such as Say, believe that production, or the supply side of the economy, is the most important factor in growing an economy. Keynesians argue that growth comes only with increased demand.

Why keep money?

In his 1936 masterpiece *The General Theory of Employment*, John Maynard Keynes (p.99) attacked Say's law, focusing on the role of money within the economy. Say had suggested that all money earned is spent on purchasing other commodities. In other words, the economy works as if it were based on a system of barter. Keynes, however, suggested that people might sometimes hold money for reasons other than for buying goods. They might, for instance, want to save some of their income. If these savings were not borrowed by others (such as through a bank) and invested in the economy (as capital for running a business, perhaps) the money would no longer be circulating. As people hold on to their money, demand for goods eventually becomes lower than the value of the goods produced. This state of "negative demand" is known as "demand deficiency", and Keynes said it would lead to pervasive unemployment.

Given the dire state of the world economy during the Great Depression of the early 1930s, Keynes's argument seemed a powerful one, especially when contrasted with a world based on Say's law, which said that unemployment would only occur in some industries, for a short time. ∎

Jean-Baptiste Say

The son of a French Protestant textile merchant, Jean-Baptiste Say was born in Lyons, France, in 1767. At the age of 18 he moved to England, where he spent two years apprenticed to a merchant before returning to Paris to work at an insurance company. He welcomed the French Revolution of 1789, both for its ending of the religious persecution of the protestant Hugenots, and for its removal of an essentially feudal economy, opening up more prospects for commerce.

In 1794, Say became editor of a political magazine in which he promoted the ideas of Adam Smith. In 1799, he was invited to join the French government, but Napoleon rejected some of his views and Say's work was censored until 1814. During this time he made a fortune by setting up a cotton factory. In his later years he lectured on economics in Paris. He died after a series of strokes in 1832, aged 66.

Key works

1803 *A Treatise on Political Economy*
1815 *England and the English*
1828 *Complete Course of Practical Political Economy*

BORROW NOW, TAX LATER

BORROWING AND DEBT

IN CONTEXT

FOCUS
Economic policy

KEY THINKER
David Ricardo (1772–1823)

BEFORE
1799 Britain introduces income tax during war with revolutionary France. Public debt approaches 250 per cent of national income.

AFTER
1945 Following World War II, government spending, taxation, and borrowing rise in developed economies to meet new welfare commitments.

1974 US economist Robert Barro revives the idea of Ricardian equivalence, which says that people spend in the same way regardless of whether their government taxes or borrows.

2011 The European debt crisis intensifies, sparking debate about the limits of taxation and public borrowing.

Should government spending be financed by **borrowing or taxation**?

↓   ↓

| If the government **borrows** now… | If the government **increases tax** now… |

↓   ↓

| … people will know that they will pay **more tax** later to repay the debt. | … people will have to **pay more tax**. |

↓   ↓

It makes no difference whether the government chooses to tax now, or "borrow now, tax later".

S hould government spending be financed by borrowing or taxation? This question was first addressed in detail by British economist David Ricardo during Britain's expensive Napoleonic wars against France (1799–1815). In his 1817

book *Principles of Political Economy and Taxation*, Ricardo argued that the method of financing should make no difference. Taxpayers ought to realize that government borrowing today will lead to more taxation in the future. In either case they will be

New classical macroeconomics

US economists Robert Barro, Robert Lucas, and Thomas Sargent formed the school of new classical macroeconomics in the early 1970s. Its key tenets are the assumption of rational expectations and market clearing – the idea that prices will spontaneously adjust to a new position of equilibrium. New classical theorists claim that this applies in the labour market: wage levels are set through the mutual adjustment of supply (number of people seeking work) and demand (number of people needed). Under this view, everyone who wants to work can, if they accept the "going wage". Therefore, all unemployment is voluntary. Rational expectations claims that people look to the future as well as the past when making decisions, so they cannot be fooled by a government when it chooses to borrow or tax.

taxed, so they should set aside savings that are equivalent to the amount they would have been taxed today in order to meet that eventuality. Ricardo suggested that people understand a government's budget constraints and continue to spend in the same way regardless of its decision to tax or borrow, because they know these will ultimately cost them the same. This idea became known as Ricardian equivalence.

Imagine a family with a gambling father who resorts to taking money from his sons. The father tells his sons that he will let them keep their money this month, because he has borrowed from his friend Alex. The happy-go-lucky younger son, Tom, spends his extra cash. The wise older son, James, realizes that next month, Alex's loan will have to be repaid with interest, at which point his father will probably ask him for money. James hides away today's extra cash, knowing he will have to give it to his father in a month. James has recognized that his overall wealth hasn't changed, so he has no reason to alter his spending today.

Ricardo was theorizing, and did not suggest that Ricardian equivalence would ever be apparent in the real world. He believed that ordinary citizens suffer from the same fiscal illusion as Tom in our example, and will spend the money on hand. However, some modern economists argue that citizens suffer no such illusions.

The modern debate

The idea re-emerged in an article by US economist Robert Barro (1944–) in 1974, and modern analysis has focused on examining the conditions under which people spend regardless of taxation or borrowing. One assumption is that people are rational decision-makers and have perfect foresight; they know that spending now means taxes later. However, this is unlikely to be the case. Borrowing and lending must also take place at identical interest rates, without transaction costs.

A further problem is that human life is finite. If people are self-interested, they are unlikely to care about taxes that will be imposed after they die. Barro suggested, however, that parents care about their children and often leave bequests, partly so that their children can pay any tax liabilities that arise after the parents' deaths. In this way, individuals factor into their decision-making the impact of taxes that they expect to be imposed even after they die.

Government spending

Ricardian equivalence, which is sometimes known as debt neutrality, is a hot topic today because of the high spending, borrowing, and taxation of modern governments. Ricardo's insight has been used by new classical economists to argue against Keynesian policies – government spending to increase demand and drive growth. They claim that if people know that a government is spending money to lift an economy out of depression, their rational expectations will ensure they anticipate greater taxes in the future, so they will not blindly respond to the increased amount of money in the system now. However, the practical evidence – for or against – is inconclusive. ∎

THE ECONOMY IS A YO-YO

BOOM AND BUST

IN CONTEXT

FOCUS
The macroeconomy

KEY THINKER
Jean-Charles Sismondi (1773–1842)

BEFORE
1776 Adam Smith argues that natural market forces create an economic equilibrium.

1803 Jean-Baptiste Say claims that the market will balance supply and demand naturally.

1817 Welsh social reformer Robert Owen identifies over-production and under-consumption as the causes of economic downturns.

AFTER
1820s French economist Charles Dunoyer identifies the cyclical nature of the economy.

1936 John Maynard Keynes urges governments to spend in order to avoid economic fluctuations.

Skyscrapers are often built during times of excessive optimism, a sure sign that the economy is overheating. By the time they are finished, the economy has often crashed.

Business cycles are the shift between strong economic growth, described as a boom or expansion period, and periods of economic decline or stagnation. They are often referred to as cycles of boom and bust. The Swiss historian Jean-Charles Sismondi was the first to identify the occurrence of periodic economic crises, but it was the work of a later economist, the Frenchman Charles Dunoyer (1786–1862) who revealed their cyclical form. Sismondi challenged the "market knows best" orthodoxy of Adam Smith (p.39), Jean-Baptiste Say (p.51), and David Ricardo (p.57). They believed that if the market is left to its own devices, an economic equilibrium is quickly and easily achieved, leading to full employment. Sismondi thought a sort of equilibrium would eventually be reached, but only after a "frightful amount of suffering."

Before Sismondi published his *New Principles of Political Economy* in 1819, economists had either overlooked short-term economic booms and busts or had attributed them to external events, such as war. Sismondi showed that short-term economic movements are due to the natural results of market forces – over-production and under-consumption – caused by growing inequality during boom times.

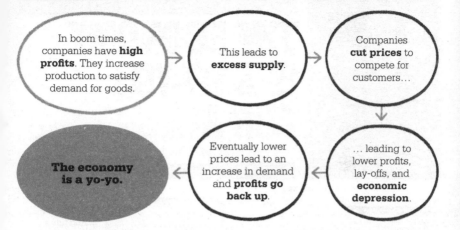

In boom times, companies have **high profits**. They increase production to satisfy demand for goods.

This leads to **excess supply**.

Companies **cut prices** to compete for customers…

… leading to lower profits, lay-offs, and **economic depression**.

Eventually lower prices lead to an increase in demand and **profits go back up**.

The economy is a yo-yo.

Fuelling the boom

As economies grow and businesses do well, workers are able to demand wage rises and buy more of the goods they produce. This fuels the economy's boom. As more and more goods are sold, companies expand, hiring more workers to produce more goods. The new workers then have money to buy goods and the boom continues.

Competition means that all companies will increase production until supply finally outstrips demand, Sismondi argued. This forces companies to cut prices in order to attract custom, triggering falling profits, falling wages, and lay-offs among the workforce – in other words, an economic crash followed by a recession. Companies begin to recover once prices become cheap enough to stimulate demand and credit becomes more available, starting the cycle all over again.

An early crisis that confirmed these economic cycles was the Panic of 1825. This stock-market crash was one of the first documented crises caused solely by internal economic events. It was precipitated by speculative investments in Poyais – a fictional country invented by a con man to attract investments – and the repercussions were felt in markets across the world.

Sismondi argued against the laissez-faire approach of Adam Smith and claimed that government intervention is necessary to regulate the progress of wealth and avoid these periodic crises.

The discovery of these cycles enabled economists to analyse the economy in a new way, and to devise strategies for trying to avoid crashes and recessions. Keynes built on Sismondi's and Dunoyer's work to develop his own theories, which were to make up one of the world's dominant economic approaches in the 20th century. ∎

Bull and bear markets

As whole economies grow and contract, markets within them rise and fall. Markets that show sustained price rises are sometimes known as bull markets; those in which prices are falling as bear markets. These labels are usually applied to assets such as shares, bonds, or houses. Bull markets – for example, a rising stock market – often occur during periods of economic growth. Investors become more optimistic about economic prospects and buy shares in companies, so fuelling rising asset values. As the economy falters, the process goes into reverse. Investors become "bearish" and start to sell assets as the market falls. US stocks were in a bull market in the 1990s with the dot-com boom. A major bear market took place during the Great Depression of the 1930s.

TRADE IS BENEFICIAL FOR ALL
COMPARATIVE ADVANTAGE

IN CONTEXT

FOCUS
Global economy

KEY THINKER
David Ricardo (1772–1823)

BEFORE
433 BCE The Athenians impose trade sanctions on the Megarians, in one of the first recorded trade wars.

1549 John Hales, an English politician, expresses the widely held view that free trade is bad for the country.

AFTER
1965 US economist Mancur Olson shows that governments respond more to the appeal of a concentrated group than one that is more dispersed.

1967 Swedish economists Bertil Ohlin and Eli Heckscher develop Ricardo's trade theory to examine how a comparative advantage might change over time.

The ideas of the renowned 18th-century British economist David Ricardo were clearly shaped by the world he inhabited and by his personal life. He lived in London, England, at a time when mercantilism (pp.22–23) was the dominant economic view. This held that international trade should be heavily restricted. As a result, governments introduced policies that aimed to increase exports and decrease imports, in an attempt to enrich the nation through an inflow of gold. In England, the policy dated back to Elizabethan times. Ricardo thought that in the long run such protectionist policies were more likely to restrict the ability of the country to increase its wealth.

Early trade protection

Ricardo was particularly concerned by the introduction of a British tax known as the Corn Laws. During the Napoleonic Wars (1799–1815) it was not possible to import wheat from Europe so the price of wheat in Britain had risen. As a result of this price increase, many landowners increased the proportion of their lands dedicated to growing crops. However, as the war began to falter in 1812, the price of wheat fell back. As a result, the landowners – who also controlled Parliament – passed the Corn Laws at the end of the war in 1815 to restrict the importation of foreign wheat and place a "floor," a bottom price, on grain.

The laws protected farmers but also pushed the price of bread beyond what poorer people could pay at a time when newly returned soldiers and sailors were unable to find work.

Ricardo vigorously opposed the Corn Laws, despite being a wealthy landowner himself. He claimed that the laws would make Britain poorer, and developed a theory that has become the mainstay for all those wishing to justify free trade between countries.

Making a product **entails costs**.
One of these costs is time.

↓

Even if Country A can do everything better than Country B, it will profit most by **focusing on the things it does best**. It is too costly to sacrifice time on something it does less well.

↓

This allows Country B, which is good (but not the world's best) at making the products Country A does not make, a chance to make them **without undue competition**.

↓

Both countries benefit from a comparative advantage, which makes the most efficient use of their time and resources.

↓

Overall, **more goods are produced**, giving consumers a wider range of products at lower prices.

↓

Trade is beneficial for all.

Comparative advantage

Adam Smith (p.39) had pointed out that the climate differences between Portugal and Britain meant they would benefit from trade. A worker in Portugal could produce more wine than a worker in Britain, who in turn could produce more wool than a worker in Portugal. Any person or state able to produce more per unit of resources than a competitor is said to have an "absolute advantage". Smith said that both Britain and Portugal would profit most by specializing in what they did best and trading the surplus. Ricardo's contribution was to extend Smith's argument to examine whether countries would benefit from specializing and trading when one party had an absolute advantage in both goods. Would »

David Ricardo

Considered one of the world's greatest economic theorists, David Ricardo was born in 1772. His parents moved to England from Holland, and at the age of 14 Ricardo began working for his father, a stockbroker. Aged 21, Ricardo eloped with a Quaker, Priscilla Wilkinson. Religious differences between the families resulted in both sides abandoning the couple, so Ricardo started his own stockbroking firm. He made a fortune betting on a French defeat at Waterloo (1815) by buying English government bonds. Ricardo mixed with notable economists of his day, including Thomas Malthus (p.45) and John Stuart Mill (p.63). He retired from the stock exchange in 1819, and became a member of Parliament. He died suddenly of an ear infection in 1823, leaving an estate worth more than $120 million in real terms today.

Key works

1810 *The High Price of Bullion*
1814 *Essay on the Influence of a Low Price of Corn*
1817 *On the Principles of Political Economy and Taxation*

it be worth trading if one country could produce both more wine and more wool per worker than the other country?

Another way of looking at this is to consider whether a person who is better at making both hats and shoes than someone else should split his time between the two jobs, or choose one job and then trade with the less-skilled worker, who makes the other product (see diagram, below). Suppose that the superior worker is 20 per cent better at making hats, but 50 per cent better at making shoes – it will be in the interest of both of them if he works exclusively at making shoes (the product he really excels in), and the inferior man works in making hats (the product he is least bad at making).

The logic behind this argument is to do with the relative costs of making a product, in terms of the amount of production time taken or lost. Because the superior worker is so good at making shoes, the cost of his making hats is high – he would have to forfeit a lot of valuable shoe production. Although in absolute terms the inferior worker is worse at making shoes and hats than the superior worker, his relative cost when making hats is lower than for the superior worker. This is because he forfeits less shoe production per hat than the superior worker would. The inferior worker is therefore said to have a "comparative advantage" in hats, while the superior worker has a comparative advantage in shoes. When countries specialize in goods for which they have a comparative advantage, more goods are produced in total, and trade delivers more and cheaper goods to both nations. Comparative advantage resolves a paradox highlighted by Adam Smith – that countries that are inferior at producing goods (they are said to have an "absolute disadvantage" in them) can nonetheless export them profitably.

20th-century advantage

What determines comparative advantage? Swedish economists Eli Heckscher and Bertil Ohlin argued that it comes from countries' relative abundance of capital and labour. Capital-rich countries will have a comparative advantage in capital-intensive products such as machines. Labour-rich countries will have a comparative advantage in labour-intensive products such as farming goods. The result is that countries tend to export goods that use their abundant factor of production; capital-abundant nations such as the USA are most likely, therefore, to export manufactured goods. Heckscher and Ohlin's analysis led to another prediction. Not only would trade tend to reduce the differences in prices of goods in different countries, it would also reduce wage differences: the specialization in labour-intensive sectors by labour-abundant economies would tend to push up wage rates, while an effect in the other direction would be seen in the capital-abundant country. So despite the overall increase in the short run, ultimately there may be losers as well as winners, and consequently opposition to the opening up of trade.

The cries for protectionism are as loud today as they were in Ricardo's time. In 2009, China accused the USA of "rampant protectionism", for imposing heavy taxes on imported Chinese car tyres. The decision to increase tariffs came after pressure from

If Worker A is 20 per cent better at making hats, but 50 per cent better at making shoes, he should focus on shoes. That is the most profitable way to use his time.

Worker B is not better than Worker A at anything, but he is better at making hats than shoes. If he makes hats, he will have a competitive advantage and can trade with Worker A for shoes.

US workers, who had seen tyre imports grow from 14 to 46 million from 2004–08, reducing US tyre output, causing factory closures, and creating unemployment. However, the USA had previously accused China of unfairly subsidizing its own tyre industry, so tensions mounted. China's response was to threaten retaliatory increases in import taxes on US cars and poultry. Tariffs produce effects that ripple through economies. Any protection gained for US tyre producers from the tariffs on tyres, for example, was counteracted by other negative impacts. Higher tyre prices increased the costs of US cars, making them less competitive, and reducing the numbers bought by US consumers. The retaliation by China also damaged US export industries. The jobs of some US tyre workers may have been saved, but in the wider economy, many more jobs were lost.

Protectionism today

The US economist Mancur Olson has helped to explain why politicians continue to impose policies that are likely to damage the overall economy, even though the costs are widely known. He points out that those against the tariffs – a small number of large domestic producers and their workers – suffer a visible impact from cheap imports. However, the potentially larger number of consumers who have to pay higher prices because of tariffs, and those workers in affiliated industries who might lose their jobs through knock-on impacts, are dispersed around the economy.

Contemporary trade

Today, most economists support the basic Ricardian position on trade, and, in particular, believe that it helped today's industrialized countries. US economists David Dollar and Aart Kraay have argued that over the last few decades, trade has helped developing countries to grow and reduce poverty. They claim that the countries that cut their tariffs have grown faster, and have seen less poverty.

Other economists have questioned whether trade always helps developing countries. The US economist Joseph Stiglitz argues that developing countries

Goods made in Asia are transported to Western countries in vast container ships. It is estimated that 75 per cent of goods in a typical US shopping trolley are exported to the USA from Asia.

often suffer from market failures and institutional weaknesses that might make a too rapid liberalization of trade costly for them.

There are also contradictions between theory and practice. When the government of India removed tariffs on imports of cheap palm oil from Indonesia, for instance, it had the positive effect of raising the living standards of hundreds of millions of Indians, in line with Ricardo's theory, but it destroyed the livelihoods of 1,000,000 farmers who grew peanuts for oil, which was now passed over for palm oil. In a perfect Ricardian world the peanut farmers would simply transfer into the production of other goods, but in practice they can't, because their investment in capital is immobile – a machine that processes peanuts has no other use.

Ricardo's critics argue that in the long run these kinds of impacts might hamper the industrialization and diversification of poorer countries. Moreover, although rich industrialized countries became successful traders, they did not practice free trade when they were first developing. How countries build up comparative advantage over the long run may be more complex than Ricardo's model suggests. Some argue that Europe and then later the Asian Tigers (pp.162–65) built it up through trade protection in which skills were developed before trade opened up. ■

INDUSTRIAL
ECONOMIC R
1820–1929

By the early 19th century, the effects of the Industrial Revolution were spreading from Britain to Europe and across North America, transforming agricultural nations into industrial economies. The change had been rapid and dramatic, bringing about a fundamental shift in the structure of economies. The focus had shifted from the merchants who traded in goods, to the producers, the owners of capital. As well as a new way of thinking about the economy, capitalism also brought with it new social and political issues.

Distorting the market
Most noticeable of the social changes was the emergence of a new "ruling class" of industrialist producers, and a steady growth in the number of firms producing goods, many of which were offering shares of their business for sale on the stock markets. These provided the competitive market that was the focus of the "classical" view of economics, in which the operations of the market are central. However, as market economies developed and grew, new problems began to emerge. For example, as Adam Smith

(p.39) had warned in 1776, there was a danger that large producers would dominate the market and operate either as monopolies or as cartels, fixing prices at a high level and keeping production low. Although regulation could prevent such practices, in instances where only a few producers operated, they could easily develop strategies to distort the competitiveness of the market.

Smith had assumed that men behaved rationally in an economy, but this also came into question as investors rushed to buy shares in companies whose worth had been exaggerated. This caused bubbles, contradicting the idea of a stable economy based on reasoned behaviour. Despite this, some economists, such as Léon Walras (p.77) and Vilfredo Pareto (p.81), argued that the market economy would always tend towards equilibrium, which would in turn determine the levels of production and prices. Their contemporary Alfred Marshall (p.75) explained supply and demand and how these and prices interact in a system of perfect competition.

The question of price was one that concerned many economists at the

AND
EVOLUTIONS

time, as it affected both producers and consumers in the new capitalist society. Taking their lead from the moral philosophers of the previous generation, they began to see the value of goods in terms of their utility (the satisfaction they would give), rather than the labour that added value to raw materials. The idea of marginal utility – the gain brought about by the consumption of a particular product – was explained in mathematical terms by William Jevons.

Marx's theory of value

The theory that the value of a product is determined by the labour involved in producing it still had some adherents, particularly as it concerned not the producers or consumers so much as the workforce producing the goods for capitalist employers. Looking at value in this light, Karl Marx argued that the inequalities of a market economy amounted to an exploitation of the working class by the owners of capital. In the *Communist Manifesto* and his analysis of capitalism *Capital*, Marx argued for a proletarian revolution to replace capitalism with what he saw as the next stage in economic development: a socialist state in which the means of production are owned by the workers, and an eventual abolition of private property.

Although Marx's ideas were subsequently adopted in many parts of the world, market economies continued to operate elsewhere. Generally, economists continued to defend capitalism as the best means of ensuring prosperity – although tempered to some extent with measures to compensate for its injustices. Following a mathematical approach to economics that focused on supply and demand, and as a reaction against the ideas of socialism, an Austrian School of economic thought emerged, stressing the creative power of the capitalist system.

The free-market economy was soon to receive some hard knocks, after the Wall Street Crash of 1929. However, the theories of neoclassical economists, and the Austrian School in particular, later resurfaced as the model for economies in the Western world in the late 20th century, and even came to replace most of the world's communist planned economies. ∎

PHONE CALLS ARE DEARER WITHOUT COMPETITION
MONOPOLIES

IN CONTEXT

FOCUS
Markets and firms

KEY THINKER
John Stuart Mill (1806–73)

BEFORE
c.330 BCE Aristotle's *Politics* describes the impact of a monopoly.

1776 Adam Smith warns of the dangers of monopolies in *The Wealth of Nations*.

1838 French economist Antoine Cournot analyses the impact on price of a reduction in the number of firms.

AFTER
1890 Alfred Marshall develops a model of monopoly.

1982 US economist William Baumol publishes *Contestable Markets and the Theory of Industry Structure*, redefining the nature of competition.

A monopoly is a situation where one firm has control of a particular market, such as the mobile phone market. The firm may be the only supplier of a product or service, or it may have a dominating market share. In many countries, a firm is said to have a monopoly if it controls more than 25 per cent of a market.

The suggestion that monopolies can cause the price of goods to be higher than they would be if many companies were supplying them has existed for millennia. It dates back at least as far as Aristotle (384–322 BCE), who warned about the problem in a story about the Greek philosopher Thales of Miletus. The public taunted Thales for practising philosophy, which they said was a useless profession that made no money. To prove them wrong, Thales bought up all the local olive presses in the winter when they were cheap, and then – using his monopoly power – sold them at very high prices in the summer when the presses were needed. In doing so he made himself rich. For Thales, the moral was that philosophers could be rich if they wanted. For economists, the story warns of the potential power of monopoly.

Market power

In 1848, the English political scientist John Stuart Mill published his *Principles of Political Economy*. It drew together much of the thinking about whether a lack of competition caused prices to rise. The general view was that some industries were likely to tend towards a lack of competition. This trend was created either through artificial means, such as the introduction of a tax by governments on imported goods, or through natural means, as a consequence of firms growing ever larger. Large firms had begun to dominate the market because late 19th-century industry required ever-increasing amounts of capital. The firms that could grow, by capturing enough of the market to finance the necessary

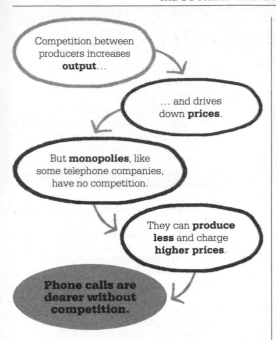

Competition between producers increases **output**...

... and drives down **prices**.

But **monopolies**, like some telephone companies, have no competition.

They can **produce less** and charge **higher prices**.

Phone calls are dearer without competition.

John Stuart Mill

Born in London in 1806, John Stuart Mill grew up in a wealthy family that was to become a great intellectual dynasty. His father was an over-demanding parent, who educated Mill at home on a difficult and accelerated programme that included Greek from the age of three. The aim was for Mill to carry on and develop his father's work on philosophy. The pressure of his upbringing was at least partly responsible for the mental health problems Mill suffered in his early 20s.

One of the great minds of the day, he was willing to speak out in defence of difficult and unpopular causes such as the French Revolution and women's rights. He was also an eloquent opponent of slavery. A 20-year affair with Harriet Taylor, whom he credited with inspiring much of his written work, caused scandal in his own private life. He died in 1873, aged 66.

Key works

1848 *Principles of Political Economy*
1861 *Utilitarianism*
1869 *The Subjection of Women*

investment, had the ability to use their market power to drive their smaller competitors out of business and to charge higher prices.

During the Industrial Revolution, coal, railways, and water supply all showed a tendency towards concentrated ownership. In mining, the ownership of the land was concentrated in just a few hands. In the case of railways and water supply, there was no alternative to a limited number of firms offering services, because the scale of the infrastructure required was so great that if there were any more than a few firms no one would be able to cover their costs. Like Adam Smith (p.39) before him, Mill believed that these features of markets did not inevitably lead to monopoly. The most likely outcome was collusion between firms, allowing them to fix high prices. Such arrangements would lead to high costs for consumers in the same way as monopolies.

Monopoly workers

Mill realized that it is not only within the goods market that a lack of competition is able to push prices up. Monopoly effects can emerge in the labour market too. He pointed to the case of goldsmiths, who earned much higher wages than workers of a similar skill because they » were perceived to be trustworthy – a characteristic that is rare and not easily provable. This created a significant barrier to entry, so that those working with gold could demand a monopoly price for their services. Mill realized that the goldsmiths' situation was not an isolated case. He noted that large sections of the working classes were barred from entering skilled professions because they entailed many years of education and training. The cost of supporting someone through this process was out of reach for most families, so those who could afford it were able to enjoy wages far above what might be expected. Similarly, some historians have viewed the guilds of the medieval era as an example of privileged craftsmen attempting to shut out competition from other workers.

From the late 1890s, British economist Alfred Marshall (p.75) rigorously analysed the effects of monopolies on prices and on consumers' welfare. Marshall was interested in determining whether the higher price and lower output that result from monopolies cause a loss in total welfare for society. In his *Principles of Economics*, Marshall formulated the concept of consumer surplus. This is the difference between the maximum amount that a consumer would be willing to pay for a good and the amount he actually pays. Suppose the consumer buys an apple for 20 pence when he would have been willing to pay 50 pence. His consumer surplus from the purchase of the apple is 30 pence. In a market with many firms, they compete on price and together supply an amount of apples that generates a certain amount of overall consumer surplus. For an apple sold to the last consumer, his willingness to pay will equal the price and no more apples can be sold. The welfare loss of monopoly comes from the fact that fewer apples are sold compared to the amount that would have been sold in perfectly competitive markets. Essentially, this means that there are apples that could be supplied to the market, that would generate consumer surplus, but they never appear on the market.

Advantages of monopoly

Monopolies also create more complex price and welfare effects. Marshall suggested that a monopolist might actually cut its prices to attract customers to its phone network, for example, as people are likely to keep using the service once it is connected, even though rival technologies such as mobile phones offer alternatives that are at least as good.

Some economists have pointed out that monopolies can have benign effects. In many markets, a monopoly would have

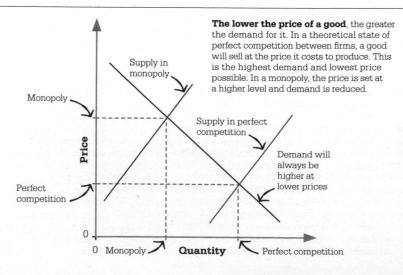

The lower the price of a good, the greater the demand for it. In a theoretical state of perfect competition between firms, a good will sell at the price it costs to produce. This is the highest demand and lowest price possible. In a monopoly, the price is set at a higher level and demand is reduced.

lower costs than the total costs of a set of smaller firms because a monopolist would spend less on advertising and make full use of economies of scale. For these reasons, a monopolist may enjoy higher profits even when its price is lower than would be the case if many firms – with higher costs – were competing. In this case, the lower prices might help consumers and help to drive economic growth.

In a similar fashion, large firms can attempt to gain monopoly profits, driving out rivals by aggressively cutting prices in the short run. Economists call this predatory pricing. In the long run, it can hurt consumers as the market becomes monopolized. However, in the 1950s and 60s, US economist William Baumol claimed that it does not matter if there is a monopoly as long as there are no barriers to entering and exiting the market – the mere threat of competition means that the monopoly will set the price at a competitive level. This is because a higher price might attract new entrants to the market, who would take market share from the monopoly. For this reason, prices may be no higher under a monopoly than in a market with many competing firms.

Natural monopolies

One argument that began to take shape during Marshall's lifetime is that some monopolies are "natural" because of the enormous cost advantages of having a single firm. Many public utilities are natural monopolies, including telephone networks, gas, and water. The fixed cost of setting up a network of gas distribution pipes is huge, compared to the cost of pumping an extra amount of gas.

This idea led to an acceptance of national monopolies in the public utilities in many countries. Even so, governments began to intervene in these markets to counteract the possible monopoly effects. The problem is that in the case of a natural monopoly, the fixed costs are so high that compelling the firm to charge a competitive price might make the firm unprofitable. Solutions to this problem include the wholesale nationalization of industries or the establishment of regulatory organizations

Operators work the switchboards of the AT&T company in New York in the 1940s. Because of the company's size and dominance, it was considered to be a natural monopoly.

which place limits on price increases, helping consumers but also ensuring the economic viability of the industry.

Mainstream economists argue that monopolized markets fall short of the perfectly competitive ideal. This view has led to government anti-trust policies, which seek to move markets towards competitiveness. This has meant the introduction of measures aimed at preventing monopolies from abusing their market power, including the break up of monopolies and the banning of mergers of firms that would create monopolies.

The modern Austrian School, including US economist Thomas DiLorenzo (1954–), are critical of this approach. Both argue that real market competition is not the passive behaviour of perfectly competitive firms operating in a state of equilibrium. It is about cut-throat rivalry between an often small number of large businesses. Competition takes place through price and non-price competition, through advertising and marketing, and through large firms innovating and creating new products.

Slightly apart from this school of economists, Austrian economist Joseph Schumpeter (p.91) also stressed the dynamic potential of monopoly as firms compete to create new products and dominate entire markets because of the potential profits. What economists agree on is that true competition is good for consumers. It is less certain whether or not monopoly is incompatible with this. In the early 20th century, German economist Robert Liefman claimed that "only a peculiar combination of competition and monopoly brings about the greatest possible satisfaction of wants". ∎

LET THE RULING CLASSES TREMBLE AT A COMMUNIST REVOLUTION
MARXIST ECONOMICS

IN CONTEXT

FOCUS
Economic systems

KEY THINKER
Karl Marx (1818–83)

BEFORE
1789 Revolution sweeps away the old feudal regime and aristocracy in France.

1816 German thinker Georg Hegel explains his dialectics in *The Science of Logic*.

1848 Revolutions spring up throughout Europe, led by disaffected members of the middle and working classes.

AFTER
1922 The USSR is established on Marxist principles, under Vladimir Lenin.

1949 Mao Zedong becomes the founding father of the People's Republic of China.

1989 The fall of the Berlin Wall symbolizes the collapse of Eastern Bloc communism.

Although much of economics is concerned with free-market economies, it should not be forgotten that for a large part of the 20th century, up to a third of the world was under some form of communist or socialist rule. These states had centralized, or planned, economies. Political philosophers were looking for an alternative to capitalism even as the modern free-market economies emerged. However, a truly economic argument for communism was not formulated until the middle of the 19th century, when Karl Marx (p.68) wrote his critique of capitalism.

While Marx's influence is popularly seen as political, he was, perhaps more than anything else, an economist. He believed that the economic organization of society forms the basis for its social and political organization; economics, therefore, drives social change. Marx saw history not in terms of war or colonialism, but as a progression of different economic systems, which gave birth to new forms of social organization.

With the rise of the market came merchants, and with the factory, an industrial proletariat. Feudalism had been replaced by capitalism, which in turn would be supplanted by communism. In his 1848 *Communist Manifesto*, Marx said that this would be brought about by revolution. To explain what he saw as the inevitability of this change, he analysed the capitalist system and its inherent weaknesses in the three-volume *Das Kapital* (Capital).

However, Marx was not absolutely critical of capitalism. He viewed capitalism as a historically necessary stage in economic progress, replacing systems that he considered to be outmoded: feudalism (where peasants were legally tied to their local land-owning lord), and mercantilism (in which governments control foreign trade). He almost admiringly described how it had driven technological innovation and industrial efficiency. But ultimately he believed that capitalism was only a passing stage, and an imperfect system whose flaws would inevitably lead to its downfall and replacement.

At the heart of his analysis is the division of society into the "bourgeoisie", a minority who own the means of production, and the "proletariat", the majority who make up the workforce. For Marx, this division characterizes capitalism.

Exploiting the workers

With the advent of modern industry, the bourgeoisie had effectively become the ruling class, as ownership of the means of production gave them the upper hand over the majority of the population, the proletariat. While workers produced goods and services in return for a wage, the owners of capital – the industrialists and factory owners – sold those goods and services for profit. If, as Marx believed, a commodity's value is based on the labour needed to produce it, capitalists must price the finished goods by first adding the price of labour to the initial commodity cost, then adding profit. In a capitalist system, the worker must produce more value than he receives in wages. In this way, capitalists extract a surplus value from the workers – this is profit.

To maximize profit, it is clearly in the interests of the capitalist to keep wages at a minimum, but also to introduce technology to improve efficiency, often condemning the workforce to degrading or monotonous work, or even unemployment. This exploitation of the workforce, seen by Marx as a necessary feature of capitalism, »

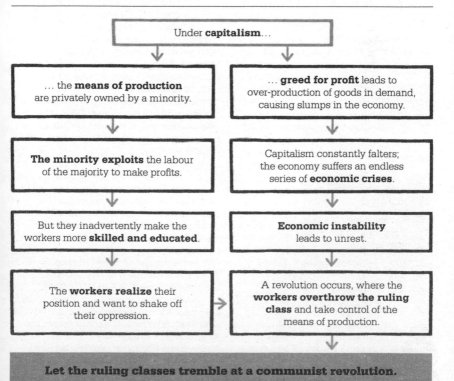

Under **capitalism**…

... the **means of production** are privately owned by a minority.

... **greed for profit** leads to over-production of goods in demand, causing slumps in the economy.

The minority exploits the labour of the majority to make profits.

Capitalism constantly falters; the economy suffers an endless series of **economic crises**.

But they inadvertently make the workers more **skilled and educated**.

Economic instability leads to unrest.

The **workers realize** their position and want to shake off their oppression.

A revolution occurs, where the **workers overthrow the ruling class** and take control of the means of production.

Let the ruling classes tremble at a communist revolution.

denies workers both an adequate financial reward and job satisfaction, alienating them from the process of production. Marx argued that this alienation would inevitably lead to social unrest.

Competition and monopoly

Another essential element of capitalism is competition between producers. To compete in a market, a firm must try not only to reduce production costs, but also to undercut its competitors' prices. In the process, some producers fail and go bankrupt, while others take over an increasing portion of the market. The tendency, as Marx saw it, was towards fewer and fewer producers controlling the means of production and a concentration of wealth in the hands of an ever smaller bourgeoisie. In the long term, this would create monopolies that could exploit not only the workers but also consumers. At the same time, the ranks of the proletariat would be swelled by the former bourgeoisie and the unemployed.

Marx saw competition as the cause of another failing of the capitalist system: the desire to jump into markets where profits are increasing encourages increased production, sometimes regardless of demand. This over-production leads not only to waste, but also to stagnation and even decline of the whole economy. By its nature, capitalism is unplanned and ruled only by the complexities of the market – economic crises are an inevitable result of the mismatch of supply and demand. Therefore, growth in a capitalist economy is not a smooth progression, but is interrupted by periodic crises, which Marx believed would become more and more frequent. The hardship created by these crises would be especially felt by the proletariat.

To Marx, these apparently insurmountable weaknesses in the capitalist economy would lead to its eventual collapse. To explain how this would come about, he used an idea proposed by the German philosopher Georg Hegel, which showed how contradictory notions are resolved in a process of dialectic: every idea or state of affairs (the original "thesis"), contains within it a contradiction (the "antithesis"), and from this conflict, a new, richer notion (the "synthesis") arises.

Marx saw the inherent contradictions within economies – personified in the conflicts between different groups or classes – as driving historical change. He analysed the exploitation and alienation of the proletariat by the bourgeoisie under capitalism as an example of a social contradiction, where the thesis (capitalism) contains its own antithesis (the exploited workers). The oppression and alienation of the workers, combined with the inherent

Karl Marx

Born in Trier, Prussia, in 1818, Karl Marx was the son of a lawyer who had converted from Judaism to Christianity. Marx studied law, but became interested in philosophy, in which he gained a PhD from Jena University. In 1842, Marx moved to Cologne and started work as a journalist, but his socialist views soon led to censorship, and he fled to Paris with his wife, Jenny.

It was in Paris that he met the German-born industrialist Friedrich Engels, with whom he wrote the *Communist Manifesto* in 1848. He moved back to Germany briefly the following year, but when the revolutions were quashed he left for London, where he spent the rest of his life. There, he devoted his time to writing, notably *Capital*, and died in poverty in 1883, despite continual financial assistance from Engels.

Key works

1848 *Manifesto of the Communist Party* (with Friedrich Engels)
1858 *Contribution to the Critique of Political Economy*
1867, 1885, 1894 *Capital: A Critique of Political Economy*

instability of a capitalist economy lurching from crisis to crisis, would result in massive social unrest. A proletarian revolution was both inevitable and necessary to usher in capitalism's successor in the historical progression (the synthesis) – communism. Marx encouraged revolution in the closing words of the *Communist Manifesto*: "The proletarians have nothing to lose but their chains. They have a world to win. Working men of all countries, unite!"

Revolution

Marx predicted that once the bourgeoisie had been overthrown, the means of production would be taken over by the proletariat. At first, this would amount to what Marx called a "dictatorship by the proletariat": a form of socialism where economic power was in the hands of the majority. However, this would be only a first step towards the abolition of private property in favour of common ownership in a communist state.

In contrast to his exhaustive analysis of capitalism, Marx wrote relatively little about the details of the communist economy that would replace capitalism, except that it should be based on common ownership, and a planned economy to ensure matching supply and demand. In so far as it removed all the iniquities and instability of capitalism, he regarded communism as the culmination of a historical progression. His criticism of the capitalist economy was met, unsurprisingly, with hostility. Most economists at the time saw the free market as a means of ensuring economic growth and prosperity, at least for a certain class of people. But Marx was not without his supporters, mainly among political thinkers, and his prediction of communist revolution proved correct – although not where he expected, in industrialized Europe and America, but in rural countries such as Russia and China.

Marx did not live to see the establishment of communist states such as the USSR and the People's Republic of China, and he could not have envisaged the reality of how inefficient such planned economies would be. Today, only a handful of communist planned economies (Cuba, China, Laos, Vietnam, and North Korea) have survived.

In 1959, Fidel Castro's revolutionaries seized power in Cuba. At first primarily a nationalist revolution, it soon became a communist one as Castro allied himself with the Soviet Union.

There is debate over just how "Marxist" the communism of these states was under the leadership of the likes of Stalin and Mao, but the collapse of communism in the Eastern bloc and the liberalization of the Chinese economy have been seen by many economists as evidence that Marx's theories were flawed.

Mixed economies

In the decades following World War II, Western Europe developed a "third way" between communism and capitalism. Many European Union states still operate mixed economies with varying degrees of state intervention and ownership, although some, most notably Great Britain, have moved away from mixed economies towards a more laissez-faire economic policy, where the state plays a smaller role. However, with communism largely discredited, and the collapse of capitalism apparently no nearer than in Marx's time, it would appear that his theory of capitalist dynamism leading to crisis and revolution were wrong. Nevertheless, Marxist economic theory has maintained a following, and recent financial crises have prompted a reappraisal of his ideas. Increasing inequality, concentration of wealth in a few large companies, frequent economic crises, and the "credit crunch" of 2008 have all been blamed on the free-market economy. While not going so far as to advocate revolution or even socialism, a growing body of thinkers – not all of them from the political Left – is taking elements of Marx's critique of capitalism seriously. ∎

THE VALUE OF A PRODUCT COMES FROM THE EFFORT NEEDED TO MAKE IT
THE LABOUR THEORY OF VALUE

IN CONTEXT

FOCUS
Theories of value

KEY THINKER
Karl Marx (1818–83)

BEFORE
1662 English economist William Petty argues that land is a free gift of nature and so all capital is "past labour".

1690 English philosopher John Locke argues that workers deserve the fruits of their labours.

AFTER
1896 Austrian Economist Eugen von Böhm-Bawerk publishes *Karl Marx and the Close of his System*, summarizing the criticisms of Marx's labour theory of value.

1942 Radical US economist Paul Sweezy publishes *The Theory of Capitalist Development*, defending Marx's labour theory of value.

Natural resources come **free from nature**.

↓

Adding labour to natural resources creates **raw materials**.

↓

Adding labour to raw materials creates **machines and commodities**.

↓

Adding labour to machines and commodities **creates goods**.

↓

The value of a product comes from the effort needed to make it.

The importance of labour in determining the value of goods has a history that can be traced back to the ancient Greek philosophers. For about 200 years from the mid-17th century, it dominated economic thought. In primitive, pre-industrial societies, the role of labour in determining the rate at which one good could be exchanged for

another was fairly simple. If it took a man a week to make a fishing net, he was unlikely to exchange it for a wooden spoon that had been carved in a morning. However, the issue became much more complicated with the emergence of modern industrial societies in the 18th century. The classical economists Adam Smith (p.39) and David Ricardo (p.57) had each developed a theory of value connected to labour, but it was the German philosopher Karl Marx (p.68), who set out the most famous description of the labour theory of value, in his magnum opus *Capital*.

Labour and cost

Marx's idea was that the amount of labour used to produce a good is proportional to its value. The theory is often justified by the following argument. If a haircut involves half an hour of labour, at £40 per hour, the haircut has £20 of value. If it also needs the use of scissors and brushes that cost a total of £60, and lose £1 of their value (through wear) on each haircut, the total value of the haircut is £21. Of the tools, the scissors themselves cost £20 because they took 45 minutes of labour to forge from a lump of steel – costing £12.50 – into the pair of scissors. The same reasoning can be applied to explain why the lump of steel cost £12.50, tracing time and costs for producing steel from iron ore. It is possible to trace the expenditure on all the intermediate inputs until we arrive back at the original natural resources, which are free – so all the value has been created by labour.

Marx pointed out that it is too difficult to calculate the value of any good in this way, so value should be determined by the "congealed" lump of labour that the good contains. He also said that value is determined by the "normal" amount of labour we expect its production to take. An inefficient hairdresser may take an hour to cut someone's hair, but the haircut's cost should not then rise by £20. Marx did not deny that supply and demand in the marketplace would influence the value or price of goods in the short run, but said that in the long run, the basic structure and dynamics of the value system must come from labour. ∎

When the labour theory of value dominated economic thought, it faced a number of critiques based on paradoxical questions:

If sandcastles are made by labour, why don't they have any value?
Marx's response was that not everything made by labour has value – labour can still be wasted on goods no one wants.

How can an artistic masterpiece be valued from the amount of labour hours used to make it?
The defence to this critique is that a great work of art is an exception to the rule because it is a one-off. Therefore, there is no average quantity of labour from which to derive a price.

How do vintage wines stored for 10 years increase in value without any additional labour input?
The defence here is that an additional cost does accrue to labour – that of waiting for the wine to mature.

Happiness in work

Karl Marx argued that people are driven by a desire to be connected to other humans and this is what makes us happy. We show this desire through work.

When a person makes something, that product represents his or her personality. When someone else buys that item, the maker is happy because not only has he or she satisfied the need of another person, but the buyer has also confirmed the "goodness" of the personality of the producer.

Capitalism destroys this essence of humanity, Marx claimed, because it alienates the workers from what they produce. People no longer control their output; they are merely hired to produce a product in which they have had little creative input and are unlikely to consume or even trade. The cooperative nature of society is lost because people are isolated in the competition for jobs. Marx argued that it is this separation from our work that makes us unhappy.

PRICES COME FROM SUPPLY AND DEMAND
SUPPLY AND DEMAND

IN CONTEXT

FOCUS
Theories of value

KEY THINKER
Alfred Marshall (1842–1924)

BEFORE
c.1300 Islamic scholar Ibn Taymiyyah publishes a study of the effects of supply and demand on prices.

1691 English philosopher John Locke argues that commodity prices are directly influenced by the ratio of buyers to sellers.

1817 British economist David Ricardo argues that prices are influenced mainly by the cost of production.

1874 French economist Léon Walras studies the equilibrium (balance) in markets.

AFTER
1936 British economist John Maynard Keynes identifies economy-wide total demand and supply.

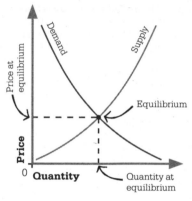

This graph, known as the Marshallian Cross, shows the relationship between supply and demand. The point at which the supply and demand curves intersect gives the price.

Supply and demand are among the fundamental building blocks of economic theory. The interplay between the amount of a product available on the market and the eagerness of consumers to buy that product creates the foundation of markets.

The importance of supply and demand in economic relationships was studied as long ago as the Middle Ages. The medieval Scottish scholar Duns Scotus recognized that a price must be fair to the consumer, but must also take into account the costs incurred in production, and therefore be fair to the producer. Subsequent economists studied the effects of supply-side costs on eventual prices, and economists such as Adam Smith (p.39) and David Ricardo (p.57) linked the price of a product to the labour required in its production. This is called the classical labour theory of value.

In the 1860s, new economic theories began to develop, challenging these ideas under the banner of the neoclassical school.

This school of thought introduced the theory of marginal utility, where the satisfaction a consumer gains or loses from having more or less of a product affects both demand and price.

British economist Alfred Marshall joined the analysis of supply with the new neoclassical approach to demand. Marshall saw that supply and demand work in tandem to generate the market price. His work was important in that he illustrated the varying dynamics of supply and demand in short-term markets (such as those for perishable goods), as opposed to long-term ones (such as for gold). He applied mathematics to economic theories and produced the "Marshallian Cross": a graph showing supply and demand as crossing lines. The point at which they intersect is the "equilibrium" price, which perfectly balances the needs of supply (the producer) and demand (the consumer).

The law of supply

The amount of products a firm chooses to produce is determined by the price at which it can sell them. If the assorted costs of production (labour, materials, machines, and premises) amount to more than the market is willing to pay for the product, production will be seen as unprofitable and be reduced or stopped. If, on the other hand, the market price for the item is substantially more than the costs of production, the company will seek to expand production to make as much profit as possible. The theory assumes that the firm has no influence over the market price and must accept what the market offers.

For example, if the costs of producing a computer amount to £200, production will be unprofitable if the market price of the computer drops under £200. Conversely, if the market price of the computer is £1,000, the firm producing it will seek to produce as many as possible to maximize profits. The law of supply can be visualized using a supply curve (see opposite), where every point of the curve provides the answer to how many units a firm will be willing to sell at a particular price.

Producers supply goods to market to meet **consumer demands**.

↓

If goods are not supplied in large enough quantities to meet demand, **prices rise**.

↓

Supply is increased (producers make more) to satisfy demand.

↓

However, at some point, **supply surpasses** demand.

↓

At this point, **prices begin to fall**…

↓

… until the **market settles** at a price that balances supply and demand.

↓

Prices come from supply and demand.

Furthermore, there must be a distinction between fixed and variable costs. The above example assumes that production can be increased with the unit cost of production remaining stable. However, this is not the case. If the computer factory can produce only 100 machines per day, yet there is demand for 110, the producer must judge whether it makes sense to open a completely new factory, with the vast additional costs this » incurs, or whether it makes more sense to sell the computers at a slightly higher price to reduce demand to only 100 per day.

The nature of demand

The law of demand sees matters from the viewpoint of the consumer rather than the producer. When the price of a good increases, demand inevitably falls (except for essential goods such as medicines). This is because some consumers will no longer be able to afford the item, or because they decide that they can gain more enjoyment by spending the money elsewhere.

Using the same example as previously, if the computer costs only £50, the volume of sales will be high as most people will be able to afford one. On the other hand, if it costs £10,000, the demand will be very low, as only the very wealthy will be able to afford them. As prices increase, demand falls.

There is a limit to how low prices can fall to stimulate demand. If the price of the computer falls to below £5, everyone will be able to afford to buy one, but nobody needs more than two or three computers. Consumers realize that their money is better spent on something else, and demand flattens out.

Price is not the only factor that affects demand. Consumer tastes and attitudes are also a major factor. If a product becomes more fashionable, the whole demand curve shifts to the right; consumers demand more of the product at each price. Given the static position of the supply curve, this drives up the price. Because consumer tastes can be manipulated through techniques such as advertising, producers can influence the shape and position of the demand curve.

 When the demand price is equal to the supply price, the amount produced has no tendency either to be increased or to be diminished; it is in equilibrium.
Alfred Marshall

Producers of goods such as Coca-Cola may influence demand through advertising that promotes the product and the brand. As demand rises, the price of the product may also rise.

Finding an equilibrium

While consumers will always seek to pay the lowest price they can, producers will look to sell at the highest price they can. When prices are too high, consumers lose interest and move away from the product. Conversely, if prices are too low, it no longer makes financial sense for the producer to continue to make the product. A happy medium must be reached – an equilibrium price acceptable to both consumer and producer. This price is found at the point where the supply curve intersects the demand curve, producing a price at which consumers are happy to pay and producers are happy to sell.

Many factors complicate these relatively simple laws. The position and size of the market are crucial in price determination, as is time. The price at which producers are happy to sell is not just influenced by the costs of production.

For instance, consider a market stall selling fresh produce. The farmer arrives having already paid for the costs of production, buying the seeds, the labour involved in planting and harvesting the crop, and his transport to the market. He knows that to make a profit, he must sell each apple for £1.20. Therefore, at the start of the day, he decides to market his apples at £1.20. If his sales are going well, he may feel he can make more money and raise his price to £1.25. This may cause a slowdown in sales, but if he manages to sell his entire stock he will be happy.

However, if the end of the day is nearing and he finds that he still has quite a few apples left, he might decide to drop his price to £1.15, to avoid being left with an excess of apples that are likely to rot before his next chance to sell them.

In this example, the costs of production are fixed and the urgency of selling the crop is the pressing factor. This is useful in illustrating the differences between short- and long-term markets. The farmer will decide how many apples to plant for his next harvest, based on his sales this time, and in this way the market should eventually arrive at equilibrium.

The farmer's market is also limited by distance. There is only a certain radius within which it makes economic sense to sell his products. For instance, the cost involved in shipping his apples overseas would make his prices uncompetitive with domestic producers. This means that, to some extent, the farmer is at liberty to set his prices slightly higher, because his customers cannot travel to seek alternatives.

The opposite scenario to the fruit-farmer is the market for a global commodity such as gold. In this long-term market, the holder of the gold is under no time pressure to sell. He can be confident that it will maintain its value. The larger the market and the more widespread the knowledge of the market, the more likely it is that the commodity has found its equilibrium price. This makes any small change in market price significant, and any change will spark a flurry of buying and selling.

Although these examples introduce further complexity into the market, they hold true to the basic rule that suppliers will only sell at a price they find acceptable, while buyers will only buy at a price they find reasonable.

The examples all relate to a market in which physical goods are traded, but supply and demand is relevant throughout economic reasoning. The model is applicable to the labour market, for instance. Here the individual is the supplier, selling his or her labour, and employers are the consumers, looking to buy labour as cheaply as possible. Money markets are also analysed as a supply and demand system, with the interest rate acting as the price.

Economists call Marshall's work "partial equilibrium" analysis, because it shows how a single market reaches equilibrium or balance through the forces of supply and demand. However, an economy is made up of many different interacting markets. The question of how all these can come together in a state of "general equilibrium" is a complex problem that was analysed by Léon Walras (p.77) in the 19th century. ■

Alfred Marshall

Born in London, England, in 1842, Alfred Marshall grew up in the borough of Clapham before going to Cambridge University on a scholarship. There, he studied mathematics and then metaphysics, concentrating on ethics. His studies led him to see economics as a practical means of implementing his ethical beliefs.

In 1868, Marshall took up a lectureship specially created for him in moral science. His interest in this continued until a visit to the USA in 1875 made him focus more upon political economy. Marshall married Mary Paley, his former student, in 1877 and became principal of University College, Bristol, UK. In 1885, he returned to Cambridge as professor of political economy, a post he held until his retirement in 1908. From about 1890 until his death in 1924, Marshall was considered the dominant figure in British economics.

Key works

1879 *The Economics of Industry* (with Mary Paley Marshall)
1890 *Principles of Economics*
1919 *Industry and Trade*

A SYSTEM OF FREE MARKETS IS STABLE
ECONOMIC EQUILIBRIUM

IN CONTEXT

FOCUS
Markets and firms

KEY THINKER
Léon Walras (1834–1910)

BEFORE
1881 Francis Edgeworth publishes a mathematical assessment of economics in *Mathematical Psychics*.

AFTER
1906 Vilfredo Pareto develops a new theory of equilibrium that takes account of the compatibility of individual incentives and constraints.

1930s John Hicks, Oskar Lange, Maurice Allais, Paul A Samuelson, and others continue to develop the theory of general equilibrium.

1954 Kenneth Arrow and Gérard Debreu provide a mathematical proof of general equilibrium.

There has long been something appealing for economists about the idea that the economy may behave with the same mathematical predictability of scientific laws such as Newton's laws of motion. Newton's laws reduce the whole complex, teeming, physical universe to three simple, reliable mathematical relationships. Is it possible to find similar relationships in the complex, changing world of markets?

In 1881, a British professor named Francis Edgeworth published *Mathematical Psychics*, an early mathematical work on economics. He realized that economics deals with relationships between variables, which means that it can be translated into equations. Edgeworth thought about economic benefits in utilitarian terms. In other words, believing that outcomes could be measured in terms of units of happiness, or pleasure.

Other economists were also intrigued by the idea of a mathematical approach. In Germany, the economist Johann von Thünen developed equations for a fair working wage and the most profitable use of land. In France, Léon Walras, an academic who would later be described as "the greatest of all economists", was trying to discover a complete mathematical, scientific framework for the entire discipline. Walras was ardent in his conviction that it was possible to discover economic laws that would make economics a "pure moral science" (describing human behaviour) that went hand in hand with the "pure natural science" of Newton. His general equilibrium theory was devised to explain the production, consumption, and prices across an entire economy.

Supply and demand

Walras began by focusing on how exchanges worked – how the prices of goods, the quantity of goods, and the demand for goods interact. In other words, he was trying to pin down just how supply and demand tally. He believed that the

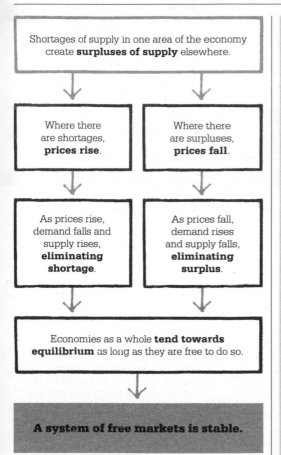

Shortages of supply in one area of the economy create **surpluses of supply** elsewhere.

Where there are shortages, **prices rise**.

Where there are surpluses, **prices fall**.

As prices rise, demand falls and supply rises, **eliminating shortage**.

As prices fall, demand rises and supply falls, **eliminating surplus**.

Economies as a whole **tend towards equilibrium** as long as they are free to do so.

A system of free markets is stable.

value of something for sale depends essentially on its *rareté* – which means "rarity", but was used by Walras to express just how intensely something is needed. In this respect, Walras differed from many of his contemporaries, including Edgeworth and William Stanley Jevons, who believed that utility – either as pleasure or usefulness – is the key to value.

Walras began to construct mathematical models to describe the relationship between supply and demand. These revealed that as price escalates, demand falls and supply climbs. Where demand and supply match, the market is in a state of equilibrium, or balance. This reflected the same kind of simple balancing forces that were evident in Newton's laws of motion. **»**

Léon Walras

Marie Esprit Léon Walras was born in Normandy, France, in 1834. As a young man, he was captivated by bohemian Paris, but his father persuaded him that one of the romantic tasks of the future was to make economics a science. Walras was convinced – though he maintained his bohemian life until, destitute, he went to Lausanne as economics professor in 1870. It was there he developed his theory of general equilibrium.

Walras believed that the organization of society was a matter of "art" outside the scientific realm of economics. He had a strong sense of social justice and campaigned for land nationalization as a prelude to equal land distribution. In 1892, he retired to the town of Clarens overlooking Lake Geneva, where he fished and thought about economics until he died in 1910.

Key works

1874–77 *Elements of Pure Economics*
1896 *Studies in Social Economics*
1898 *Studies in Applied Economics*

General equilibrium

To illustrate this equilibrium, imagine that today the current market price of mobile phones is $20. In a local market, stall holders have 100 phones for which they want $20. If 100 buyers visit the market, each willing to pay $20, the market for cheap mobiles is in equilibrium, because the supply and demand are perfectly balanced with no shortages or surpluses. Walras went on to apply the idea of equilibrium to the whole economy in order to create a theory of general equilibrium. This was based on the assumption that when goods are in surplus in one area, the price must be too high. Prices are judged "too high" by comparison, so if one market's prices are "too high", there must be another where prices are "too low", causing a surplus in the higher-priced market.

Walras created a mathematical model for the whole economy, including goods such as chairs and wheat and factors of production such as capital and labour. Everything was interlinked and dependent on everything else. He insisted that interdependency is key; price changes do not take place in a vacuum – they only occur because of a change in supply or demand. Moreover, when prices change, everything else also changes. One small change in one part of the economy can ripple through the entire economy. For example, suppose that a war breaks out in a major oil-producing country. Prices of oil

An auctioneer takes bids at a cattle auction. Walras imagined an auctioneer who provides perfect information for the market. He announces prices, and a sale only takes place at the point of equilibrium.

 There was… a set of prices, one for each commodity, which would equate supply and demand for all commodities.
Kenneth Arrow

across the world will rise, which will have far-reaching effects on governments, firms, and individuals – from increased prices at the petrol stations and increased heating costs at home, to being forced to cancel a now-expensive holiday or business trip.

Towards equilibrium

Walras succeeded in reducing his mathematical model of an economy to a few equations containing prices and quantities. He drew two conclusions from his work. The first was that a state of general equilibrium is theoretically possible. The second was that wherever an economy started, a free market could move it towards general equilibrium. So a system of free markets could be inherently stable.

Walras showed how this might happen through an idea he called *tâtonnement* (groping), in which an economy "gropes" its way up to an equilibrium just as a climber gropes his way up a mountain. He thought about this by imagining a theoretical "auctioneer" to whom buyers and sellers submit information about how much they would buy or sell goods at different prices. The auctioneer then announces the prices at which supply equals demand in every market, and only then does buying and selling begin.

Flaws in the model

Walras was keen to point out that this was simply a mathematical model, designed to help economists. It was not intended to be taken to be a description of the real world. His work was largely ignored by his contemporaries; many of whom believed that real-world interactions are too complex and chaotic for a true state of equilibrium to develop.

Where prices are judged to be too high
in one market, this will lead to an excess in supply in that market. Prices adjust to eliminate excesses in supply or demand across an economy in a process that Léon Walras called *tâtonnement*.

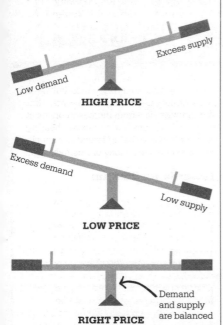

HIGH PRICE
Low demand / Excess supply

LOW PRICE
Excess demand / Low supply

RIGHT PRICE
Demand and supply are balanced

On a technical level, Walras's complex equations were too difficult for many economists to master, which was another reason why he was ignored, although his student Vilfredo Pareto (p.81) later developed his work in new directions. In the 1930s, two decades after Walras's death, his equations came under the scrutiny of the brilliant Hungarian-born American mathematician, John von Neumann. Von Neumann exposed a flaw in Walras's equations, showing that some of their solutions produced a negative price – which meant sellers would be paying buyers.

However, Walras's ideas have been rescued by the work of US economists Kenneth Arrow and Lionel W McKenzie and French economist Gérard Debreu (p.123) who, in the 1950s, developed a sleeker model (pp.122–25). Using

rigorous mathematics, Arrow and Debreu derived conditions under which Walras's general economic equilibrium would hold.

They found that when people's decisions about buying and selling are "rational" – in the sense that they are consistent – then it is possible for all the markets in an economy to be in equilibrium. A requirement for consistency is the "transitivity" of people's preferences: if you prefer apples over oranges, and oranges over grapes, then you must prefer apples over grapes.

Computable economies
Improvements to computers in the 1980s allowed economists to calculate the effects of interactions between multiple markets in actual economies. These computable general equilibrium (CGE) models applied Walras's idea of interdependence to particular situations, to analyse the impact of changing prices and government policies.

The attraction of CGE is that it can be used by large organizations – such as governments, the World Bank, and the International Monetary Fund – to make quick and powerful calculations showing the state of the whole economy, as well as seeing the effects of changing different parameters.

Today, analysis of partial equilibrium – considering the forces that bring supply and demand into balance in a single market – is the first thing that an economics student learns. Walras's insights about general equilibrium also continue to generate work at the cutting edge of economic theory. For most economists, equilibrium and the existence of forces that return an economy to this state remain fundamental principles. These ideas are perhaps the essence of mainstream economic analysis. ∎

 The equilibrium…
re-establishes itself
automatically as soon
as it is disturbed.
Léon Walras

MAKE ONE PERSON BETTER OFF WITHOUT HURTING THE OTHERS
EFFICIENCY AND FAIRNESS

IN CONTEXT

FOCUS
Welfare economics

KEY THINKER
Vilfredo Pareto (1848–1923)

BEFORE
1776 Adam Smith's *The Wealth of Nations* relates self-interest to social welfare.

1871 British economist William Jevons says that value depends entirely on utility.

1874 French economist Léon Walras uses equations to determine the overall equilibrium of an economy.

AFTER
1930–50 John Hicks, Paul Samuelson, and others use Pareto optimality as the basis of modern welfare economics.

1954 US economist Kenneth Arrow and French economist Gérard Debreu use mathematics to show a connection between free markets and Pareto optimality.

A government wants to **improve the welfare** of its people...

↓

... but **individual welfare** is unmeasurable in absolute (not relative) terms.

↓

A reasonable aim would be to reach a state of **Pareto efficiency**...

↓

... where **each individual trades** to improve their own welfare...

↓

... until they reach a compromise, or equilibrium, where you can't make one person better off without hurting the others.

I n the 19th century, a group of British philosophers known as the utilitarians introduced the idea that the happiness of individuals can be measured and added up, or aggregated. Italian economist Vilfredo Pareto disagreed. In his *Manual of Political Economy*, he introduced a weaker definition of social welfare that has come to dominate modern economics. His argument is based on a ranking of relative happiness known as "ordinal utility", rather than an absolute measurement of happiness ("cardinal utility").

Pareto said that individuals know their own preferences and will do what suits them best. If everyone follows their own tastes, constrained as they are by the obstacles they face, society will soon reach a point where no one can be made better off without hurting someone else. This state is known as Pareto optimality, or Pareto efficiency.

Pareto efficiency

Suppose a couple named Jane and John both like rice. If we have a sack of rice, any division of it between them – even one where one person gets all the rice – would be optimal, because only taking rice *away* from a person is said to hurt them. In this way Pareto efficiency is different from fairness.

In most situations, there are many goods and tastes. For instance, if John likes rice but not chicken, and Jane likes chicken but not rice, an allocation in which John had everything would be Pareto inefficient: a transfer of chicken from John to Jane would help Jane without hurting John. Often preferences aren't so clear cut: both might like chicken and rice but to different degrees. In that case, Jane and John can exchange just small amounts of chicken and rice until an optimal allocation emerges.

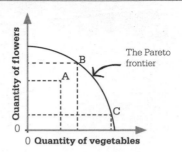

Pareto efficiency can be used to determine efficient production. If two people own a garden, and one prefers flowers while the other prefers vegetables, the garden can be planted with flowers, vegetables, or a combination of both. Any point on the Pareto frontier, such as B or C, is Pareto efficient. Any point under the line, such as A, is inefficient.

We can all agree

Using Pareto efficiency reduces the need to judge between conflicting interests. Avoiding such judgements is the hallmark of positive economics (describing how things are), as opposed to normative economics (prescribing how they should be). Pareto argued that free markets are efficient in his sense of the term. This formalized Adam Smith's idea that self-interest and free-market competition operate for the common good (pp.34–39). ∎

Vilfredo Pareto

Born in France in 1848, Vilfredo Pareto was the son of an Italian marquis and a French mother. The family moved to Italy when he was four, and

Pareto was schooled in Florence, then in Turin, where he did a PhD in engineering. While working as a civil engineer he became interested in economics and free trade. In 1893, he was recommended by his friend, the Italian economist Maffeo Pantaleoni, to succeed Léon Walras (p.77) to the chair of political economy at the University of Lausanne in Switzerland. He took up the post at the age of 45, and it was there that he made his major

contributions to the field, including his theories on income distribution.

Pareto continued to teach until 1911. His works were prolific, covering sociology, philosophy, and mathematics as well as economics. He died in Geneva in 1923.

Key works

1897 *Course of Political Economy*
1906 *Manual of Political Economy*
1911 *Mathematical Economics*

THE BIGGER THE FACTORY, THE LOWER THE COST
ECONOMIES OF SCALE

IN CONTEXT

FOCUS
Markets and firms

KEY THINKER
Alfred Marshall (1842–1924)

BEFORE
1776 Adam Smith explains how large firms can lower unit costs through labour division.

1848 John Stuart Mill suggests that only large firms can adapt successfully to certain business changes, and that this can lead to the creation of natural monopolies.

AFTER
1949 South African economist Petrus Johannes Verdoorn shows that increasing growth creates increasing productivity through economies of scale.

1977 Alfred Chandler publishes *The Visible Hand: the Managerial Revolution in American Business*, which describes the rise of giant corporations and mass production.

Alfred Chandler described the development of large US corporations, such as those in the motor industry, into vast production-line industries.

From the beginning of the Industrial Revolution, when manufacturing shifted from small-scale outfits to large factories, it became apparent that bigger firms could produce at a lower cost. As a firm grows and produces more, it uses more machinery, labour, and raw materials, so a bigger factory has higher total costs. But it can also produce more for a lower unit cost. This fall in average costs is known as economies of scale.

In 1890, British economist Alfred Marshall (p.75) explored this effect in *Principles of Economics*. He pointed out that when firms increase their output, all they can do in the short run is alter the number of workers to increase production – nothing else. As extra workers add less to output than the workers before them, costs per unit rise. Yet in the long run, if a firm is able to double the size of its factory, workforce, and machines, it will be able to take advantage of the specialization of labour and costs will fall.

In the 1960s, US economist Alfred Chandler (1918–2007), showed how the growth of large corporations caused a new Industrial Revolution at the start of the 20th century. Large enterprises came to dominate industries, producing more goods at lower cost and driving competitors out of business. These large firms often enjoyed a "natural monopoly". ■

THE COST OF GOING TO THE MOVIES IS THE FUN YOU'D HAVE HAD AT THE ICE RINK
OPPORTUNITY COST

IN CONTEXT

FOCUS
Theories of value

KEY THINKER
Friedrich von Wieser (1851–1926)

BEFORE
1817 David Ricardo argues that the value of a commodity is determined by the amount of labour hours used to produce it.

AFTER
1920 Alfred Marshall argues in *Principles of Economics* that both supply and demand have a role in determining price.

1949 Ludwig von Mises explains in *Human Action* how prices convey important information in markets.

1960 Italian economist Piero Sraffa questions the opportunity cost measure of value in *Production of Commodities by Means of Commodities*.

 Economics brings into view that conflict of choice which is one of the permanent characteristics of human existence.
Lionel Robbins

E conomists at the end of the 1800s were still wrestling with what determined the value of a product. By 1914, Austrian economist Friedrich von Wieser was convinced that the value of something was determined by what had to be given up in order to get it. In a world where people have infinite wants and yet have only a fixed amount of resources to meet those wants, he argued that scarcity would create the need for choices. He called this concept "opportunity cost" in *Foundations of Social Economy* (1914). In 1935, the British economist Lionel Robbins argued that a tragedy of human life is that the consequence of choosing to do one thing is that something else has to be given up.

True cost
This means that the cost of going to the movies, for example, is not really the cost of admission to the cinema but also the enjoyment you give up from your next best choice of activity. So although there is a monetary consequence of choosing one course of action, opportunity cost means more. You can't watch a movie and ice skate at the same time. Sometimes there is what can be called an opportunity cost even if there is no monetary cost. Weiser thought that ultimately the price of a product was determined by how much it was desired and this is measured by what people were willing to give up to get it, rather than how much it cost to produce. ∎

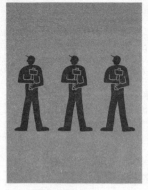

WORKERS MUST IMPROVE THEIR LOT TOGETHER
COLLECTIVE BARGAINING

IN CONTEXT

FOCUS
Society and the economy

KEY THINKER
Beatrice Webb (1858–1943)

BEFORE
1793 Friendly societies, an early kind of union, are given legal recognition in the UK.

1834 Workers in the USA and Europe begin to unite in national organizations.

1870s Union power in France and Germany becomes firmly allied to socialist movements.

AFTER
1920s and 30s Trade unions fight for workers' rights during the Great Depression.

1955 US unions unite under a single umbrella: the AFL–CIO.

1980s Union membership and collective bargaining begins to decline in the face of privatized public services and measures by right-wing governments to curb union power.

Public sector workers demonstrate in Madrid, Spain, in 2010 to protest against job cuts. Today, trade unions are stronger in the public sector than the private sector in most countries.

The term "collective bargaining" was coined by British socialist reformer Beatrice Webb in 1891 to describe the process by which workers organize into unions, which negotiate pay and conditions with employers on the workers' behalf. Webb and her husband, Sidney, campaigned against poverty and their books brought about change at government level. In 1894, they published *History of Trade Unionism*, documenting the rise of the unions during the Industrial Revolution in Britain, when large numbers of workers were thrown together in the new factories. Conditions were harsh, job security almost non-existent, and wages often close to the breadline. The Combination Acts of 1799 and 1800 outlawed trade unions, and any worker who combined with another to gain a wage increase or a decrease in hours was sentenced to three months in jail. After the acts were repealed in 1824, trade unions formed rapidly, especially in the textile industry. A series of strikes led to a new law, limiting union rights to meetings for collective bargaining purposes.

As union membership in Europe increased throughout the 19th century, a struggle developed between those who saw unions as following in the tradition of crafts guilds,

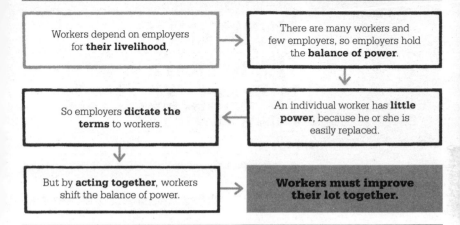

Workers depend on employers for **their livelihood**,	→

There are many workers and few employers, so employers hold the **balance of power**.

So employers **dictate the terms** to workers. ← An individual worker has **little power**, because he or she is easily replaced.

But by **acting together**, workers shift the balance of power. → **Workers must improve their lot together.**

---

negotiating for better working conditions for their members, and those who saw unions as the vanguard of a revolution, fighting for a better world for all working people.

A continuing struggle

Collective bargaining was widely adopted because it works for employers as well as workers. It dramatically simplifies the process of agreeing conditions, because one agreement can often be applied industry-wide.

However, since the 1980s, trade unions and the power of collective bargaining have shrunk dramatically. US economist Milton Friedman (p.117) has argued that unionization gives higher wages for union members at the expense of jobs and depresses wages in industries that are not unionized. Perhaps for this reason or more political ones, governments have often sought to curtail union power by outlawing sympathetic strikes.

The globalization of production has also isolated groups of workers within countries. The terms under which people work on a global product are often locally determined between workers and the company, rather than set industry-wide across the whole country. ∎

Beatrice Webb

Born in Gloucestershire, UK, in 1858, Beatrice Webb was the child of a radical member of parliament. She grew up with a keen interest in social questions and became fascinated in the structural problems underlying poverty. In 1891, she met her lifelong partner, Sidney Webb, and the pair became central to the British Labour movement. They formulated the idea of "the national minimum" – a minimum level of wages and quality of life below which a worker could not be allowed to fall. They also founded the London School of Economics and the magazine *The New Statesman*. The Webbs helped to shape the trade union movement. They created a blueprint for the UK's National Health Service and welfare systems around the world. Beatrice Webb died in 1943.

Key works

1894 *History of Trade Unionism* (with Sidney Webb)
1919 *The Wages of Men and Women*
1923 *The Decay of Capitalist Civilization*

SOCIALISM IS THE ABOLITION OF RATIONAL ECONOMY
CENTRAL PLANNING

IN CONTEXT

FOCUS
Economic systems

KEY THINKER
Ludwig von Mises (1881–1973)

BEFORE
1867 Karl Marx sees scientific socialism as organized like an immense factory.

1908 Italian economist Enrico Barone argues that efficiency can be achieved in a socialist state.

AFTER
1929 US economist Fred Taylor says that mathematical trial and error can achieve equilibrium under socialism.

1934–35 Economists Lionel Robbins and Friedrich Hayek emphasize the practical problems with socialism – such as the scale of computation required and the absence of risk-taking.

 In the socialist commonwealth, every economic change becomes an undertaking whose success can be neither appraised in advance nor later retrospectively determined. There is only groping in the dark.
Ludwig von Mises

The German philosopher Karl Marx described socialist economic organization in his great work *Capital* in 1867 (pp.66–69). A socialist economy, he argued, required state ownership of the means of production (such as factories). Competition was wasteful. Marx proposed running society as if it were one enormous factory, and believed that capitalism would lead inevitably to revolution.

Economists took Marx's ideas seriously. When Italian economist Vilfredo Pareto (p.81) used mathematics to demonstrate how free-market competition produces efficient outcomes, he also suggested that these could be achieved by a central planner under socialism. His compatriot, the economist Enrico Barone, took this notion further in *The Ministry of Production in a Collectivist State* (1908). Just a few years later, Europe was engulfed by World War I, which many saw as a catastrophic failure of the old order. The Russian Revolution of 1917 provided an example of a socialist takeover of the economy, and the war's defeated powers – Germany, Austria, and Hungary – saw socialist parties take power.

Free-market economists seemed unable to offer theoretical counter-arguments to socialism. But then in 1920, Austrian economist Ludwig von Mises raised a fundamental objection, claiming that planning under socialism was impossible.

Calculating with money

Von Mises's 1920 article *Economic Calculation in the Socialist Commonwealth* carried a simple challenge. He said that production in the modern economy is so complex that the information provided by market prices – which is generated through the rivalry of many producers focused on making profits – is essential to planning. We need prices and profits to establish where demand lies and guide investment. His ideas started a debate between capitalism and socialism, called the "socialist calculation" or "systems debate".

Imagine planning a railway between two cities. Which route should it take, and should it even be built at all? These decisions require a comparison of benefits and costs. The benefits are savings in the transport expenses of many different users. The costs include labour hours, iron, coal, machinery, and so on. It is essential to use a common unit to make this calculation: money, the value of which is based on market prices. Yet, under socialism, genuine money prices for these items no longer exist – the state has to make them up. Von Mises said that this was not such a problem for consumer goods. It is not difficult to decide, based on consumer tastes, whether to devote land to producing 1,000 litres of wine or 500 litres of oil. Nor is it a problem for simple production, as in a family firm. One person can easily make a mental calculation as to whether to spend the day building a bench, making a pot, picking fruit, or building a wall. However, complex production requires formal economic calculation. Without such help, von Mises claimed, the human mind "would simply stand perplexed before the problems of management and location".

Market prices

In addition to using money prices as a common unit with which to evaluate projects, economic calculation under capitalism has two other advantages. First, market prices automatically reflect the valuations of everyone involved in trade. Second, market prices reflect production techniques that are both technologically and economically

Modern production is **complex and various**.

↓

Only **prices and profits** can efficiently guide investment.

↓

Under socialism, the **state owns** the means of production.

↓

Without private ownership and rivalry, there is **little information or incentive** for efficient production.

↓

Socialism is the abolition of rational economy.

feasible. Rivalry among producers means only the most profitable production techniques are selected.

Von Mises argued that genuine market prices rely on the existence of money, which must be used at all stages – for buying and selling the goods involved in production, and for buying and selling them in consumption. Money is used in a more limited way in the socialist system: for paying wages and buying consumer goods. But money is no longer needed at the state-owned production-end of the economy, just as it is not needed for the internal workings of a factory. Von Mises considered alternatives to money, such as Marx's idea of valuing products by the »

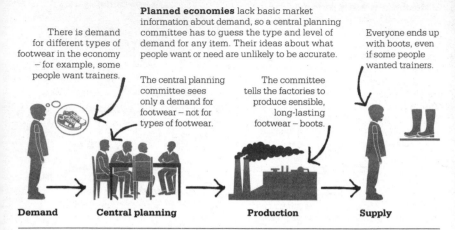

There is demand for different types of footwear in the economy – for example, some people want trainers.

Planned economies lack basic market information about demand, so a central planning committee has to guess the type and level of demand for any item. Their ideas about what people want or need are unlikely to be accurate.

The central planning committee sees only a demand for footwear – not for types of footwear.

The committee tells the factories to produce sensible, long-lasting footwear – boots.

Everyone ends up with boots, even if some people wanted trainers.

Demand   **Central planning**   **Production**   **Supply**

number of hours of labour that have gone into making them. But such a measure ignores the relative scarcity of different materials, the different qualities of the labour, or the actual (as opposed to labour) time that the production process takes. Only market prices take all these factors into account.

Changing prices

Von Mises, and his followers in the Austrian School of economists, did not believe that societies reach equilibrium, where they "naturally" hover around a certain level, or state of balance. He argued that economies are in constant disequilibrium; they are always changing, and participants are surrounded by uncertainty. Furthermore, a central planner cannot simply adopt the prices that previously prevailed under a market system. If central planning relies on prices from a different system, how could socialism possibly supersede the market economy?

Von Mises's challenge sparked several responses. Some economists claimed that a central planner could equate supply and demand through trial and error, similar to the process that Léon Walras (p.77) had suggested for establishing equilibrium in a market economy. However, this mathematical approach was really no different from the arguments of Barone, and any discussion of mathematical equilibrium was considered unrealistic by the Austrian School.

Von Mises's supporters, Lionel Robbins and Friedrich Hayek (p.105), added that such computation was not practical. Moreover, the socialist system could not replicate the risk-taking in the face of uncertainty undertaken by entrepreneurs in the market system. In 1936, economists Oskar Lange and Abba Lerner proposed a system of "market socialism" whereby many separate firms are owned by the state and seek to maximize profits, given prices set by the state. Hayek, the Austrian School's new champion, led the response to market socialism (pp.102–05), arguing that only the free market could provide the necessary incentives and information.

Socialism in action

For some of its life, the Soviet Union operated a form of market socialism. At first it appeared to do well, but the economic system suffered from persistent problems. There were periodic attempts at reform, shifting targets from output to sales, and trying to give more discretion to state firms. But state firms often hid resources from central planners, met targets through shortcuts that did not meet customer needs, and neglected tasks outside their plans. There was considerable waste and output fell well short of targets. When the system collapsed, the Austrian School's concerns about incentives and information seemed to have been justified by events.

Von Mises was equally critical of any form of government intervention in the market economy. He claimed that intervention produces adverse side effects which lead to further intervention, until, step-by-step, society is led into full-blooded socialism. In the market economy, firms make profits by serving consumers, and in his opinion – and that of the Austrian School – there should be no restrictions on such a worthwhile activity. The Austrian School does not accept the concept of market failure, or at least sees it as trumped by government failure. It believes monopoly is caused by governments rather than by private enterprise. Externalities (outcomes that are not reflected in market prices) such as pollution, are taken into consideration by consumers, or solved by voluntary associations, or the responses of people whose property rights are affected by the externality.

For the Austrian School, one of the worst forms of government intervention is interference in the money supply. They claim that when governments inflate the supply of money (by printing more money, for example) it leads to interest rates that are too low, which in turn result in bad investments. The only thing to do when a bubble bursts is to accept the commercial failures and ensuing depression. They recommend abolishing central banks, and

Socialist economies saw themselves as vast production lines assembling everything the economy needed. During World War II, this command style of production line worked relatively efficiently.

basing money on a real commodity standard, such as gold. The Austrian School are firm believers in laissez-faire (hands-off) government.

In 1900, there were five leading schools of economics. Marxism, the German Historical School (which was also critical of the market system), and three versions of the mainstream free-market approach: the British School (led by Alfred Marshall), the Lausanne School (centred on general equilibrium through mathematical equations), and the Austrian School, led by Carl Menger. The British and Lausanne schools became mainstream economics, but the Austrian School trod an uncompromising path. Only recently, following the 2008 financial crisis and the retreat of socialism, has it begun to grow in popularity. ■

Ludwig von Mises

The leader of the Austrian School, Ludwig von Mises was the son of a railway engineer. He was born in Lemberg, Austria–Hungary, in 1881 and studied at the University of Vienna, where he regularly attended the seminars of the economist Eugen von Böhm-Bawerk. From 1909–34, von Mises worked at the Vienna Chamber of Commerce, serving as principal economic adviser to the Austrian government. At the same time he also taught economic theory at the university, where he attracted a dedicated following but never became professor. In 1934, concerned by Nazi influence in Austria, he took a professorship at the University of Geneva. In August 1940, shortly after the German invasion of France, he emigrated to New York, USA, and taught economic theory at New York University from 1948–67. He died in 1973.

Key works

1912 *The Theory of Money and Credit*
1922 *Socialism: An Economic and Sociological Analysis*
1949 *Human Action: A Treatise on Economics*

CAPITALISM DESTROYS THE OLD AND CREATES THE NEW
CREATIVE DESTRUCTION

IN CONTEXT

FOCUS
Economic systems

KEY THINKER
Joseph Schumpeter (1883–1950)

BEFORE
1867 Karl Marx states that capitalism moves forward by crisis, repeatedly destroying a whole range of productive forces.

1913 German economist Werner Sombart argues that destruction opens the way for creation, just as a shortage of wood led to the use of coal.

AFTER
1995 US economist Clayton M Christensen distinguishes between disruptive and sustaining innovation.

2001 US economists Richard Foster and Sarah Kaplan argue that even the most exceptional corporations cannot beat the capital markets indefinitely.

When a recession bites and companies and jobs start to disappear, there is often a demand for government intervention to counteract these effects. The Austrian economist Joseph Schumpeter, writing in the depths of the Great Depression in the 1930s, disagreed. He insisted that recessions are how capitalism moves forwards, weeding out the inefficient and making way for new growth, in a process originally described by Karl Marx (p.68) as "creative destruction".

Schumpeter believed that entrepreneurs are at the heart of capitalist progress. Where Adam Smith (p.39) saw profit arising from the earnings of capital, and Marx from the exploitation of labour, Schumpeter said that profit comes from innovation – which does not derive from capital or labour. He saw the entrepreneur as a new class of person, an "upstart" outside the capital-owning or working class, who innovates, creating new products and forms of production in uncertain conditions.

The entrepreneur's creative response to economic change makes him or her stand out from the owners of existing firms, who only make "adaptive responses" to minor economic change. Forced to borrow to bring their innovations to market, entrepreneurs take risks and inevitably meet with resistance. They disturb the old system and open up new opportunities for profit. For Schumpeter, innovation creates new markets far more effectively than Smith's "invisible hand" or free-market competition.

Breaking through
Schumpeter argued that, although a new market may grow after an innovation, others soon imitate and begin to eat into the profits of the original innovator. In time, the market begins to stagnate. Recessions are a vital way of moving things forward

To survive, capitalists continually seek **new profits** through the pursuit of **new markets**.

↓

The pursuit of new markets leads to **innovations**.

↓

As **capital (money) shifts** to new markets and innovations...

↓

... existing sectors of industry are **devastated**.

↓

Capitalism destroys the old and creates the new.

again, clearing away the dead wood, even if the process is painful. In recent years, business strategists such as US economist Clayton M Christensen have distinguished between two types of innovations. "Sustaining" innovations maintain an ongoing system, and are often technological improvements. On the other hand, "disruptive" innovations upset the market and really get things moving, changing the market through product innovation. For example, although Apple did not invent the technology of the digital music player, it combined a high-design product (iPod) with a music download program (iTunes) to provide a new way of accessing music.

Marx believed that creative destruction gave capitalism huge energy, but also explosive crises that would destroy it. Schumpeter agreed, but argued that it would destroy itself due to its success, not failure. He saw monopolies as the engine of innovation, but said these were doomed to grow into over-large corporations, whose bureaucracy would eventually stifle the entrepreneurial spirit that had given them life. ∎

Joseph Schumpeter

Born in 1883 in Moravia, then part of the Austro-Hungarian Empire, Joseph Schumpeter was the son of a German factory owner. His father died when he was four, and Schumpeter moved with his mother to Vienna. There she married an aristocratic Viennese general, who helped launch the brilliant young economist on a whirlwind career that saw him become a professor of economics, the Austrian Minister for Finance, and President of the Biedermann Bank.

After the bank collapsed in 1924, and Austria and Germany succumbed to nazism, Schumpeter moved to the USA. He became a lecturer at Harvard, where he acquired a small cult following. Schumpeter died in 1950 at the age of 66.

Key works

1911 *The Theory of Economic Development*
1939 *Business Cycles*
1942 *Capitalism, Socialism and Democracy*
1954 *History of Economic Analysis*

WAR AND DEPRESSIO

1929–1945

In the years following World War I, confidence in traditional economic thinking was put to the test by events in Europe and North America. Social and political unrest had led to a communist revolution in Russia, while hyperinflation had made the German economy collapse.

During the 1920s, the USA enjoyed such prosperity that in 1928 President Herbert Hoover said, "We in America are nearer to the final triumph over poverty than ever before in the history of any land." One year later, the Wall Street Crash took place: shares collapsed, and thousands of firms folded. By 1932, more than 13 million Americans were unemployed. The USA recalled the huge loans they had previously made to Europe, and European banks collapsed. For much of the decade, many countries worldwide were in a severe depression. It was during this period that the British economist Lionel Robbins formulated his often-quoted definition of economics as "the science of scarce resources".

A new approach
Trust in the free market's ability to provide stability and growth was shaken, and economists looked for new strategies

to tackle economic ills, particularly unemployment. Some began to examine the institutional problems of developed capitalist economies. US economists Adolf Berle and Gardiner Means, for example, showed how managers were running corporations for their own benefit rather than for the firm's. The most pressing need was to find a means of stimulating the economy, for which a completely new approach was needed. The answer came from British economist John Maynard Keynes (p.99), who recognized the failings of a totally free market – one that is untouched by any form of intervention. Where previous generations had trusted the market's own workings to right the system's shortcomings, Keynes advocated state intervention, and specifically government spending, to boost demand and lift economies out of depression.

At first, his ideas were met with skepticism, but they later gained support. His model envisaged the economy as a machine that could be regulated by governments through adjusting variables such as the money supply and public spending. In 1933, Keynes's arguments provided a rationale for US President

NS

Franklin D Roosevelt to kick-start the US economy with the stimulus policies known as the New Deal. Government money was used to fund huge infrastructure projects and all banks were taken under federal control. The New Deal formed the basis for economic policy in America and Europe following World War II.

Norwegian economist Ragnar Frisch drew attention to the two different ways in which an economy could be studied – in part (microeconomics) or as a whole system (macroeconomics). The new field of econometrics (mathematical analysis of economic data) emerged as a useful tool in economic planning and forecasting. Modern macroeconomics took its approach from Keynes, and his approach was widely admired. However, despite the Keynesian solution to the depression of the 1930s, the idea of state intervention was still seen by many economists as unhealthy interference with the market economy. Some Americans saw it as alien to the "American way", while European economists associated it with socialism. Keynes himself saw it as part of a British Liberal tradition, in which the hard facts of economics are tempered by social considerations.

Global differences

Economics developed certain national characteristics, with different schools of thought developing along broadly cultural lines. In Austria, a radical school of thought evolved that supported an absolutely free market, based largely on the work of Friedrich Hayek (p.105). His stance was as much anti-communist as it was pro-capitalist. He argued that the freedom and democracy of the West was bound up with its free-market economies, while the tyranny of communist regimes, with their planned, centralized economies, removed this freedom. Others took this view further, arguing that competitive markets are essential to growth, as evidenced by the higher standards of living in Western capitalist countries.

The migration of many German and Austrian thinkers to Britain and the USA during the 1930s led these ideas to become widespread. Later on, as faith in Keynesian economics began to wane, a new generation of economists reintroduced the idea that markets should be left to their own devices. ∎

UNEMPLOYMENT IS NOT A CHOICE

DEPRESSIONS AND UNEMPLOYMENT

IN CONTEXT

FOCUS
The macroeconomy

KEY THINKER
John Maynard Keynes (1883–1946)

BEFORE
1776 Scottish economist Adam Smith argues that the "invisible hand" of the market will lead to prosperity.

1909 British social campaigner Beatrice Webb writes her *Minority Report*, saying that the causes of poverty are structural, and cannot be blamed on the poor.

AFTER
1937 British economist John Hicks presents his analysis of the Keynesian system.

1986 US economists George Akerlof and Janet Yellen explain involuntary unemployment through their efficiency wage models.

I n 1936, John Maynard Keynes published his ground-breaking work *The General Theory of Employment, Interest, and Prices*, often referred to simply as *The General Theory*. The book was important because it forced people to consider the workings of the economy from a completely different perspective. It made Keynes one of the world's most famous economists.

Ever since the Scottish economist Adam Smith (p.39) had published *The Wealth of Nations* in 1776, outlining what came to be known as classical economics, the economy had been viewed as a perfectly balanced collection of individual markets and decision-makers. The consensus among economists was that the economy would spontaneously and naturally achieve a state of equilibrium, with all those who wanted to work finding employment.

Keynes was to turn much of the basic cause-and-effect of the classical model on its head. He also argued that the macroeconomy (the total economy) behaved quite differently from the microeconomy (a section of the economy). Originally tutored in the classical school, Keynes claimed that he struggled to escape from its habitual modes of thought. His success in doing so, however, led to a radical economic approach that suggested an entirely different set of causes for unemployment, and equally different solutions.

For a century prior to the publication of *The General Theory*, poverty, rather than unemployment, was the enduring problem. Until the 1880s, countries such as Britain and USA, which were undergoing rapid growth as a result of the Industrial Revolution, enjoyed general advances in living standards but pockets of grinding poverty remained.

The idle poor

Economists had long seen poverty as the greatest social policy issue, but by the end of the 19th century, the unemployment of workers began to cause increasing concern.

The difficulty lies not in the new ideas but in escaping from the old ones.
John Maynard Keynes

At first, it was thought the problem was caused by illness or some defect in the character of the worker, such as idleness, vice, a lack of enterprise, or a lack of a work ethic. This meant that unemployment was seen as a problem for individuals who were for some reason unable to work, rather than a problem for society in general. It was certainly not seen as an issue that public policy needed to concern itself with.

In 1909, British social campaigner Beatrice Webb (p.85) produced *The Minority Report of the Royal Commission on the Poor Laws*. This was the first document to lay out the concept and policies of a welfare state, and it claimed that "the duty of so organizing the national labour market as to prevent or minimize unemployment should be placed upon a Minister". The term "involuntary unemployment" came into use for the first time. With this came the idea that unemployment is caused not by the shortcomings of individuals, but by surrounding economic conditions outside of their control.

Involuntary unemployment

By 1913, the concept of involuntary unemployment was understood as defined by the British economist Arthur Pigou: it was a situation where workers in an industry were willing to provide more labour at the current wage level than was being demanded. Even today, this definition would be regarded as a good representation of the involuntary nature of unemployment, in that it suggests that the workers have been left with no choice about whether they work or not. At this time, the classical view of unemployment still dominated. This held that unemployment was largely voluntary, that it existed because workers chose not to work at the going wage rate, or would rather be involved in some "non-market activity", such as childcare. Those holding this view insisted that any involuntary unemployment would be dealt with by automatic and self-correcting mechanisms of the free market.

Under the classical view, involuntary unemployment could not persist for long: the play of markets would always quickly return the economy to full employment. There is evidence to suggest that Keynes originally had some sympathy with this view. In *A Treatise on Money* (1930), he wrote that firms have three choices when prices fall faster than costs: to put up with the losses, close the business, »

Classical economics states that **unemployment is always a choice** – there are jobs if people are prepared to work for lower wages.

But wages change slowly, so during recessions, as prices fall, the value of wages rise – and firms **demand less labour**.

As demand in the economy slumps, workers are **trapped in unemployment** and firms are trapped in under-production.

Unemployment is not a choice.

or embark on a struggle with the employees to reduce their earnings per unit of output. Only the last of these, Keynes said, was capable of restoring real equilibrium from the national point of view.

However, after the 1929 stock market crash in the USA and the Great Depression that swept across the world in its aftermath, Keynes changed his mind. The financial collapse of Wall Street trapped the economies of the world in a cycle of falling production – it fell by 40 per cent in the USA. By 1931, US national income had fallen from a pre-crash level of $87 billion to $42 billion; by 1933, 14 million Americans were unemployed. Their gaunt figures haunted the landscape, and the rapid fall in living standards is evident in the images of poverty and desperation from that era. Witnessing this devastation inspired Keynes to write *The General Theory*.

The Great Depression

Keynes took the world of the Great Depression as his starting point. The normal workings of the market seemed unable to create the pressure necessary to correct the problem of high, persistent, involuntary unemployment in the economy. In general, the number of people in work

Anxious crowds gather on Wall Street, New York, on 29 October 1929, the day the stock market crashed. Half the value of US shares was wiped out in a day, starting the Great Depression.

is determined by the level of real wages – the level of wages relative to the prices of goods and services on offer. In times of recession, prices of goods tend to fall faster than levels of wages, because demand for goods lowers and prices fall, whereas workers resist cuts in their wage packets. This causes the real wage to rise. At this higher level of real wages, the number of people willing to work will increase and the number of workers demanded by firms will fall because they are more expensive. The result is unemployment.

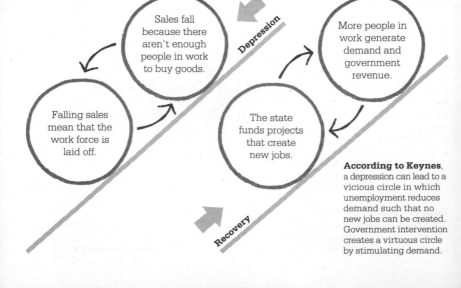

Sales fall because there aren't enough people in work to buy goods.

Depression

More people in work generate demand and government revenue.

Falling sales mean that the work force is laid off.

The state funds projects that create new jobs.

Recovery

According to Keynes, a depression can lead to a vicious circle in which unemployment reduces demand such that no new jobs can be created. Government intervention creates a virtuous circle by stimulating demand.

Sticky wages

One way to eliminate unemployment would be for the excess labour (the people not working) to create pressure on money wages to fall, by being willing to work for less than the going wage. Classical economists believed that markets were flexible enough to adjust and bring down real wages. But Keynes suggested that money wages might be "sticky" and would not adjust: involuntary unemployment would persist. Keynes argued that workers were unable to price themselves back into work by accepting lower wages. He pointed out that after a collapse in demand, such as that seen in the Great Depression, firms might notionally be willing to employ more workers at lower real wages, but in reality they cannot. This is because the demand for output is constrained by a lack of demand in the whole economy for the goods they make. Workers want to supply more and firms want to make more, because otherwise factories and machinery lie idle. A lack of demand has trapped workers and firms into a vicious cycle of unemployment and under-production.

The government's role

Keynes saw that the solution to the problem of involuntary unemployment lay outside of the control of both the workers and the firms. He claimed that the answer was for governments to spend more in the economy, so that the overall demand for products would rise. This would encourage firms to take on more workers and as prices rose, real wages would fall, returning the economy to full employment. To Keynes, it did not matter how the state spent more. He famously said that "the treasury could fill old bottles with banknotes and bury them... and leave it to private enterprise on well tried principles of laissez-faire to dig the notes up again". As long as the government injected demand into the economy, the whole system would start to recover.

Real wages

The General Theory is not easy to understand – even Keynes said he found it "complex, ill-organized, and

The unemployment rate in several countries between 1919 and 1939 is shown here. Most economies recovered in the 1920s only to suffer soaring unemployment with the onset of the Great Depression in 1930.

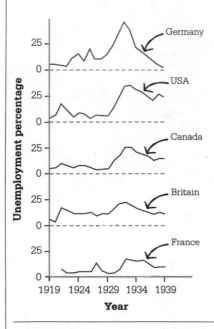

sometimes obscure" – and there is still considerable debate about exactly what Keynes meant, particularly by the difference between involuntary and voluntary unemployment. One explanation for high unemployment being involuntary is based on the idea that a firm's demand for labour is determined by the real wage that firms have to pay. Workers and firms can only negotiate what the money wage is for that job or that industry – they have no control over the price level in the wider, general economy. In fact, lower wages will generally reduce both the cost of production and therefore the prices of goods as well, meaning the real wage will not fall by the level required to remove the unemployment. In this way, the unemployment is involuntary because workers are powerless to do anything about it. There is a commonly held view that trade unions can resist the »

US President Franklin D Roosevelt invested in vast new infrastructure projects, such as the Hoover Dam on the Colorado River. Even so, the government was not pursuing Keynesian policies.

inflation, which would also cause a reduction in real wages, is resisted less strongly because it affects all of the workers equally.

Economic theories known as efficiency wages models ask why firms don't cut

adjustment of wages to the level required for full employment through the process of collective action, so that those who are unemployed are prevented from getting work. Keynes placed this type of unemployment in the voluntary category, arguing that workers in total are agreeing openly, or tacitly, not to work for less than the current wage. Keynes's reasoning was different from that of later economics, which became dominated by mathematical modelling. Much of macroeconomics in the post-war period was about clarifying what Keynes said and framing it in terms of more formal models and equations. British economist John Hicks (p.101) formulated Keynesian ideas in terms of a financial model known as the ISLM model. After the war, this became the standard macroeconomic model and it is still one of the first things taught to economics students.

New interpretations

Modern considerations of Keynes's work suggest that what workers are most concerned with is their wage relative to other workers. Workers have an idea of their position in a theoretical "league table" of pay, and will fiercely fight any wage reductions that would push them further down the table. It is interesting to note that a general increase in the price level through wages to increase profits, and suggest that firms are reluctant to do so because a wage cut would demotivate the existing workers, who would see their relative position in the league table undermined. The net effect of cutting wages would in fact be a loss in profits, because the benefit of lower wages is more than offset by the reduction in productivity that results from low morale or skilled workers leaving. In this way, workers cannot choose to price themselves into work. Related "New Keynesian" models of wage determination provide other explanations for rigid wages.

Classical resurgence

Keynesianism became discredited in the 1970s as European economies ran into trouble. Classical ideas about

 If by a regularization of national demand we prevent… the involuntary idleness of unemployed men, we make a real addition to the national product.
Sidney Webb
Beatrice Webb

unemployment were revived by the so-called "new classical" school of economists, who once again denied the possibility of persistent involuntary unemployment. The US economist Robert Lucas (1937–) was one of the leaders of the assault on Keynesianism. When he was asked how he would describe an accountant who was driving a taxi because he could not find a job as an accountant, Lucas replied, "I would describe him as a taxi driver, if what he is doing is driving a taxi." For the modern classicists, the market always clears and workers always have a choice whether to work or not.

Efficiency wage theorists might agree that all workers who want jobs in a recession might be able to get one, but they think that some workers – like the accountant – are under-utilized and are not maximizing their value to the economy. As a taxi driver, the man is still an involuntarily unemployed accountant. When demand in the economy returns to a normal level, he will return to his most productive and efficient occupation: accountancy. Fundamental difference in views about the ability of markets to adjust lie at the heart of the debate between Keynesians and the classical economists.

Classical reality

Keynes would probably have agreed with the American Nobel Prize-winning economist Joseph Stiglitz, who said that during the Great Depression in the USA, one quarter of the unemployed workforce of Chicago might be said to have chosen to be unemployed, because they could have migrated west to California to pick fruit on farms, along with the millions of others who did so. He said that nonetheless, this still represents a massive failure of the market, and if classical theory suggests that there is nothing more to be done than commiserate with the unemployed on their bad luck, we would be better off not consulting the theory at all. ∎

Is an accountant driving a taxi an out-of-work accountant or an in-work taxi driver? Keynesians might say that he is involuntarily unemployed. New classical economists say he has got a job.

John Maynard Keynes

Born in 1883, the year that Karl Marx died, John Maynard Keynes was an unlikely saviour of the working class. Raised in Cambridge, England, by academic parents, he led a life of privilege. He won a scholarship to Cambridge University, where he studied mathematics, then spent time working in the India Office of the British government, and published his first book: *Indian Currency and Finance.*

Keynes was an adviser at both the Paris Peace Conference after World War I and at the Bretton Woods Conference in 1944. He always did several things at once (while writing *The General Theory*, he built a theatre), and he counted leading writers and artists among his friends. Keynes made his fortune on the stock market, and used much of it to support his artist friends. He died of heart problems in 1946.

Key works

1919 *The Economic Consequences of the Peace*
1930 *A Treatise on Money*
1936 *The General Theory of Employment, Interest and Money*

GOVERNMENT SPENDING BOOSTS THE ECONOMY BY MORE THAN WHAT IS SPENT
THE KEYNESIAN MULTIPLIER

IN CONTEXT

FOCUS
The macroeconomy

KEY THINKER
John Maynard Keynes (1883–1946)

BEFORE
1931 British economist Richard Kahn sets out an explicit theory to explain the multiplying effects of government spending suggested by John Maynard Keynes.

AFTER
1971 Polish economist Michal Kalecki further develops the notion of the multiplier.

1974 US economist Robert Barro revives the idea of "Ricardian equivalence" (that people alter their behaviour to adjust to government budget shifts). This implies there are no multiplier effects from government spending.

 Besides the primary employment created by the initial public works expenditures, there would be additional indirect employment.
Don Patinkin
US economist (1922–95)

Macroeconomics seeks to explain the working of entire economies. In 1758, the French economist François Quesnay (p.29) demonstrated how large amounts of spending by those at the top of the economic tree – the landlords – was multiplied as others received money from them and re-spent it.

In the 20th century, British economist John Maynard Keynes looked specifically at why prices and labour do not revert to equilibrium, or natural levels, during depressions. Classical economics – the standard school of thought from the 18th to the 20th centuries – says that this should naturally occur through the normal working of the free market. Keynes concluded that the fastest way to help an economy recover was to boost demand through an increase in short-term government spending.

A key idea here was that of the multiplier, discussed by Keynes and others, notably Richard Kahn, and then developed mathematically by John Hicks. This says that if a government invests in large projects (such as road building) during a recession, employment will rise by more than the number of workers employed directly. National income will be boosted by more than the amount of government spending.

This is because the workers on the government projects will spend a proportion of their income on things made by other people around them, and this spending creates further employment. These newly

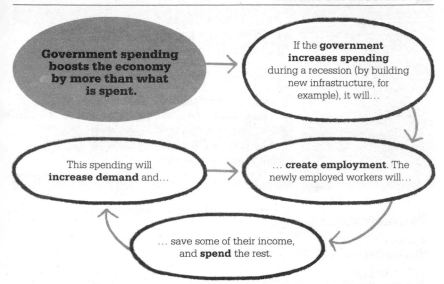

Government spending boosts the economy by more than what is spent.

If the **government increases spending** during a recession (by building new infrastructure, for example), it will…

This spending will **increase demand** and…

… **create employment**. The newly employed workers will…

… save some of their income, and **spend** the rest.

employed workers will also spend some of their income, creating yet more employment. This process will continue, but the effect will lessen on each round of spending, as each time some of the extra income will be saved or spent on goods from abroad. A standard estimate is that every £1 of government spending might create an increase in income of £1.40 through these secondary effects.

In 1936, British economist John Hicks devised a mathematical model based on the Keynesian multiplier, known as the ISLM model (Investment, Savings, the demand for Liquidity, and the Money supply). It could be used to predict how changes in government spending or taxation would impact on the level of employment through the multiplier. During the post-war period it became the standard tool for explaining the working of the economy.

Some economists have attacked the principle of the Keynesian multiplier, claiming that governments would finance spending through taxation or debt. Tax would take money out of the economy, so create the opposite effect to that desired, while debt would cause inflation, lessening the purchasing power of those vital wages. ■

John Hicks

The son of a journalist, John Hicks was born in Warwick, England, in 1904. He received a private-school education and a degree in philosophy, politics, and economics from Oxford University, all funded by mathematical scholarships. In 1923 he began lecturing at the London School of Economics alongside Friedrich Hayek and Ursula Webb, an eminent British economist who became his wife in 1935. Hicks later taught at the universities of Cambridge, Manchester, and Oxford. Humanitarianism lay at the heart of all his work, and he and his wife travelled widely after World War II, advising many newly independent countries on their financial structures. Hicks was knighted in 1964 and awarded the Nobel Prize in 1972. He died in 1989.

Key works

1937 *Mr. Keynes and the Classics*
1939 *Value and Capital*
1965 *Capital and Growth*

WE WISH TO PRESERVE A FREE SOCIETY

ECONOMIC LIBERALISM

IN CONTEXT

FOCUS
Society and the economy

KEY THINKER
Friedrich Hayek (1899–1992)

BEFORE
1908 Italian economist Enrico Barone shows how a central government planner can replace the free market if it can calculate prices.

1920 Ludwig von Mises refutes Barone's argument.

1936–37 Oskar Lange argues against von Mises's position.

AFTER
1970s Hayek's arguments for free markets gain ground.

1991 US historian Francis Fukuyama says free-market capitalism has defeated all possible alternatives.

Late 2000s Criticisms of government bank bailouts prompt a revival of interest in Hayek's ideas.

Mainstream economics has always had its critics. Its focus on mathematical formulae and its sometimes sweeping assumptions have led economists to challenge both its methods and its lack of empirical evidence. Many of these critics have been from the political Left, who see the mainstream as providing a glossy support for an unjust free market.

One minority tradition, the Austrian School, has argued quite differently. Vociferous defenders of the free market, but critical of the mainstream, they have carved out a unique place within the discipline. Most prominent of these radicals was an Austrian-British economist, Friedrich Hayek. Hayek vies with John Maynard Keynes (p.99) for the title of the 20th century's most influential economist, and he made a range of contributions to political and economic thought. These covered economics, law, political theory, and neuroscience. His writings maintained a closely argued, consistent set of principles, which he saw as being in the tradition of classical liberalism: support for free markets; support for private property; and deep pessimism about the ability of governments to shape society.

Creating dictatorships
The argument for which Hayek is best remembered appeared in 1944 in *The Road to Serfdom*. At the time, there was a growing enthusiasm for government intervention and central planning. Hayek argued that all attempts to impose a collective order on society are doomed to failure. He said they would lead, inexorably, to the totalitarianism of fascism or Stalinist communism. Since all planning necessarily acts against the "spontaneous order" of the market, it can only occur with a degree of force, or coercion. The more that a

Firms **do not know everything** about the entire economy.

↓

But each firm has information about production and the market's demands that are **relevant to itself**.

↓

Firms make decisions based on these facts and **act on them**, for example by changing output.

↓

Prices move in response to these individual actions, and so **reflect total market information**.

↓

This produces a free market that governments should protect, because we wish to preserve a free society.

government draws up plans and imposes them, the more coercion is needed. As governments are poorly informed about the detailed workings of the market, planning is bound to steadily fail in its aims, while becoming increasingly coercive to compensate for those failings. At that point, a society would lurch towards a totalitarian state, in which all freedom was extinguished, however moderate the planners' initial goals.

Economists of the Left had argued that a centrally planned economy was not only possible, but more efficient than a free market. Their first significant opponent, in 1920, was another member of the Austrian School, Ludwig von Mises (p.89). He argued that socialism – here defined as central planning – is not economically viable. It offers no rational means of pricing commodities, since it relies on the *diktat* (unquestionable

command) of one central planner or committee to perform the allocation decisions that in a free market are undertaken by many hundreds of thousands of individuals. The amount of information needed to assess the scarcities and surpluses of a market and set prices correctly is so huge that the attempt is doomed to failure. Socialism, wrote von Mises, is the "abolition of the rational economy". Only a free market with private property can provide the basis for the decentralized pricing decisions a complex economy requires.

Socialism defended
Polish economist Oskar Lange, however, disagreed with von Mises. He famously responded to von Mises's claims in a 1936 article, *On the Economic Theory of Socialism*, using a development of general equilibrium theory. This theory, which was not perfected until after World War II, is a mathematical representation of a market economy stripped to its bare essentials. All imperfections in markets have been removed, and all participants in the market are fully informed and concerned only with their self-interest. On this basis, Lange said, a central planning board could fix the initial set of prices for the economy, and then allow all those in society to trade freely, adjusting their demand and supply around the prices given. The planning board could then »

The totalitarian state of North Korea suffers regular shortages and famine. Economists of the Austrian school claim that this is the inevitable result of central planning that ignores markets.

The free flow of information between individual sellers and vendors (left) results in the correct pricing of goods, according to Hayek. Centrally planned economies, on the other hand, impose the view of one person or committee (right), curtailing individual freedom to communicate and firms' ability to trade.

adjust prices according to demand and supply. The outcome, he argued, would be efficient. A planner could also reduce income inequalities and constrain the market's tendency to short-term thinking.

Lange had taken the usual assumptions of microeconomics (that supply and demand determine price), and turned them on their head. His work later formed the basis for welfare economics, which looks at how free markets can achieve socially desirable aims.

The Austrian School

However, Hayek and his colleagues offered quite a different version of the free market's virtues. They did not assume that markets lack imperfections or that individuals are completely informed. To the contrary, they argued, it is because individuals and firms are poorly informed and society imperfect that the market mechanism is the best way to distribute goods. This view became an important tenet of the Austrian School of thought.

In a situation of continual ignorance, Hayek argued, the market is the best available means not to provide information, but to acquire it. Each individual and every firm knows their own situation best: they have goods and services people demand, they can plan for the future, and they

see the prices that are relevant to them. Information is specific, and dispersed among all those in society. Prices move in response to actions by individuals and firms, and so come to reflect the entire amount of information available to society as a whole.

Hayek maintains that this "spontaneous order" is the best available means to organize a complex modern economy, given that knowledge about society can never be perfect. Attempts to impose collective restraints on this order represent a reversion to primitive, instinctual orders of society – and the free market must be defended against this.

Collective tyranny

The idea of spontaneous order came to dominate Hayek's thinking, and his writing turned increasingly to political questions. These were discussed most fully in *The Constitution of Liberty* (1960), which argues that government should act only to preserve the spontaneous workings of the market, in as far as this is possible. Private property and contracts are legally sacrosanct, and a free society must observe rules that bind all parties – including the state itself. Beyond this, the state can, if the need arises, act against those collectivist forces threatening to undermine the rule of law. Hayek was broadly in favour of democracy, but critical of its inclination in some cases towards a "democratic tyranny of the collective".

Birth of neoliberalism

Following World War II, the necessary rebuilding of countries led to a Keynesian consensus, which proposed increased government intervention in the economy. At the same time, Hayek and others in the Austrian School formed the Mont Perelin Society, which acted as a guiding influence on the free-market think-tanks that arose during the breakdown of the Keynesian consensus in the 1970s. A similar new approach to economic policy sprang up in South America, but it was its adoption by the governments of Margaret Thatcher in the UK and Ronald Reagan in the USA that made it globally significant. This was neoliberalism, and it followed closely the ideas of the once-maligned Austrian School.

Nationalized industries were privatized, and governments rolled back their intervention in the workings of the market. The Soviet Union collapsed, giving further impetus to the apparent triumph of Hayekian themes in politics. Across the world, even those parties once most adamantly opposed to free markets came to believe that there was no viable alternative, including Britain's Labour Party – who had been the direct target of Hayek's *Road to Serfdom*.

Mainstream economists strongly influenced by free-market thinking, such as Milton Friedman, have risen to influence. By 2000, a "new consensus" prevailed in macroeconomics that emphasized the limited role of the state.

New relevance

Despite the apparent triumph of Austrian themes in economics, and Hayek's 1974 Nobel Prize, the distinctive methods and theory of the Austrian School remained largely confined to the fringes. However, the collapse of the global financial system in 2007–08 and the subsequent bank bailouts have provoked a renewed interest in its doctrines. Austrian School economists have been prominent in attacking bank bailouts, claiming that they represent an unwarranted interference in the market. The Free Banking School, which calls for an end to the government monopoly of the money supply, takes its cue from a 1976 Hayek paper, *Denationalization of Money*, and its ideas have gained ground. Keynesian programmes of increased government spending have been similarly criticized. With mainstream economics in a continuing state of turmoil, the Austrian School is set to achieve fresh influence. ∎

Friedrich Hayek

Friedrich August von Hayek was born in Vienna, Austria, to a family of intellectuals. By the age of 23, he had received doctorates in law and politics, in addition to spending a year in the Italian army during World War I. Initially drawn to socialism, he attended Ludwig von Mises's seminars while in Vienna, and with von Mises's support founded the Austrian Institute of Business Cycle Research. In 1923, he travelled to New York for a year, and the accuracy of US newspaper accounts of the war compared to those in Austria led to his deep distrust of governments.

In 1931, he moved to London to teach at the London School of Economics, and became embroiled in a very public, two-year argument with John Maynard Keynes. Hayek became a British citizen in 1938, but in 1950 left London for the University of Chicago. He died aged 93 in Freiburg, Germany, in 1992.

Key works

1944 *The Road to Serfdom*
1948 *Individualism and Economic Order*
1988 *The Fatal Conceit*

INDUSTRIALIZATION CREATES SUSTAINED GROWTH
THE EMERGENCE OF MODERN ECONOMIES

IN CONTEXT

FOCUS
Growth and development

KEY THINKER
Simon Kuznets (1901–85)

BEFORE
1750s French economist François Quesnay states that wealth comes from agriculture, not from industry.

1940 British-Australian economist Colin Clark argues that economic growth involves a shift from agriculture to manufacturing and to services.

AFTER
1967 US economist Edward Denison highlights the important contribution of technological change and productivity growth to economic growth.

1975 US economists Hollis Chenery and Moshe Syrquin find evidence that as agriculture declines, economies grow, and then industry and services increase.

With **new technology** and the growth of manufacturing…

↓

… people increasingly move from rural areas **to the cities** for work.

↓

Industrialized work requires **more skill and education** than agricultural work.

↓

Workers benefit from learning, and contribute towards **cultural change and business growth**.

↓

Succeeding generations **continue to benefit** from these cultural and industrial advances.

↓

Industrialization creates sustained growth.

The Russian-born economist Simon Kuznets described the emergence of the modern economy as a controlled revolution – in which the factory replaces the farm. The resulting higher living standards require economic and social changes that run deeper than might at first be suggested by a simple, numerical rate of growth. Kuznets called this process "modern economic growth", and showed how success in achieving this is what sets rich countries apart from the rest.

The key characteristic of Kuznets' growth theory is that income per person grows rapidly, even in the face of an expanding population: there are more people and they are richer. This expansion is driven by the spread of factories and machines. With an increase in capital to sustain industrial growth, workers are redeployed out of small family enterprises into impersonal firms and factories. Yet new technologies and large-scale production methods cannot be exploited if people are illiterate, superstitious, or tied to the village. For Kuznets, this growth causes profound social changes, with an increase in urbanization and a weakening of religion.

The steam hammer, invented in 1837, was one of the machine tools that increased the pace of industrialization, allowing machines to build machines.

Industrial Revolution

Britain was the first country to achieve modern economic growth. The Industrial Revolution of the 18th century put Britain on the path to becoming an advanced industrialized nation. Steam power and inventions reshaped production. Workers left the fields and entered the factories. Cities grew. New means of transport and communication technologies allowed British firms to penetrate the global economy. Its own economy did not transform overnight, but the changes – technological, social, and institutional –

kept going. They led to unprecedented improvements in the living standards of a growing population.

The spread of true modern economic growth has been limited. Among the rich nations, including the USA, Australia, and Japan, the process continues today. After a first wave of industrialization, these economies have typically evolved away from heavy industry and towards the service sector, which will inevitably involve further kinds of social change. ∎

Simon Kuznets

Simon Kuznets was born in Pinsk, in present-day Belarus, in 1901. His involvement with economics began early – he became head of a Ukrainian statistical office while still only a student. After the Russian Revolution, Kuznets' family left for Turkey, then the USA; he followed them in 1922.

Kuznets enrolled at Columbia University in New York, earning a PhD in 1926. He then worked at the National Bureau of Economic Research, where he developed the modern system of national income accounting used to this day by governments worldwide. In 1947, Kuznets helped set up the International Association for Research in Income and Wealth, advising many governments. He taught widely, and in 1971 won the Nobel Prize for his analysis of Modern Economic Growth. He died in 1985, aged 84.

Key works

1941 *National Income and Its Composition, 1919–1938*
1942 *Uses of National Income in Peace and War*
1967 *Population and Economic Growth*

POST-WAR ECONOMIC

1945–1970

The years immediately following World War II were, inevitably, a time for rebuilding economies. Even before the end of the war, politicians and economists had started planning for peace. They were keen to avoid the problems that had followed World War I and to establish a peaceful world of international economic cooperation.

The League of Nations, an international organization set up to maintain peace, had collapsed at the beginning of the war, and in 1945 it was replaced by the more robust United Nations (UN). One of the UN's first tasks was to vote on proposals drawn up by delegates to the UN Monetary and Financial Conference, now better known after its location – Bretton Woods, in New Hampshire, USA. Here, delegates from the Soviet Union, the UK, and the USA agreed on the founding of major new institutions, such as the International Monetary Fund (IMF), the International Bank for Reconstruction and Development (IBRD), and the General Agreement on Tariffs and Trade (GATT).

Post-war Keynesianism

The British delegate at Bretton Woods was John Maynard Keynes (p.99), whose 1919 book, *The Economic Consequences of the Peace*, had warned what might happen after World War I as a result of economic policy. Keynes's work had inspired US President Franklin D Roosevelt to lift the USA out of the Great Depression of the 1930s by the state spending package of the New Deal. It was not surprising that his ideas were equally influential after World War II. In the USA, Keynesian policies were enthusiastically advocated by economists such as Canadian-American John Kenneth Galbraith and quickly adopted by the liberal-democrat government. In Britain, the incoming Labour government brought in measures that set up a welfare state. The rebuilding of the economies of Japan and Germany was to mark a turning point in their histories. Germany, in particular, experienced an "economic miracle", the *Wirtschaftswunder*, under Chancellor Konrad Adenauer. The success of their social market economy, tempering free-market economics with government intervention, became the model for many Western European economies in the second half of the 20th century. However, other countries were not moving along the same lines. Much of Asia was under communist rule, and the Iron Curtain

S

now separated Europe into East and West. This was the era of the Cold War between the Soviet bloc and the West. The spread of communist regimes prompted a reaction among many economists in the West, especially those with experience of their tyranny.

Free-market revival

Influenced by Austrians such as Ludwig von Mises (p.89) and Friedrich Hayek (p.105), the USA's Chicago School of economists took a conservative stance against the prevailing mood of Keynesianism. They advocated a move back to a free-market system with less government interference. The roots of this idea lay in the neoclassical economics of the turn of the 20th century, which focused its analysis on supply and demand. Economists of the Chicago School turned to science for inspiration. Kenneth Arrow used mathematics to prove the stability and efficiency of markets, and Bill Phillips (p.121) used ideas from physics to describe the trade-off between inflation and unemployment. Some Western economists, such as Maurice Allais, introduced ideas from psychology in the 1950s and 60s. This inspired new models

of decision-making that challenged the belief in "rational economic man" first described by Adam Smith.

Huge advances in communication technologies made the world seem a smaller place during the post-war decades, and economists became more aware than ever before of the international nature of economics. Although the USA and Europe still dominated economic thinking outside the communist states, more notice was being taken of the developing countries, not just as a source of raw materials, but as economies in their own right.

Globalization continued apace, and economists began to examine the reasons for the gap between rich and poor countries, and how this could be narrowed. Ideas for development moved from capital investment to debt relief, but it became clear that the problems were more complex, involving politics, culture, and economics. At the same time, economists began increasingly to suggest that perhaps economic prosperity was not the only – or even the best – way to measure a country's well-being. ■

IN THE WAKE OF WAR AND DEPRESSION, NATIONS MUST COOPERATE

INTERNATIONAL TRADE AND BRETTON WOODS

IN CONTEXT

FOCUS
Global economy

KEY EVENT
The Bretton Woods agreements are signed in New Hampshire, USA, in July 1944.

BEFORE
1930s The world economic system collapses during the Great Depression, and cooperation between economies breaks down.

1944 John Maynard Keynes publishes his plans for an "international currency union" to regulate world trade.

AFTER
1971 US President Nixon cuts the link between the dollar and the price of gold, ending the Bretton Woods system.

2009 The Bank of China says the dollar is unable to act as a credible reserve currency because of conflicts between the USA's domestic and international policies.

The gold standard was a monetary system that backed paper money with gold, thereby guaranteeing its value. It came into effect in Britain in 1821, and was adopted internationally in 1871.

The system provided a stable anchor for the international monetary system by fixing the exchange rates of various currencies relative to the price of gold. It also acted as a mechanism for making gold transfers between countries to reflect new balances of trade and capital flows. However, World War I placed exceptional demands on government financing, and the system began to break down.

Some countries suspended their gold standard membership to allow substantial borrowing and expenditure, often financed simply by printing money. The war's end did not see a smooth return to the status quo – countries such as Germany had exhausted their gold reserves and could not return to membership, while other nations re-entered the standard at wildly variable rates.

Abandoning gold

During the Great Depression of the 1930s, nations left the gold standard in droves as they tried to expand their economies by devaluing their currencies to promote exports. At the same time, international trade, which had been fairly unrestricted before the war, became subject to an increasing range of restrictions, as countries tried to maintain their position in a shrunken world market. These policies helped to prolong the Depression, as each new restriction or devaluation further reduced the world market.

After World War II, the Allied powers turned to the question of post-war economic reconstruction. A conference was held in June 1944 at Bretton Woods, New Hampshire, USA, where delegates agreed to a US plan

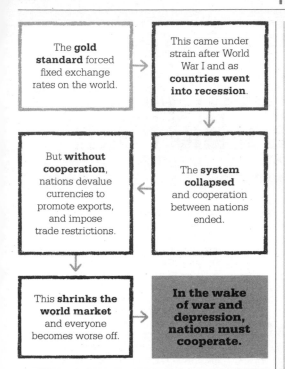

The **gold standard** forced fixed exchange rates on the world.

→ This came under strain after World War I and as **countries went into recession**.

↓

The **system collapsed** and cooperation between nations ended.

← But **without cooperation**, nations devalue currencies to promote exports, and impose trade restrictions.

↓

This **shrinks the world market** and everyone becomes worse off.

→ **In the wake of war and depression, nations must cooperate.**

to peg currencies against the dollar. The dollar, in turn, was to be maintained by the US government at a fixed rate of exchange with the price of gold.

This system was overseen by a new International Monetary Fund (IMF), which would be responsible for providing emergency funding, while the International Bank for Reconstruction and Development (now part of the World Bank group) was established to provide funding for development projects. In 1947, a General Agreement on Tariffs and Trade (GATT) aimed to rebuild international trade. Together these new organizations sought to renew economic cooperation among nations, the lack of which had been so costly between the wars.

This system held for nearly 30 years of exceptional economic growth, but it was structurally flawed. Continuous US trade deficits (where imports exceed exports) helped keep the system working, but dollars flooded abroad until the stockpiles exceeded US gold reserves, pushing the price of gold in dollars above the fixed price of gold. As US government expenditure increased, the strain worsened. In 1971, President Nixon suspended the dollar–gold link, ending the Bretton Woods system. ∎

The International Monetary Fund

Created by the Bretton Woods agreement, the International Monetary Fund (IMF) is today one of the world's most controversial international bodies. It was established initially as an emergency fund for countries experiencing financial difficulties arising from balance of payments deficits, debt crises, or often both. More than 180 member countries contribute towards a central fund, depending on the size of their economy, and they can apply for cheap loans from that fund. When the Bretton Woods fixed-exchange system was abandoned in 1971, the IMF's role changed. It began to impose strict conditions on its loans. From the late 1970s, these were heavily influenced by neoliberal ideas (pp.102–05), which advocated privatization and cutting government spending. Economists have criticized the IMF for making crises worse, such as the East Asian crisis of the late 1990s.

Traders watch as the crisis caused by the collapse of the Thai baht spreads across Asia in 1997. The Thais had given in to pressure from the IMF to float the baht.

ALL POOR COUNTRIES NEED IS A BIG PUSH

DEVELOPMENT ECONOMICS

One of the central questions for economists is "how did poor nations become rich?" After World War II, this question re-emerged with new force. The crumbling of colonial empires had spawned young, independent nations, whose living standards were falling further and further behind those of their former masters. Many of them were experiencing rapid population growth and needed a corresponding growth in the goods and services they produced in order to improve living standards.

Europe had quickly recovered from the war, aided by the Marshall Plan – a huge infusion of funds from the US government that funded the rebuilding of infrastructure and industries. The Polish economist Paul Rosenstein-Rodan argued that to make economic progress, the newly independent countries of the 1950s and 60s needed a "big push" in investment, just as Europe had received from the Marshall Plan.

Another related idea was that countries pass through a series of stages, taking them from traditional societies to mass consumer-based economies. Walt Rostow, the US economist who put forward this theory, said that for traditional nations to develop, massive capital investments would be required: it is the big push that triggers a take-off into self-sustained growth. This eventually transforms poor countries into mature economies, with high living standards for the majority of the population. The question of how the investments needed for a big push might be made became the central question of the new field of development economics.

Building simultaneously

Rosenstein-Rodan argued that in less-developed countries the market fails to funnel resources efficiently into beneficial investments that generate growth. This is because big projects such as roads, ports, and factories are complementary: the existence of one makes the others more economically viable. This can lead to a logical dilemma: the first investment might only be profitable once a second has been made, but the second investment is only viewed as profitable if the first has been made. For instance, a factory needs a power station nearby to be economically viable, but the power station is only profitable if there is a factory to buy its power. Two outcomes are possible: one in which there is no factory and no power station, another in which there are both.

The same kind of argument applies to more complex mixes of production. Imagine that a huge shoe factory is built in an underdeveloped economy. It makes £10 million worth of shoes, and the sales revenues go into wages and profits. However, this factory is only viable if all the incomes it generates (for its workers) are spent on shoes, whereas in fact people spend their money on a range of goods. Suppose people spend 60 per cent of their incomes on bread, 20 per cent on clothes, 10 per cent on paraffin, and 10 per cent on shoes. If factories making bread, clothes, paraffin, and shoes were built in exactly this ratio, the incomes generated from these enterprises would be spent on each industry's products in the same proportion. Only when these industries exist together, in the right proportions, do they become viable.

Essential linkages

The German economist Albert Hirschman used the term "linkage" to describe the interconnections between industries. For instance, a paint plant helps the development of a car industry by increasing the supply of paint. Hirschman called this a "forward linkage". The expansion of the paint industry also increases demand for the chemicals used to make paint, and so increases the profitability of chemicals factories. This is known as a "backward linkage". In practice, industries have multiple forward and backward linkages to other industries, creating a complex web of interactions, which can lead to the economic viability of an entire diversified production base.

The big push involves countries going from having nothing to having everything. From having no power station and no factory, developing economies suddenly need to have both. Starting from a position where they have no industrial sectors, they must establish all of them at once. But because each investment requires others, it is difficult for individual entrepreneurs to lead the push. For this reason, Rosenstein-Rodan and others like him argued that the big push has to come from the state, not from private markets.

In line with this thinking, post-war governments across the developing world became involved in large investment programmes, undertaking industrial and infrastructure projects as part of national development plans. Less-developed nations were viewed as having dual economies, consisting of traditional agricultural »

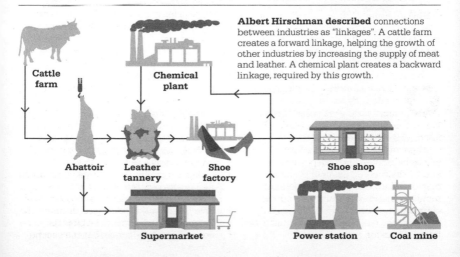

Albert Hirschman described connections between industries as "linkages". A cattle farm creates a forward linkage, helping the growth of other industries by increasing the supply of meat and leather. A chemical plant creates a backward linkage, required by this growth.

Cattle farm

Chemical plant

Abattoir Leather tannery Shoe factory Shoe shop

Supermarket Power station Coal mine

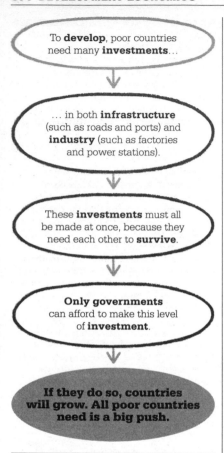

To **develop**, poor countries need many **investments**…

↓

… in both **infrastructure** (such as roads and ports) and **industry** (such as factories and power stations).

↓

These **investments** must all be made at once, because they need each other to **survive**.

↓

Only governments can afford to make this level of **investment**.

↓

If they do so, countries will grow. All poor countries need is a big push.

---

sectors (containing a lot of unproductive labour) alongside modern sectors made up of new industries. The idea was that the big push would siphon off excess labour from the rural areas and deposit it in the new industrial enterprises. This way of thinking provided the rationale for large infusions of foreign aid, intended as the fuel for the investment drive.

State-directed investment has led to beneficial industrialization in some places. Some Southeast Asian countries saw industrial expansion and fast income growth; their successful tying together of an activist state and big business became known as the Developmental State model. However, the conditions in which

the Marshall Plan was enacted in 1948 were different from those in the newly independent nations of the 1950s; many attempts at a big push ran into trouble.

Inefficient investment

At early stages the investments needed for economic development may seem obvious. Even so, coordinating an investment drive across many industries is a huge task. Governments can only create viable industries if they know the correct balance of production – the right share of shoes, clothes, and bread – which is implied by the composition of consumer demand. It is only possible to exploit the interactions between different kinds of production when there is detailed knowledge of the forward and backward linkages between industries. Not all governments have the expertise, information, or political clout to do this successfully.

What many countries ended up with was bloated, inefficient, state-owned industries that failed to trigger take-off into sustained growth. Industrialization was frequently attempted behind trade tariffs – foreign goods were shut out of the domestic market in the hope that this would give fledgling industries a chance to develop. The state's protection of firms from foreign competition generated "rent-seeking" – wasteful lobbying of the government by commercial interest groups seeking to preserve their privileges. Often this led to cosy relationships between governments hampered competition and innovation.

During the 1970s, the big push came under intellectual attack by economists who believed that developing economies were not fundamentally different from developed ones. They said economically rational behaviour and the power of price signals were as valid in poor as in rich countries. Investment was important, but it needed to be correctly distributed around the economy. Markets, not governments, were the best arbiter of where to invest.

This new wave of thinking held that developing economies were hampered not by the inherent inefficiency of their markets, but by the wrong policies. Too much state involvement had undermined the price mechanism (where prices are set by supply and demand), and had disrupted its ability to allocate resources efficiently. Good policy involved "getting prices right" and allowing the market mechanism to operate freely, so that resources would be put to the best use. The way forward was to roll back the boundaries of the state, remove rent-seeking, and let the price mechanism take over.

In the 1980s, this revision in thinking led to the rise of free-market development policy. The World Bank and the International Monetary Fund (IMF) introduced "structural adjustment programmes" to inject market principles into African economies. The so-called "shock therapy", used in Eastern Europe by these institutions after the fall of communism, was aimed at rapidly establishing market systems. However, these free-market experiments eventually came under attack for making poverty worse while also failing to build dynamic, diversified economies.

Market-friendly policies

Today, disillusionment with structural adjustment has led to a new consensus, fusing the insights of the early development thinkers with a more sanguine view of markets. Markets are now seen as vital in poor countries for creating incentives for mobilizing resources in a profitable way. At the same time, economists such as American Joseph Stiglitz have pointed to market

❝ Complementarity of different industries provides the most important set of arguments in favour of a large-scale planned industrialization.
Paul Rosenstein-Rodan ❞

failures at the small-business level that commonly restrain developing countries. For instance, profitable investments can't be made when small firms can't get loans. The state may have a role to play in correcting these failures, and in this way help the price mechanism to function more smoothly. This consensus, sometimes called the market-friendly approach, sees the state and markets as complementary.

However, at the start of the 21st century, there was a resurgence of more explicit big push ideas. In 2000, the United Nations drew up development targets for 2015 that included universal primary education, the eradication of hunger, and the reduction of child mortality rates. This involves promises by donor countries to keep up aid flows, and requires large, coordinated investments across a range of sectors and infrastructure projects. ∎

Post-war development in Latin America

Bolivia's oil industry enjoyed record investments from its government in 2011. Privatized in the 1990s, the industry was renationalized in 2006.

After World War II, many Latin American governments intervened in their economies to promote industrialization across a broad range of sectors. They restricted imports and set up new industries to produce the same goods, imposing tariffs and exchange controls to stifle foreign competition.

Governments also invested directly in the infrastructure that industry needed, helped by foreign aid and technical assistance. This process was known as Import Substitution Industrialization, and it

was most successful in countries that had internal markets that were large enough to allow heavy industry to sit alongside consumer-oriented enterprises in a viable way, such as Brazil and Venezuela.

Critics argue that Latin American countries should have focused on strengthening the sectors in which they had a comparative advantage, encouraging firms to become internationally competitive and to export their products.

GOVERNMENTS SHOULD DO NOTHING BUT CONTROL THE MONEY SUPPLY
MONETARIST POLICY

IN CONTEXT

FOCUS
Economic policy

KEY THINKER
Milton Friedman (1912–2006)

BEFORE
1911 Irving Fisher formalizes the quantity theory of money, which proposes that prices are directly related to the size of the money supply.

1936 John Maynard Keynes questions the effectiveness of policies to control the money supply.

AFTER
1970s Robert Lucas develops models that assume "rational expectations".

1970s–80s Many countries adopt formal monetary growth targets, by which governments attempt to control growth in the size of the money supply in order to keep down inflation.

The Great Depression saw millions of Americans migrate west in search of work on farms. Milton Friedman blamed the slump on the Federal Reserve's reduction in the money supply.

W riting in the 1930s, John Maynard Keynes (p.99) argued that policies aimed at controlling the money supply were often ineffective. He believed that altering interest rates or the money supply did not affect the economy in a predictable way. Instead, governments could better use fiscal policy – changing the mix of government spending and taxation – to protect against unemployment or inflation. By 1945, his views were widely accepted.

From the 1950s, however, US economist Milton Friedman began to challenge Keynes with the idea that "money matters". Friedman believed that money affects output in the short run, and prices only in the long run. He argued that monetary policy has a valuable role to play in managing the economy: an idea now known as monetarism.

In 1963, Friedman published *A Monetary History of the United States, 1867–1960* with his colleague Anna Schwartz. They tracked the role of money in business cycles, finding that fluctuations in monetary growth preceded fluctuations in output growth. In particular, they attributed the Great Depression of 1929–33 to the incompetence of the Federal Reserve, the US central bank, allowing or causing the quantity of money to fall by more than one third.

Theory of consumption

Keynes's case for government spending in a slump was based partly on his ideas about consumption. He argued that as people's income rises, their consumption also goes up, but not by as much. In a slump, people hoard money, which prolongs the slump. State spending in such a situation increases incomes, and has a large, predictable effect on consumption, restoring the economy to full employment.

In 1957, Friedman published *A Theory of the Consumption Function*, an important work that began to challenge the Keynesian orthodoxy. Friedman argued that people distinguish between "permanent income" – their stable long-term earnings, which they feel confident to consume – and "transitory income", which is less permanent, can be positive or negative, and which does not affect their consumption. Those with high incomes will have high transitory income, and consume only a small share of their total income; those with the lowest incomes will have negative transitory income, and will consume more than their income. But if you add all their incomes together, the positive and negative transitory incomes largely cancel each other out. Friedman's theory seemed to fit the evidence well. In a cross-section of the population, consumption did not rise much with income. But, measured over time and looking at the total population (so that transitory income effects cancelled out), consumption did rise with income. Friedman concluded that Keynes's model of consumption was wrong. State spending would be treated as transitory income, and would simply "crowd out" private spending. Unending slumps caused by inadequate consumption would not happen.

Quantity theory of money

Friedman aimed to show that monetary policy works: a change to the amount of money in the economy has a predictable effect on total incomes. Keynes had suggested that this relationship was unstable, because people held money for different reasons; some of these reasons were what he called "speculative" and hard to pin down. To help prove the quantity theory right, Friedman needed to show that the demand for money is stable. He had to come up with a testable theory about the demand for money.

In 1956, Friedman published *The Quantity Theory of Money: A Restatement*. He treated money as a good, a "temporary abode of purchasing power". The market demand for a good depends on people's overall budget and its relative price against other competing goods, as well as buyers' tastes. Friedman thought that the demand for money would be influenced by various »

Milton Friedman

Born in Brooklyn, New York, in 1912, Milton Friedman was the son of Hungarian immigrants. He was taught by the USA's top economists – at Rutgers, New Jersey, for his bachelor's degree; Chicago for his master's; and Columbia, New York, for his PhD. At Chicago, he met economics student Rose Director. They married in 1938, and collaborated throughout their careers. From 1935 to 1946, he worked as a statistician and economist in New York and Washington. From 1946 to 1976, he taught at the University of Chicago. It was there that he became a major figure. His fame increased with the 1980 TV series and book *Free to Choose*. He was an advisor to US presidents Richard Nixon and Ronald Reagan. He died in 2006.

Key works

1957 *A Theory of the Consumption Function*
1963 *A Monetary History of the United States, 1867–1960* (with Anna Schwartz)
1967 *The Role of Monetary Policy* Presidential address to the American Economic Association

factors. First, it would increase with the general level of prices, as money is wanted for its purchasing power over real goods. It would also be influenced by people's "real" wealth or their permanent income, and the returns on money, bonds, equities, and durable goods. Finally, demand for money would be influenced by "tastes", which in this context means factors such as economic uncertainty, which leads people to want to hold money.

Given a well-defined level of demand for money, an extra supply of money would not be required by consumers: they would already be holding the money that they needed. They would therefore spend any extra cash. Prices do not adjust instantly in the short run, so this would lead to higher output. But in the long run, prices would adjust and the only effect of the extra money would be higher prices. Friedman's approach can therefore be seen as a revival of the quantity theory of money, a formula that states $MV = PT$, where "M" is the money supply and "V" represents how quickly money circulates. "P" is the price level, and by multiplying this by "T", the number of transactions, we arrive at the total value of transactions. Roughly, this equation says that if V and T are constant then a higher money supply means a higher price level. In the long run, money has no "real" effects on the economy.

Natural unemployment

The word "monetarism" was first used in 1968, the year that Friedman presented a new account of the Phillips Curve (p.121). This showed the supposedly stable relationship between inflation and unemployment, which allowed governments to choose between less inflation with more unemployment, or more inflation with less unemployment. Friedman denied that such a trade-off exists except in the very short run. He said there is a single "natural rate" of unemployment, which consists of unemployed workers temporarily in the process of looking for jobs. In practice, the economy is at full employment when unemployment is at this natural rate. If governments spend money to reduce unemployment below the natural rate, pushing up inflation, wage-earners will further inflate their wage demands. Two things can then happen. Unemployment can return to the natural rate, at the new, higher inflation rate. Or the government tries to maintain the lower unemployment level, but at the cost of a spiral of accelerating inflation.

The **demand for money** can be predicted by looking at people's behaviour.

↓

The **supply of money** can be controlled by the government.

↓

Government spending cannot reduce unemployment below its natural rate without causing inflation.

↓

Inflation damages **economic efficiency** and should be avoided.

↓

Money should grow at a modest, constant rate in order to keep inflation low.

↓

Governments should do nothing but control the money supply.

Between 1975 and 1999, the US government set yearly targets for growth in the money supply. However, it regularly grew by more than the upper limit to the government target.

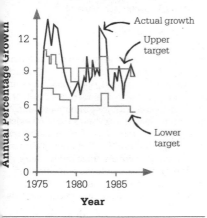

The conclusion was clear: it is futile for governments to try to stabilize employment through fiscal policy. Increasing the money supply likewise only leads to higher prices. In the long run, the Phillips Curve is a straight vertical line at the natural rate of unemployment.

The time lag between monetary changes and output changes is often only a few quarters. Price movements can take between one to two years or more to come through. These lags are considerably variable. For this reason, Friedman advised governments against trying to use monetary policy to actively manipulate markets, as it is easy to misread what is happening in the economy. They should follow a simple rule: ensure that money, however it is defined, increases by a constant amount – 2–5 per cent (depending on the definition of money chosen) annually.

The new classical macroeconomics school, led by US economists Robert Lucas and Thomas Sargent, put forward a revised version of this argument based on rational expectations of future economic policy. Friedman's model treated expectations as if they only adapted to past mistakes. Lucas and Sargent argued that people's expectations are forward-looking. People can see what governments might plan, so any government attempt to reduce unemployment below the natural rate will lead immediately to higher inflation. In other words, the Phillips Curve is vertical in the short run as well – governments don't ever have the power to reduce unemployment.

Monetarism in practice

It did not take long for Friedman's warnings to be proved correct. In the 1970s, the supposed Phillips Curve trade-off fell apart, as both inflation and unemployment increased together – a phenomenon known as stagflation. Governments started to introduce targets for growth in the money supply into their planning. Germany, Japan, the USA, the UK, and Switzerland adopted monetary targeting in the 1970s. However, it proved hard to control monetary growth. One problem was which form of money to target. Most central banks targeted a broad version of money, which included bank time deposits (deposits that cannot be withdrawn for a fixed period of time). However, this proved hard to control.

Attention then focused on the narrow monetary base, namely notes, coins and reserves held at the central bank. This was easier to control, but did not seem to enjoy a stable relationship with so-called broad money.

Monetarist experiments were largely unsuccessful, but the impact of monetarism was significant. It grew from a policy prescription about the money supply to a programme aimed at reducing government involvement in all aspects of the economy. Few today would disagree that "money matters". Monetary policy receives as much attention as fiscal policy, and is usually aimed at controlling inflation. But the purest form of monetarism and its policy implications rely on controversial assumptions: that there is a predictable demand for money and that the money supply can easily be controlled by the authorities. In the 1990s, countries moved away from monetary targeting. Many began to use the exchange rate to control inflation, or to tie interest rate policy directly to inflation trends. ∎

THE MORE PEOPLE IN WORK, THE HIGHER THEIR BILLS
INFLATION AND UNEMPLOYMENT

IN CONTEXT

FOCUS
Economic policy

KEY THINKER
Bill Phillips (1914–75)

BEFORE
1936 John Maynard Keynes attempts to explain unemployment and recessions.

1937 British economist John Hicks turns Keynes's insights into a mathematical model.

AFTER
1968 Milton Friedman argues that the Phillips Curve should account for people's expectations of inflation, and that there is a "natural" rate of unemployment.

1978 Economists Robert Lucas and Thomas Sargent attack the Phillips Curve.

From 1980s New Keynesian macroeconomics rehabilitates the possibility of stabilizing the macroeconomy (the whole economy).

F or 30 years after World War II, the world's more developed economies enjoyed their longest ever period of growth. Unemployment was low, incomes rose, and economists thought they had overcome the crises of the 1930s.

If **unemployment is high**, the government can boost demand by increasing its spending.

↓

This causes **prices to rise** (inflation) and unemployment to fall.

↓

But as more people are needed for employment, **wages rise**, pushing up other prices.

↓

The more people in work, the higher their bills.

This confidence stemmed from a belief in the power of government intervention to manage the economy, which was powerfully summarized in the Phillips Curve. In 1958, New Zealander Bill Phillips published *The Relationship Between Unemployment and the Rate of Change of Money Wages*, showing a link between wage inflation and unemployment in the UK from 1861–1957. Years of high inflation were years of low unemployment, and vice versa.

Inflation or employment?
Later work showed similar, stable relationships for other developed countries.

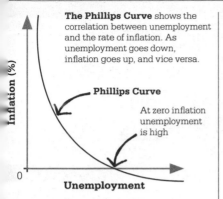

The Phillips Curve shows the correlation between unemployment and the rate of inflation. As unemployment goes down, inflation goes up, and vice versa.

Phillips Curve

At zero inflation unemployment is high

Governments realized that there was a trade-off between inflation and unemployment. They could pick their preferred point along the Phillips Curve, choosing either low unemployment and high inflation, or low inflation and high unemployment, and adjust their policies to suit. By increasing or reducing their spending, and tightening or slackening monetary policy (the money supply and interest rates), they could regulate aggregate demand (total spending) to fix the economy on the curve. The economy was treated like a giant machine. All major questions about the macroeconomy – the country's whole economic system – could seemingly be reduced to technical fixes, rather than battles over ideology.

The curve fitted well with the Keynesian macroeconomics (pp.94–99) that was prevalent at the time. When unemployment was high, it was assumed that the dip in labour and product markets would drag wages and prices downwards. Inflation would be low. When employment was high, additional demand in the economy – perhaps from government spending – did not increase output and employment, but pulled prices and wages upwards. Inflation would rise. However, by the 1970s this stable relationship appeared to have collapsed. Unemployment and inflation rose together, in a condition known as "stagflation". US economist Milton Friedman (p.117) explained it in a way that came to dominate macroeconomic theory. He said that as well as showing a relationship between actual prices and unemployment, the Phillips Curve needed to take account of expectations of inflation. People realized that when the government increased spending to boost the economy (and raise employment), inflation would surely follow. Consequently, any increase in government spending during periods of high unemployment was taken as a sign of impending inflation, and workers asked for wage rises ahead of prices actually rising. In the long run, claimed Friedman, there is no trade-off between unemployment and inflation. The economy is fixed at a "natural rate" of unemployment. Government attempts to stabilize the economy had merely pushed up expectations of future inflation, and actual inflation had risen as a result.

Friedman's challenge cleared the way for an assault on Keynesian macroeconomics, and governments turned to ways of improving the supply of capital and labour, rather than focusing their efforts on regulating demand. ∎

Bill Phillips

Born in New Zealand in 1914, Alban William Phillips moved to Australia in his early twenties, working for a time as a crocodile hunter. He travelled to China in 1937, fled when the Japanese invaded, and arrived in the UK in 1938 to study engineering. On the outbreak of World War II, Phillips joined the RAF. Captured by the Japanese in 1942, he spent the rest of the war in a prison camp. In 1947, he took up sociology, and enrolled at the London School of Economics, but switched to economics at post-graduate level. He became a professor there in 1958. In 1967, he moved to Australia to teach, but had a stroke two years later, and retired to New Zealand.

Key works

1958 *The Relationship Between Unemployment and the Rate of Change of Money Wages*
1962 *Employment, Inflation and Growth: An Inaugural Lecture*

THEORIES ABOUT MARKET EFFICIENCY REQUIRE MANY ASSUMPTIONS
MARKETS AND SOCIAL OUTCOMES

By the 1860s and 70s, mainstream economics had developed a distinctive set of claims about the world, offering mathematical models that allowed economists to assess individual behaviour in certain market conditions. These models were taken from the rapidly developing mathematics that described the natural world. This development, sometimes called a "marginalist revolution", involved a claim that value is determined by people's preferences and resources, rather than by a more objective or absolute standard, and it allowed pressing theoretical questions to be posed in new ways. Did Adam Smith's "invisible hand" of the market really guide self-interested individuals to the best available outcomes? Were markets more, or less, efficient than other ways of guiding society? Could completely free markets even exist?

Stable markets
French economist Léon Walras (p.77) was one of the pioneers of this revolution in theory. He attempted to show that markets, left to their own devices, can achieve a stable outcome for the whole of society, perfectly balancing the demands of consumers and firms with the supply of goods and services. It was known that a single market could achieve this balance, or equilibrium, but it was not clear that a whole set of markets could do the same thing.

The problem of "general equilibrium" was rigorously solved in 1954 by French mathematician Gérard Debreu and US economist Kenneth Arrow. Applying advanced mathematics, they showed that under certain circumstances a set of markets could achieve an overall equilibrium. In a sense, Arrow and Debreu had reworked Adam Smith's argument that free markets would lead to social order. But Smith made

Market prices reflect demands for and supplies of each commodity.

↓

So in theory, prices **completely reflect** both consumers' preferences and the limits to an economy's resources.

↓

This implies that markets lead to an **"efficient" economic outcome**.

↓

But this only happens if you **make assumptions** that rarely occur in the real world.

↓

Theories about market efficiency require many assumptions.

Gérard Debreu

Born in Calais, France, in 1921, Gérard Debreu was educated at the École Normale Supérieure in Paris during the German occupation. After a period of service in the French army, Debreu returned to his studies of mathematics and developed an interest in economic problems. In 1949, a fellowship allowed him to visit some of the top universities in the USA, Sweden, and Norway, bringing him up to date with economic developments that were then unknown in France. In the USA, he became part of the highly influential Cowles Commission, which had been convened in the 1930s to pursue the mathematical treatment of economic issues. He worked at the US universities of Stanford and Berkeley, teaching economics and mathematics. In 1983, he was awarded the Nobel Prize. He died in 2004.

Key works

1954 *Existence of an equilibrium for a competitive economy* (with K Arrow)
1959 *Theory of Value: An Axiomatic Analysis of Economic Equilibrium*

a stronger claim than the purely factual one that markets tend towards a point of stability. He also said that this equilibrium was desirable because it entailed a free society.

Pareto-efficient outcomes
Modern economists measure desirability using a concept known as "Pareto efficiency" (pp.80–81). In a Pareto-efficient situation, it is impossible to make one person better off without making another person worse off. An improvement takes place in an economy if goods change hands in such a way that at least one person's welfare increases and no one's falls. Arrow and Debreu connected market equilibrium with Pareto efficiency. In doing so, they rigorously probed Smith's ultimate »

An Edgeworth box is a way of showing the distribution of goods in an economy. In this example, the economy contains two people – Ben and Sarah – and two goods – 20 apples and 10 pears. Each point in the box represents a possible distribution of apples and pears between Ben and Sarah. The central line is the contract curve, which represents the possible allocation of goods that could be reached by Ben and Sarah after trading with each other. Trading to points on this curve leads to Pareto efficiency.

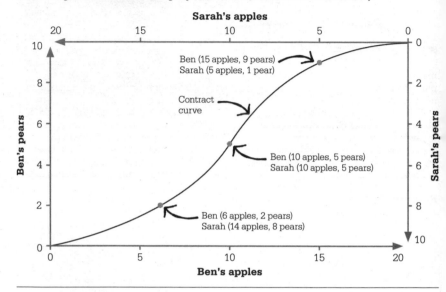

contention that market outcomes are good. They did this by proving two theorems, known as the "fundamental theorems of welfare economics".

The first welfare theorem holds that any pure free-market economy in equilibrium is necessarily "Pareto efficient" – that it leads to a distribution of resources in which it is impossible to make someone better off without making someone else worse off. Individuals begin with an "endowment" of goods. They trade with

 How this coordination [of supply and demand] takes place has been a central preoccupation of economic theory since Adam Smith.
Kenneth Arrow

each other and reach an equilibrium, which the theorem holds will be efficient.

Pareto efficiency is a weak ethical criterion. A situation in which one rich person has all of a desired good and everyone else has none of it would be Pareto efficient because it would be impossible to remove some of the good from the rich person without making him worse off. So this first welfare theorem says that markets are efficient but says nothing about the critical issue of distribution.

The second welfare theorem deals with this problem. In an economy there are typically many Pareto-efficient allocations of resources. Some will be fairly equal distributions, some highly unequal. The theorem says that any of these Pareto-efficient distributions can be achieved using free markets – a concept represented by economists as a "contract curve". However, to achieve a particular one of these allocations, an initial redistribution of individual endowments needs to be

> ❝ An allocation of resources could be efficient in a Pareto sense and yet yield enormous riches to some and dire poverty to others.
> **Kenneth Arrow** ❞

made. Then trading can begin and the particular Pareto-efficient allocation of resources occurs.

The practical implication here is that a government can redistribute resources – through the levying of taxes – and can then depend upon the free market to ensure the eventual allocation is efficient. Equity (fairness) and efficiency go hand in hand.

Real-world limits

Arrow and Debreu's results depend on stringent assumptions: when these don't hold, efficiency may be compromised, a situation that economists call "market failure". For the theorems to hold, individuals have to behave according to economic rationality. They need to respond perfectly to market signals, something that is clearly not the case in reality. The behaviour of firms has to be competitive, whereas in practice the world is full of monopolies.

In addition, welfare theorems don't hold when there are economies of scale, such as in situations in which there are large firms with high set-up costs – for example, in the case of many public utilities companies. A further important condition for the efficiency of equilibrium is that there should be no "externalities". These are costs and benefits that do not register in market prices. For example, the noise from a motorcycle workshop might hurt the productivity of a firm of accountants next door, but the workshop owners do not take this broader cost into account because it doesn't affect their private costs. Externalities hamper efficiency. Also, if individuals don't have full information about prices and about the characteristics of the goods they are buying, then markets are likely to fail.

What the theorems tell us

It is tempting to ask what is the point of this model if its assumptions are so removed from reality as to be inapplicable to any situation, but theoretical models aren't intended to be faithful descriptions of reality: if they were, Arrow and Debreu's model would be useless. Instead, their theorems answer a central question: under what conditions do markets bring efficiency? The stringency of these conditions, then, tells us by how much and in what ways real economies stray from the benchmark of full efficiency. Arrow and Debreu's conditions point to what we might do to move closer to efficiency. For instance, we might try to price pollution to deal with externalities, to break up monopolies to make markets more competitive, or to create institutions to help inform consumers about the goods that they buy.

The work of Arrow and Debreu formed the foundation of much post-war economics. Attempts were made to refine their findings and to investigate the efficiency of economies under different assumptions. Large macroeconomic models, both theoretical and empirical, were built using Arrow and Debreu's general equilibrium approach. Some have criticized the equilibrium approach for failing to take into account the chaotic, truly unpredictable nature of real-world economies. These voices have become louder recently, with the failure of these kinds of models to predict the 2008 financial crash. ∎

Equilibrium models failed to predict the crisis of 2008, which began when Lehman Brothers Bank collapsed and fired all its staff. This led to criticisms of the models' basic assumptions.

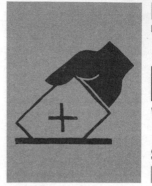

THERE IS NO PERFECT VOTING SYSTEM
SOCIAL CHOICE THEORY

IN CONTEXT

FOCUS
Welfare economics

KEY THINKER
Kenneth Arrow (1921–2017)

BEFORE
1770 French mathematician Jean-Charles de Borda devises a preferential voting system.

1780s English philosopher and social reformer Jeremy Bentham proposes a system of utilitarianism – aiming for the greatest happiness of the greatest number.

1785 Nicolas de Condorcet publishes *Essay on the Application of Analysis to the Probability of Majority Decisions*, in which he sets out the original voting paradox.

AFTER
1998 Indian economist Amartya Sen is awarded the Nobel Prize for his work on welfare economics and social choice theory.

Voters are to **choose between** candidates A, B, and C.

⬇

A **majority** of people might prefer...

⬇

... **A** to B...

⬇

... and **B** to C...

⬇

... but **also C to A**.

⬇

It is impossible to devise a voting system that truly reflects the preferences of an electorate.

At a first glance, the mathematics of voting may seem to have little to do with economics. However, in the area of welfare economics, and in social choice theory in particular, it plays a crucial role. Social choice theory was developed by US economist Kenneth Arrow in the 1950s. He saw that in order to evaluate the economic well-being of a society, the values of its individual members have to be taken into account. In the interests of making collective decisions that determine the welfare and social state of a society, there must be a system for individuals to express their preferences, and for these to be combined.

The collective decision-making process is dependent on a fair and efficient system of voting. However, in *Social Choice and Individual Values* (1951), Arrow demonstrated that there is a paradox at work.

Voting paradox

The so-called voting paradox was first described almost 200 years earlier by the French political thinker and mathematician Nicolas de Condorcet (1743–94). He found that it is possible for a majority of voters to prefer A over B, and B over C, and yet at the same time express a preference for C over A. For example, if one-third of voters rank the choices A-B-C, another third B-C-A, and the remaining third C-A-B, then a majority clearly favour A over B, and B over C. Intuitively, we would expect that C is at the bottom of the list of options. But a majority also prefer C over A. Making a fair collective decision in such cases is clearly problematic.

Arrow showed that a voting system that truly reflects the preferences of the electorate is not just problematic, but impossible. He proposed a set of fairness criteria that need to be satisfied by an ideal voting system. He then demonstrated that it was not possible for any one system to satisfy all these conditions. In fact, when a majority of reasonable assumptions are met, there is a counter-intuitive outcome. One of the criteria for fairness was that there should be no "dictator" – no individual who determines the collective decision. Yet paradoxically, when all the other conditions are adhered to, just such a dictator emerges.

The right to vote at the ballot box, shown here in 19th-century France, is entrenched in Western civilization and almost universal, but the truly perfect voting system is elusive.

The well-being of many

Arrow's paradox (also known as the general possibility theorem) is a cornerstone of modern social choice theory, and Arrow's fairness criteria have formed the basis for devising fair methods of voting that take into account the preferences of individuals.

Social choice theory has now become a major field of study in welfare economics, evaluating the effects of economic policies. This field, which began as the development of abstract theorems, has been applied to concrete economic situations in which governments and planners have to continuously weigh up the well-being of many. Much of this has profound implications for the fundamental economic problems of the allocation of resources and the distribution of wealth. ∎

What are social welfare functions?

There are various methods of assessing the well-being of a society. The 19th-century utilitarians thought that peoples' individual levels of utility, or happiness, could be added up, rather like incomes, to measure overall welfare. Later economists developed "social welfare functions" in an attempt to do the same, but these didn't necessarily involve the measurement of utility. Kenneth Arrow and others formulated these functions as a means of turning individual preferences into rankings of possible social states (their economic position in society). There is an ethical dimension to social welfare thinking. A simple form of utilitarianism emphasizes the maximization of total happiness less its distribution. Another, proposed by US philosopher John Rawls (1921–2002), maximizes the well-being of the least well-off person in society.

MAKE MARKETS FAIR
THE SOCIAL MARKET ECONOMY

IN CONTEXT

FOCUS
Society and the economy

KEY THINKERS
Walter Eucken (1891–1950)
Wilhelm Röpke (1899–1966)
Alfred Müller-Armack (1901–78)

BEFORE
1848 Karl Marx and Friedrich Engels publish the *Communist Manifesto*.

1948 German economists Walter Eucken and Franz Böhm establish the journal ORDO, which gives its name to ordoliberalism, a movement that advocates the social market economic model.

AFTER
1978 Chinese premier Deng Xiaoping introduces capitalist elements into the Chinese economy.

1980s Milton Friedman's monetarist arguments against government intervention are adopted by the USA and UK.

I n the aftermath of World War II, West Germany had to rebuild its economy and political system from scratch. Chancellor Konrad Adenauer carried out this task in 1949, following the Allied occupation. The model he chose had its roots in the ideas of Franz Böhm and Walter Eucken of the Freiburg school of the 1930s, which resurfaced in the 1940s as "ordoliberalism". Its chief advocates were Wilhelm Röpke and Alfred Müller-Armack.

These economists aimed to achieve what Müller-Armack called a social market economy: not just a "mixed economy", with government providing a bare minimum of necessary public goods, but a middle way between free-market capitalism and socialism that aimed for the best of both worlds. Industry remained in private ownership, and was free to compete, but government provided a range of public goods and services, including a social security system with universal health care, pensions, unemployment benefit, and measures to outlaw monopolies and cartels (agreements between firms). The theory was that this would allow the economic growth of free markets, but at the same time produce low inflation, low unemployment, and a more equitable distribution of wealth.

Economic miracle

The mixture of free markets with elements of socialism worked dramatically well. Germany experienced a *Wirtschaftswunder* ("economic miracle") in the 1950s that transformed it from post-war devastation into a major developed nation. Similar social market economies developed elsewhere, notably in Scandinavia and Austria. As Europe made moves towards economic union, the social market economy was extolled as the model for the European Economic Community in the 1950s. Many

A **free-market** economy…	A **socialist** economy…
… encourages **economic growth** and development.	… ensures more **equal distribution of** wealth.
It can also be volatile, suffer from market failures, and **produce monopolies**.	It lessens the effects of monopolies and market failure and **stabilizes the economy**.
This can lead to **inequality**.	But it can **hamper economic growth** and development.

A social market economy aims to make markets fair, by creating a middle way.

countries in Europe thrived under some form of social market economy, but by the 1980s, some – most especially Britain – were attracted by the ideas of Milton Friedman (p.117), who advocated "smaller" government. British prime minister Margaret Thatcher criticized the European model for its state intervention and high taxes, which she believed hampered competition.

With the collapse of communism in the Eastern Bloc, the planned economies of Eastern Europe were replaced by various versions of the mixed economy. At the same time, some of the remaining communist countries made moves to introduce reform. In China, for example, premier Deng Xiaoping adopted elements of free-market economics to operate within the centralized economy, in what he described as a "socialist market economy with Chinese characteristics". His aim was to promote economic growth and become competitive on the world stage. Today, China's economy is still a long way from the European social market model, but it has made significant moves towards becoming a mixed economy. ∎

The Nordic model

While the German social market is associated with centre-right politics, the economies of Scandinavia developed along similar lines but were politically centre-left, with more emphasis on making the markets fair. The so-called Nordic model is characterized by generous welfare systems and a commitment to fair distribution of wealth, achieved through high taxes and public spending. These countries have enjoyed high living standards and strong economic growth, helped by having small populations with strong manufacturing industries and, in the case of Norway, oil.

Today, there is pressure to reduce the role of the state in order to remain internationally competitive. However, change is gradual: governments are mindful that deregulation in Iceland in the 1990s led to economic growth followed by a financial crisis.

OVER TIME, ALL COUNTRIES WILL BE RICH

ECONOMIC GROWTH THEORIES

IN CONTEXT

FOCUS
Growth and development

KEY THINKER
Robert Solow (1924–)

BEFORE
1776 Adam Smith poses the question of what makes economies prosper in *The Wealth of Nations*.

1930s and 1940s Economists Roy Harrod of the UK and Russian-American Evsey Domar devise a growth model containing Keynesian (government interventionist) assumptions.

AFTER
1980s US economists Paul Romer and Robert Lucas introduce Endogenous Growth Theory, suggesting that growth is primarily the result of internal factors.

1988 US economist Brad DeLong finds little evidence for the basic convergence prediction of the Solow model.

Cyclists in Beijing, China, eye a Ferrari parked in the cycling lane. China and India have joined the club of converging ("catch-up") countries.

I n the 1950s, US economist Robert Solow devised a model of economic growth that predicted an equalization of living standards across the globe. His assumption was that capital has diminishing returns: extra investments add less and less to output. Because poor countries have little capital, extra capital would add a lot to output, and these returns pull in investment. Countries are assumed to have access to the same technology; by using it, poor countries use the additional capital to increase output. The effect is larger than would be the case in a richer country. The upshot is that growth is higher in poor countries and their living standards catch up with those of rich countries, in an effect economists call convergence.

Since the 1950s, a few Asian countries have caught up with the West, but many African countries have fallen further behind. Solow's assumptions aren't always satisfied. Technology is not universal: even when knowledge is accessible there may be barriers to using it. Capital doesn't always flow to poor countries; for example, weak property rights and political instability can put investors off. Finally, the endogenous growth theory, developed in the mid-1980s, goes beyond Solow's model by more realistically analysing the effects of technological change. In this

Capital in developed countries is subject to diminishing returns – **extra investment results in less and less** output.

↓

But poor countries have had so little capital invested that investors can still make **high returns** on their investments.

↓

Poor countries can use this **new capital with new technologies** to provide very rapid growth.

↓

Poor countries **grow faster** than rich ones, and their living standards catch up.

↓

Over time, all countries will be rich.

theory, new techniques developed by one firm can benefit other firms. This can lead to increasing returns on investment. So, rather than convergence, the result may be divergence between countries.

Living standards

Convergence can be measured using factors other than income. Health and literacy are related to income but imperfectly so: some poor countries have relatively healthy and educated populations. Life expectancies can increase dramatically through simple medical interventions such as immunization. So, in non-income aspects of living standards, poor countries have had more success in catching up.

Despite this, many economists remain focused on explaining income differences. Attention has shifted away from a concern with capital and technology towards the institutional prerequisites needed for developing countries to converge with richer ones. ∎

Robert Solow

Robert Solow was born in New York in 1924. His experience of the Great Depression made him want to understand how economies grow and how living standards can be improved. He entered Harvard University in 1940 but in 1942 left to join the US Army, serving in World War II. On returning, he was mentored by the economist Wassily Leontief and his PhD thesis won Harvard's Wells Prize – $500 and a book publication. Solow thought he could do better than his thesis, so he never published it or cashed his cheque. In the 1950s, he took a position at the Massachusetts Institute of Technology (MIT), where he published his ideas outlining a new model of economic growth. This research inspired new fields in the study of economic growth, and earned him the 1987 Nobel Prize.

Key works

1956 *A Contribution to the Theory of Economic Growth*
1957 *Technical Change and the Aggregate Production Function*
1960 *Investment and Technical Progress*

GLOBALIZATION IS NOT INEVITABLE

MARKET INTEGRATION

IN CONTEXT

FOCUS
Global economy

KEY THINKER
Dani Rodrik (1957–)

BEFORE
1664 English economist Thomas Mun says that growth requires reductions in imports.

1817 British economist David Ricardo says that international trade makes countries richer.

1950 Raúl Prebisch and Hans Singer argue that developing countries lose out from globalization because of unequal terms of trade.

AFTER
2002 Joseph Stiglitz criticizes globalization as promoted by the World Bank and the IMF.

2005 World Bank economist David Dollar argues that globalization has reduced poverty in poor countries.

G lobalization is a term that means different things to politicians, business people, and social scientists. To an economist it means the integration of markets. Economists have long thought this a good thing.

In the 18th century, Adam Smith (p.39) attacked the old mercantilist ideas of protectionism, which aimed to restrict the inflow of foreign goods. He argued that international trade would expand the size of markets and allow countries to become more efficient by specializing in certain products. Often, market integration is seen as inevitable because it rides on the back of a wave of new technology – such as smarter phones, faster planes, and an expanding internet. But globalization is also affected by choices made by nations – sometimes conscious, sometimes accidental. Although technological change tends to bring nations together, policy choices can push them apart.

Modern globalization is not unprecedented. Globalization has waxed and waned over time as nations have made different policy choices. Sometimes these choices have added to the effect of technological progress on the integration of markets; sometimes, they have hindered it.

Market integration is the fusing of many markets into one. In one market, a commodity has a single price: the price of carrots would be the same in east Paris and west Paris if these areas were part of the same market. If the price of carrots in west Paris were higher, sellers of carrots would move from the east to the west and prices would equalize. The price of carrots in Paris and in Lisbon might be different, though, and high transport costs and other kinds of expenses might mean that it would be uneconomical for Portuguese sellers to move their stocks to France if prices were higher there. In distinct markets, the price of the same good can be different for long periods of time.

Full globalization requires the **harmonization of trade regulations and laws** across countries.

↓

Such harmonization would require either a **global government** or the erosion of countries' democracies.

↓

Neither of these is feasible and they are **not desired by electorates**.

Globalization spreads with technology, but is also **impeded by barriers** such as trade tariffs.

↓

In the past, governments have made **different choices** about the level of barriers and therefore about the path of globalization.

↓

→ **Globalization is not inevitable.**

Global market integration means that price differences between countries are eliminated, as all markets become one. One way to track the progress of globalization is to look at trends in how prices converge (become similar) across countries. When the costs of trading across borders fall, there is more potential for firms to take advantage of price differences, for Portuguese carrot sellers to enter the French market, for example. Trading costs fall when new forms of transport are invented, or when existing ones become faster and cheaper. Also, some costs are man-made: states erect barriers to trade, such as tariffs and quotas on imports. When these are reduced, the cost of international trading falls.

The rise of global trade

Long-distance trade has existed for centuries, at least since the trade missions of the Phoenicians in the first millennium BCE. Such trade was driven by growing populations and incomes, which created a demand for new products. But the underlying barriers to trade that divided up markets, such as transport costs, did not change that much. Globalization only really took off in the 1820s, when price differences started to close up. This was

caused by a transport revolution – the advent of steamships and railroads, the invention of refrigeration, and the opening of the Suez Canal, which slashed the journey time between Europe and Asia. By the eve of World War I, the global economy was highly integrated, even by late 20th-century standards, with unprecedented flows of capital, goods, and labour across borders.

From the 19th century onwards, technological change helped to integrate markets. It is this that makes globalization seem irreversible – once technology such as steam-powered transport is invented, it is not then uninvented, but tends to become economically viable in more countries. Much of this development is outside the direct control of governments. However, at a stroke, governments can put up tariffs and other types of barriers to trade that choke off imports and stymie trade.

The most dramatic policy-related reversal of globalization in modern times occurred during the Great Depression of the 1930s. As countries headed into recession, governments imposed tariffs. These were intended to switch the demand of their consumers towards domestically produced goods. In 1930, the USA enacted the Smoot–Hawley tariff, which raised »

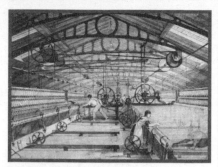

By the mid-19th century, Britain had new technology such as these mechanized looms in cotton mills, which allowed it to export and compete in multiple markets around the world.

tariffs on imported goods to record levels. These tariffs reduced demand for foreign goods. Foreign countries retaliated by imposing their own tariffs. The result was a collapse in world trade that worsened the effects of the Depression. It took decades to rebuild the world economy.

Integration

By the end of the 20th century, globalization across most markets had returned to the levels seen just before World War I. Today, markets are more integrated than ever as transport costs have continued to fall and most tariffs have been scrapped altogether.

One vision of the future of globalization involves the elimination of other kinds of barriers to trade caused by institutional differences between countries. Markets are embedded in institutions – in property rights, legal systems, and regulatory regimes. Differences in institutions between countries create trading costs in the same way that tariffs or distance do. For example, there may be different laws in Kenya and China about what happens when a buyer fails to pay. This might make it hard for a Chinese exporter to recover what it is owed in the event of a dispute, which could make the firm reluctant to enter the Kenyan market. Despite the removal of tariffs the world is far from being a single market. Borders still matter because of these kinds of institutional incompatibilities. Complete integration requires the ironing out of legal and regulatory differences to create a single institutional space.

Some economists argue that this process is underway and inevitable, and that global markets drive the harmonization of institutions across countries. Consider a multinational firm choosing a country in which to locate its factory. In order to attract the firm's investment, a government might cut business tax rates and loosen regulatory requirements. Other competing countries follow suit. The resulting lower tax revenues make countries less able to finance welfare states and educational programmes. All policy decisions become oriented towards maximizing integration with global markets. No goods or services would be provided that are incompatible with this.

Liberalizing the money markets

The liberalization of capital (money) markets, where funds for investment can be borrowed, has been an important contributor to the pace of globalization. Since the 1970s, there has been a trend towards a freer flow of capital across borders. Current economic theory suggests that this should aid development. Developing countries have limited domestic savings with which to invest in growth, and liberalization allows them to tap into a global pool of funds. A global capital market also allows investors greater scope to manage and spread their risks.

However, some say that a freer flow of capital has raised the risk of financial instability. The East Asian crisis of the late 1990s came in the wake of this kind of liberalization. Without a strong financial system and a robust regulatory environment, capital market globalization can sow the seeds of instability in economies rather than growth.

Globalization v democracy

The Turkish economist Dani Rodrik (1957–) has criticized this vision of "deep integration", arguing that it is undesirable and far from inevitable, and that in reality considerable institutional diversity persists between countries. Rodrik's starting point is that choices about the direction of globalization are subject to a political "trilemma". People want market integration because of the prosperity that it can bring. People also want democracy, and they want independent, sovereign nation-states. Rodrik argues that the three of these are incompatible. Only two are possible at any one time. How the trilemma is resolved implies different forms of globalization.

The trilemma comes from the fact that the deep, or more complete, integration of markets requires the removal of institutional variations between countries. But electorates in different countries want different types of institutions. Compared to US voters, those in European countries tend to favour large welfare states. So a single global institutional framework in which nation-states still existed would mean ignoring the preferences of electorates in some countries. This would conflict with democracy, and governments would be placed in what US journalist Thomas Friedman (1953–) has called a "golden straitjacket". On the other hand, a global institutional framework in which democracy reigned would require "global federalism" – a single worldwide electorate and the dissolution of nation-states.

Today, we are far from either the golden straitjacket or global federalism. Nation-states are strong, and persistent institutional diversity across countries suggests that the varied preferences of different populations are still important. Since World War II, Rodrik's trilemma has been resolved by sacrificing deep integration. Markets have been brought together as much as possible given nations' varied institutions. Rodrik calls this the "Bretton Woods compromise", referring to the global institutions that were established after the war (pp.110–11) – the General Agreement on Tariffs and Trade (GATT), the World Bank, and the International Monetary Fund (IMF). These

Nations may want democracy, independence, and deep global economic integration. Yet at any one time, only two out of three may be compatible with each other. In the diagram, each side of the triangle represents a possible combination.

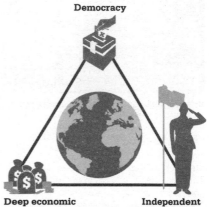

Democracy

Deep economic integration

Independent nation-state

organizations aimed at preventing a repeat of the catastrophic backlash seen in the 1930s through a form of managed integration, in which nation-states were free to pursue their own domestic policies and develop along varied institutional paths.

The liberalization era from the 1980s saw an undermining of the Bretton Woods compromise, with the policy agenda being increasingly driven by the aim of deep integration. Rodrik argues that institutional diversity should be preserved over deep integration. European electorates' desire for welfare states and public health systems is not just about economics, but also their view of justice. Institutional diversity reflects these different values. More practically, there is more than one institutional route to a healthy economy. The requirements for growth in today's developing countries may be different from those for developed nations. Imposing a global institutional blueprint runs the risk of placing countries in a straitjacket that suffocates their own economic development. Globalization may have limits, and it may be that the complete fusion of economies is neither feasible nor – ultimately – desirable. ■

SOCIALISM LEADS TO EMPTY SHOPS
SHORTAGES IN PLANNED ECONOMIES

IN CONTEXT

FOCUS
Economic systems

KEY THINKER
János Kornai (1928–)

BEFORE
1870 Economists William Jevons, Alfred Marshall, and Léon Walras focus on optimizing efficiency within budget constraints.

AFTER
1954 Gérard Debreu and Kenneth Arrow identify the conditions under which demand equals supply in all the markets of a competitive economy.

1991 The Soviet Union collapses and central planning ends.

1999 Economists Philippe Aghion, Patrick Bolton, and Steven Fries publish *The Optimal Design of Bank-Bailouts*, arguing that banks face a soft budget constraint.

In competitive markets, firms' **revenues must be higher than their costs**, or they will go bankrupt.

↓

In planned economies, if firms do not cover their costs, the state steps in to **protect them** from bankruptcy.

↓

This means that costs (materials and labour) do not have to be closely matched to **output or demand**.

↓

Socialism leads to empty shops.

After an initial dramatic rush of growth after World War II, the centrally planned economies of Eastern Europe faced increasingly obvious problems. They could mobilize resources on a large scale for well-defined tasks, such as producing military armaments, but seemed to have difficulty meeting more complex demands. Shortages abounded, as – despite planning – goods and services were not delivered on time, in the required quantity, or at an appropriate quality. The gap between the East and the West yawned wider.

Soft budget constraints
In response, a number of regimes attempted to introduce reforms to the planning system. Hungary went further than most, introducing elements of market competition from the 1960s onwards. In theory, this was supposed to introduce the benefits of the market, provoking innovation and expanding choice, while

retaining the ability of the plan to deliver broad social goods like full employment. In practice, after some initial successes the system continued to produce shortages and inefficiency.

Attempting to understand the problem, Hungarian economist János Kornai hit on the concept of the "soft budget constraint". In competitive markets, firms' decisions are normally subject to "hard" budget constraints: their revenues must at least cover their costs or they will face financial losses. This disciplines firms to economize on inputs and sell output in a way that maximizes profits. Kornai noticed that in planned economies such as Hungary's, firms were not subject to this discipline: they faced soft, not hard, budget constraints. The state cushioned firms from the threat of bankruptcy – firms that produced essential goods would never be forced to close. Even after some market reforms were implemented, the state continued to bail out failing firms. In addition, firms could use political bargaining to get away with underpaying for supplies, or avoiding taxation.

Soft budget constraints mean that firms do not have to cover costs with revenues. They tend to demand excessive amounts of inputs relative to production levels. This leads to excess demands for particular inputs, and then shortages arising from inefficiency. Shortages eventually trickle down to consumers, who find shop shelves bare. Kornai argued that shortages would mean that consumers would be subject to "forced substitution", the necessity of having to purchase the next best available good, given a shortage.

Bailouts

Inefficiencies such as these added up to serious weaknesses in planned economies. Guaranteed bailouts and a lack of budgetary discipline meant firms had little incentive to supply goods and services efficiently.

Kornai describes soft budget constraints as a "syndrome" of central planning that cannot be cured, because only a complete systemic change would bring a solution. The problem is not confined to socialist countries – Kornai has argued that major banks in the West face soft budget constraints, as they expect to be bailed out by their governments, leading to inefficiently high levels of risk-taking in the banking system. On the other hand, introducing hard budget constraints into every state or local-authority decision – such as forcing jail on an insolvent family – might be seen as unjust. In practice, even the most free-market economies contain a mix of hard and soft budget constraints. ∎

János Kornai

János Kornai is a Hungarian economist best known for his work on the planned economy. He experienced the horrors of fascism first-hand – his father died in Auschwitz – and this drove him to communism. He studied philosophy in Budapest, but changed to economics after reading Marx's *Capital*. In 1947, Kornai began working on the Communist Party newspaper, but he broke with the Party in the early 1950s, shaken by the regime's torture of an innocent friend. His critical articles resulted in his dismissal from the paper in 1955. Refused permission to leave Hungary, he worked at the Hungarian Academy of Sciences until 1985, when he took up a post at Harvard. Kornai returned to Hungary in 2001. He has criticized neoclassical economics for preferring abstract theorizing to addressing and answering the "big questions".

Key works

1959 *Overcentralization in Economic Administration*
1971 *Anti-equilibrium*
1992 *The Socialist System*

WHAT DOES THE OTHER MAN THINK I AM GOING TO DO?

GAME THEORY

IN CONTEXT

FOCUS
Decision-making

KEY THINKER
John Nash (1928–2015)

BEFORE
1928 US mathematician John von Neumann formulates the "minimax rule" that says the best strategy is to minimize the maximum loss on any turn.

AFTER
1960 US economist Thomas Schelling publishes *The Strategy of Conflict*, which develops strategies in the context of the Cold War.

1965 German economist Reinhard Selten analyses games with many rounds.

1967 US economist John Harsanyi shows how games can be analysed even if there is uncertainty about what sort of opponent you are playing against.

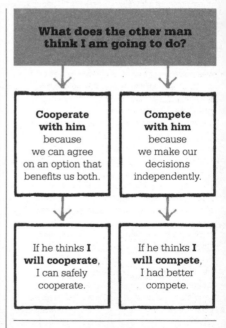

What does the other man think I am going to do?

Cooperate with him because we can agree on an option that benefits us both.

Compete with him because we make our decisions independently.

If he thinks **I will cooperate**, I can safely cooperate.

If he thinks **I will compete**, I had better compete.

C onsidering how another person might react when you do something involves making strategic calculations. Successfully negotiating your way through social and economic interactions is a bit like a game of chess, where players must choose a move on the basis of what the other player's countermove might be. Up to the 1940s, economics had largely avoided this issue. Economists assumed that every buyer and seller in the market was very small compared to the total size of the market, so nobody had any choice about the price they paid for a good or the wage they sold their labour for. Individual choices had no effects on others, it was reasoned, so they could safely be ignored. But as early as 1838, French economist Antoine Augustin Cournot had looked at

Our everyday interactions involve strategic decisions that are similar to a game of chess, where players choose their moves on the basis of how they think their opponent will respond.

how much two firms would produce on the basis of what they thought the other firm was going to do, but this was an isolated case of analysing strategic interactions.

In 1944, US mathematicians John von Neumann and Oskar Morgenstern published the ground-breaking work, *Theory of Games and Economic Behaviour*. They suggested that many parts of the economic system were dominated by a small number of participants, such as large firms, trade unions, or the government. In such a situation, economic behaviour needed to be explained with reference to strategic interactions. By analysing simple two-person games that are "zero-sum" (one person wins and the other loses), they hoped to create general rules about strategic behaviour between people in every situation. This became known as game theory.

Von Neumann and Morgenstern looked at cooperative games in which players were given a number of possible actions, each with its own particular result, or pay-off. The players were given the opportunity to discuss the situation and come to an agreed plan of action. A real example of such a game was provided by US mathematician Merrill Flood, who allowed his three teenagers to bid for the right for one of them to work as a babysitter for a maximum payment of $4. They were allowed to discuss the problem and form a coalition, but if they were unable to agree between themselves then the lowest bidder would win. To Flood, there were easy solutions to the problem, such as settling by lot or splitting the proceeds equally. However, his children were unable to find a solution and eventually one of them bid 90 cents to do the work.

Nash equilibrium
In the early 1950s, a brilliant young US mathematician named John Nash extended this work to look at what happens when players make independent decisions in non-cooperative situations – where there is no opportunity for communication or collaboration. Cooperation is a possible outcome but only if each player sees cooperation as maximizing their own individual chances of success. Nash identified the state of equilibrium in such games where neither player wants to change their behaviour. Players are choosing their best strategy on the basis that their opponents are also selecting their best strategies. Nash identified the state in such games where neither player »

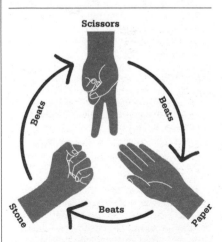

Scissors-paper-stone is an example of a simple zero-sum game in which if one player wins, then the other loses. The game is played by two players. Each player must make one of three shapes with their hand at the same instant. The shape one player makes will either match, beat, or lose to their opponent's shape: stone beats scissors, scissors beats paper, and paper beats stone. Game theorists analyse games such as this to discover general rules of human behaviour.

The prisoner's dilemma is an example of a non-cooperative game in which neither party can communicate with the other. The "Nash equilibrium" of the game is for both players to betray.

Stays silent

Betrays

Stays silent

6 months

10 years   **Free**

Betrays   **Free**   **10 years**

3 years

wants to change their behaviour as "each player's strategy is optimal against those of the others". This is now known as the Nash equilibrium.

There was an incredible blooming of game theory after World War II, much of it at the think tank RAND (the name comes from Research ANd Development). Set up by the US government in 1946, RAND was charged with putting science at the service of national security. They employed mathematicians, economists, and other scientists to research areas such as game theory, which was seen to be particularly relevant to the politics of the Cold War.

In 1950, the game theorists at RAND devised two examples of non-cooperative games. The first was published under the name "So Long Sucker". This game was specifically designed to be as psychologically cruel as possible. It forced players into coalitions, but ultimately to win you had to double-cross your partner. It is said that after trials of the game, husbands and wives often went home in separate taxis.

The prisoner's dilemma
Perhaps the most famous example of a non-cooperative game is the prisoner's dilemma. It was created in 1950 by Melvin Dresher and Merrill Flood, and builds on Nash's work. The dilemma involves two captured criminals, who are kept separate during interrogation and offered the following choices: They are told that if they both testify against each other, they will each get a medium jail sentence that will be painful but bearable. If neither will testify against the other, then they will both receive a short sentence that they will cope with easily. However, if one agrees to testify and the other does not, then the man who testifies will go free, and the man who stayed silent will receive a long sentence that will ruin his life.

The dilemma for each prisoner is this: to betray or not to betray. If he betrays his partner, he will go free or end up with a medium sentence. If he trusts his partner

Expensive technology, such as the Stealth Bomber, was developed during the Cold War. To avoid the "sucker's pay-off", game theory suggested that both sides should spend this money.

not to betray him, he could end up with a short sentence or a very long time in prison. To avoid the possibility of the "sucker's pay-off" – ending up with a long sentence – the Nash equilibrium is always to betray. What is interesting is that the "dominant" (best) strategy of mutual betrayal does not maximize welfare for the group. If they had both refused to betray, their total jail time would have been minimized.

Dresher and Flood tested the prisoner's dilemma on two of their colleagues to see whether Nash's prediction would be true. They made a game where each player could choose to trust or betray the other player. The pay-offs were designed so that there was a sucker's pay-off, but also an option for a cooperative trade that would benefit both players, a solution that reflected von Neumann and Morgenstern's earlier work involving cooperative games. The experiment was run over 100 rounds. This iterative version of the game gave players the chance to punish or reward the previous behaviour of their partner. The results showed that the Nash equilibrium of betrayal was only chosen 14 times against 68 times for the cooperative solution. Dresher and Flood concluded that real people learn quickly to choose a strategy that maximizes their benefit. Nash argued that the experiment was flawed because it allowed for too much interaction, and that the only true equilibrium point was betrayal.

Peace–war game

The iterative version of the prisoner's dilemma came to be known as the peace–war game. It was used to explain the best strategy in the Cold War with the Soviet Union. As new technologies such as intercontinental ballistic weapons were developed, each side had to decide whether to invest enormous sums of money to acquire these weapons. The new technology might lead to the ability to win a war relatively painlessly if the other side didn't develop the new weapon. The consequence of not developing it was either a huge saving of money if the other side didn't develop it either, or the sucker's pay-off of a total defeat if they did.

The importance of Nash's work in a wider context was to show that there could be an equilibrium between independent self-interested individuals that would create stability and order. In fact, it was argued that the equilibrium achieved by individuals trying to maximize their own pay-offs produced safer and more stable outcomes in non-cooperative situations than when the players tried to accommodate each other. »

John Nash

Born in 1928 into a middle-class American family, John Nash was labelled as backward at school due to his poor social skills. However, his parents recognized his outstanding academic ability. In 1948, he won a scholarship to Princeton University. His former tutor wrote a one-line letter of recommendation: "This man is a genius." At Princeton, Nash avoided lectures, preferring to develop ideas from scratch. It was there that he developed the ideas on game theory that were to earn him his Nobel Prize. In the 1950s, he worked at the RAND Corporation and MIT (Massachusetts Institute of Technology), but by now his mental state was worsening. In 1961, his wife committed him for treatment for his schizophrenia. Nash battled with the condition for the next 25 years but never stopped hoping that he would be able to add something else of value to the study of mathematics.

Key works

1950 *Equilibrium Points in N-person Games*
1950 *The Bargaining Problem*
1952 *Real Algebraic Manifolds*

Each player's strategy
is optimal against
those of the others.
John Nash

Nash shared the 1994 Nobel Prize for economics with two other economists who helped to develop game theory. Hungarian-born economist John Harsanyi showed that games in which the players did not have complete information about the motives or pay-offs of the other players could still be analysed. Since most real-life strategic decisions are made in the fog of uncertainty, this was an important breakthrough. A real-life example might be when financial markets cannot be sure of the central bank's attitude towards inflation and unemployment, and therefore cannot know whether it will increase interest rates to reduce inflation or reduce rates to increase employment. Since the profits of firms in the financial markets are determined by the rate of interest that the central bank will set in the future, firms need to be able to assess the risk of lending more or less money. Harsanyi

showed that even if the markets cannot tell which target the central bank is more concerned with, game theory can identify the Nash equilibrium, which is the solution to the problem.

The centipede game

Another economist responsible for advancing game theory was the German Reinhard Selten, who introduced the concept of sub-game perfection in games that are multi-staged. The idea is that there should be an equilibrium at each stage or "sub-game" of the overall game. This can have major implications. An example of such a game is the centipede game, where a number of players pass a sum of money between them, and each time they do so the pile of money is increased by 20 per cent. There are two ways for the game to end: the money is passed between them for 100 rounds (hence the name centipede), and then the total pot of money is shared or, at some stage one player decides to keep the pile of money that he or she has been given. Each player's choice is to cooperate by passing the money on or defect and keep the money. In the last round the player does best by defecting and taking all the pot. This implies that in the second-to-last round, defection is also a better choice –

Getting to the truth

When haggling with a buyer, a seller may start with a price many times what he is happy to accept, but in doing so risks losing the sale.

In 1960, Russian-born economist Leonid Hurwicz began to study the mechanisms by which markets work. In classical theory, it is assumed that goods will be traded efficiently: at a fair price and to the people who want them most. In the real world, markets do not work like this. For instance, Hurwicz recognized that both the buyer and seller of a second-hand car have an incentive to lie about how much each values it.

Even if both parties revealed how much they were willing to buy or sell for, and agreed to split the

difference in the price, it is unlikely that this mechanism would create an optimal outcome. Sellers will naturally claim to want a much higher price than they actually require, while buyers will offer much less than they are willing to pay. In such circumstances, they will fail to come to an agreement even though they both want to make a deal. Hurwicz concluded that if the participants could be persuaded to reveal the truth, then the benefits to both parties would be maximized.

In cooperative games, players have the chance to form alliances. In many of these games, such as a tug of war, the only chance an individual has of winning is to cooperate with others.

anticipating the future defection of your rival. By continuing this logic backwards it seems that defection dominates in every round so that the sub-game perfect choice is to defect on the first round. This result appears paradoxical, however, given that the sum of money in the first round is very small, and hardly worth defecting over.

This idea has been applied to the situation where there is a large chain store with outlets all round the country, and a rival is preparing to enter the market in one or more locations. The chain store could threaten to cut prices in the location that the new firm is thinking of entering. This threat would appear to be both credible and worthwhile as it would not cost the chain store too much profit and would deter the firm from trying to enter in that area. The optimal strategy in terms of Nash equilibrium appears to be for the chain store to fight a price war, and for the new firm not to try to enter the market. However, according to Selten, if the existing firm were forced to cut prices every time a new firm tried to enter one of its markets, the cumulative losses would be too great. Thus, by looking forwards and reasoning backwards, the threat of a price war is irrational. Selten concludes that the new firm's entry without a price war is sub-game perfect.

Bounded rationality
These paradoxes come from the assumption that individuals playing games are fully rational. Selten proposed a more realistic theory of decision-making. Although people do sometimes make decisions through rational calculation, often they do so on the basis of past experience and rules of thumb. People may not always use rational calculation. Instead, they may be what game theorists call "boundedly rational": able to choose the more intuitively appealing solutions to games that may not be sub-game perfect.

Game theory is not without its critics, who say that it tells great stories but fails the main test of any scientific theory: it can make no useful predictions about what will happen. A game might have many equilibriums. An industry resulting in a cartel might be as rational a result as one that descends into a price war. Further, people don't make decisions based on "If I do this and they do this and I do that and they do that" ad infinitum.

The US economist Thomas Schelling has addressed this issue by studying the idea that the triggers for behaviour are not simply based on mathematical probabilities. In the "coordination game", where both players are rewarded if they think of the same playing card, what card in the pack would you select if you wanted to try to match with someone else? Would you pick the ace of spades? ∎

RICH COUNTRIES IMPOVERISH THE POOR
DEPENDENCY THEORY

IN CONTEXT

FOCUS
Growth and development

KEY THINKER
Andre Gunder Frank (1929–2005)

BEFORE
1841 German economist Friedrich
List argues against free trade and for
protectionism in domestic markets.

1949–50 Hans Singer and Raúl
Prebisch claim that the terms of trade
between poor and rich countries
deteriorate over time.

AFTER
1974–2011 US sociologist
Immanuel Wallerstein develops
Frank's development theories to
devise world-system theory. This
uses a historical framework to explain
the changes that were involved in the
rise of the Western world.

R
ich countries claim that they do not
set out to keep poor countries poor –
rather that relationships between
them should help both parties. However,
in the 1960s, German economist Andre
Gunder Frank claimed that the development
policies of the Western world, along with
free trade and investment, perpetuate the
global divide. They preserve the dominance
of the rich world and keep poor countries
poor. Frank called this "dependency theory".

**Many Nigerian
oil workers** work
for foreign firms.
These firms have
poured investment
into Nigeria
but may benefit
disproportionately
from low local
wages and
valuable raw
materials.

Unbalanced trading
Rich Western countries were never junior
trading partners to a bloc of powerful
and economically advanced countries,
as poor countries are today. For this
reason, some economists have pointed
out that policies that helped the advanced
countries develop may not benefit
today's poor countries.

The liberalization of international
trade is often extolled by economists as a
guaranteed way of helping underdeveloped
economies. However, Frank's dependency
theory claims that such policies often lead
to situations where rich countries take
advantage of poorer ones. Underdeveloped
countries produce raw materials, which
are bought by richer countries, who then
produce manufactured goods that are sold
internally or between developed countries.
This leads to an unbalanced trading
system, where the majority of the poor
countries' trade is with richer, developed

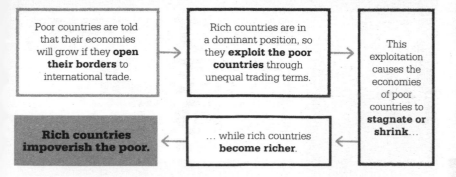

Poor countries are told that their economies will grow if they **open their borders** to international trade.

Rich countries are in a dominant position, so they **exploit the poor countries** through unequal trading terms.

This exploitation causes the economies of poor countries to **stagnate or shrink**...

Rich countries impoverish the poor.

... while rich countries **become richer**.

countries, whereas the richer countries' trade is mainly internal or with other developed nations. Only a small proportion is with the developing countries. As a result, poorer countries find themselves in a weak bargaining position – they are trading with larger, richer powers – and they are denied the favourable trading terms they need to progress.

It is argued that these forces lead to a separation of the global economy into a "core" of rich countries to which wealth flows from a "periphery" of marginalized poor countries. The economies of poor countries also tend to be organized in such a way that they discourage investment, which is a key driver of growth in the economy of any country.

When richer countries bring industry and investment to poorer countries, they claim that they will help grow the poor countries' economies. The dependency theorists claim that in reality, local resources are often exploited, workers are poorly paid, and the profits are distributed to foreign shareholders, rather than being re-invested into the local economy.

An alternative route

To avoid the kinds of dangers outlined by the dependency theorists, some poor countries have taken a different route. Far from opening themselves up to world trade, globalization, and foreign investment, they have decided to do the opposite and insulate themselves. Some argue that the rise of the Asian Tigers – Hong Kong, Singapore, Taiwan, and South Korea –

and the extraordinary economic growth of China expose flaws in the dependency view. Here were a group of developing economies for whom international trade was an engine of rapid growth and industrialization. Most recently, dependency theory has found echoes in the anti-globalization movements, which continue to question the classical approach. ∎

Unequal export: raw and manufactured goods

In 1949 and 1950, economists Hans Singer of Germany and Raúl Prebisch of Argentina independently published papers illustrating the disadvantage faced by developing countries when trading with the developed world. They observed that the terms of trade (the amount of imports a nation can buy with a given amount of exports) is worse for countries whose primary export is a raw material or commodity than for countries whose main export is manufactured goods. This can be explained by the fact that, as incomes rise, demand for food and commodities tend to remain steady.

On the other hand, higher incomes provoke stronger demand for manufactured and luxury goods. This leads to price rises, and results in the poorer country being able to afford fewer imported manufactured goods in return for the money it receives from exports.

SIMILAR ECONOMIES CAN BENEFIT FROM A SINGLE CURRENCY
EXCHANGE RATES AND CURRENCIES

IN CONTEXT

FOCUS
Global economy

KEY THINKER
Robert Mundell (1932–)

BEFORE
1953 Milton Friedman argues that freely floating exchange rates would enable market forces to resolve problems with balance of payments (the difference between the value of exports and imports).

AFTER
1963 US economist Ronald McKinnon shows that small economies would benefit from a currency union since they can mitigate shocks better than large economies.

1996 US economists Jeffrey Frankel and Andrew Rose argue that the criteria for a currency area are themselves affected by prior economic development.

By the early 1960s, the institutions of the post-war economies were well-established. Towards the end of World War II, the Bretton Woods system (pp.110–11) was set up to regulate the financial relations between the big industrial states, basing Western capitalism on a system of fixed exchange rates that controlled the flows of capital and money worldwide. International trade had recovered after the slump of the interwar years, and economic growth was rapid.

However, there were glitches in this system. First there were problems with balance of payments – the difference between what a country pays for imports and what it earns from exports. Balance of payments crises occurred because countries could not easily adjust their exchange rates within the international system. Coupled with tight labour markets and inflexible domestic prices, the previously automatic, market-led mechanisms that allowed countries to adjust to external economic shocks did not function very well. The result was a series of crises that arose when countries were unable to pay for imports by using the proceeds of their exports. Alongside this, a series of moves towards the integration of European economies began to float the possibility of a currency union between European countries. This started with the Treaty of Paris in 1951, which established common trading areas for coal and steel. In 1961, Canadian economist Robert Mundell was the first to attempt an analysis of what he called an "optimal currency area".

Currency areas
Mundell sought to answer what might at first seem an odd question: over what geographical area should one type of currency be used? At the time, this issue had barely been posed. It had simply been taken for granted that national economies used their own national currencies.

> It hardly appears within the realm of political feasibility that national currencies would ever be abandoned in favour of any other arrangement… **Robert Mundell**

The idea that this might not be the best arrangement had not really occurred to anyone. Mundell realized that while history had provided nations with their own currencies, this did not mean it had provided them with the best possible currency arrangements. There were clearly costs involved in using many different currencies, as these had to be exchanged if trade was to take place. At one extreme, having a different currency for every postcode in a city would be very inefficient. On the other hand, one currency for the entire world would be an undesirable straitjacket on so many diverse economies. Mundell asked what was the most efficient point between these two extremes.

First of all, it is important to understand why countries need different currencies. A country with its own currency can make decisions about its money supply and interest rates, and can therefore set its monetary policy tailored to its own domestic economic conditions. Also, when the exchange rates of its currency are not fixed, the exchange rate with its trading partners can adjust to offset trade imbalances. Suppose a country specializing in agriculture is trading with a manufacturing economy. A sudden increase in productivity in the manufacturing economy might cause an excess demand for agricultural products and an excess supply of manufactured goods. The manufacturing economy slips into a balance of payments deficit, importing more (by value) than it exports. The deficit causes the manufacturing country's currency to depreciate, making its exports cheaper, and therefore boosting them and restoring equilibrium.

But suppose instead that the manufacturing economy and the agricultural economy shared a currency. In this case, the type of adjustment described above would not be possible, and it might be that separate currencies would be more »

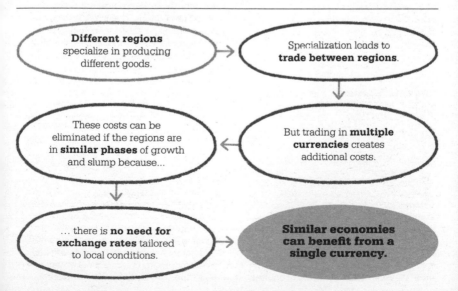

Crowds gather in Frankfurt, Germany, for the launch of the euro, the single currency of the eurozone, on 1 January 1999. For a while, the euro traded alongside national currencies.

beneficial. It might also be the case that a single economic area – such as that constituted by the manufacturing economy – is in fact made up of several nation-states. It would therefore be efficient for them to share a currency.

Business cycles

Later thinking on the subject helped clarify the conditions under which a currency area would be most economically viable. For a region to be best suited to a single currency, it would need flexible markets for capital and labour, allowing both to move freely in response to market demands. Prices and wages would, as a result, need to be flexible, adjusting to demand and supply changes and signalling to mobile capital and labour where they should move to. The different parts of the region would also need to share broadly similar business cycles, allowing the shared central bank for the single currency to act appropriately for the whole

region. There would also need to be mechanisms for dealing with situations when business cycles weren't completely synchronized across the region. The most obvious of these would be fiscal transfers – taking taxes from one area enjoying growth and redistributing to another in recession. This last condition, and the failure to implement it, was to have grave consequences for Europe.

Introducing the euro

The idea of a single currency for Europe began taking shape in 1979, when the European monetary system (EMS) was formed to stabilize exchange rates. Finally, in 1999, the eurozone (the area of the single currency) was established with 11 member states of the European Union (EU). While EU states traded heavily with each other, and their institutions had removed restrictions on the movement of labour, capital, and goods, it was felt necessary to implement further constraints on euro membership to ensure that the currency could function effectively.

Robert Mundell

Born in Kingston, Canada, in 1932, Robert Mundell studied at the University of British Columbia in Vancouver, before moving to the University of Washington in Seattle. He earned his PhD at the Massachusetts Institute of Technology in 1956. He was professor of economics at the University of Chicago from 1966–74, when he moved to Columbia University, New York.

Apart from his academic work, Mundell has acted as adviser to the governments of Canada and the USA, and to organizations including the United Nations and the International Monetary Fund. Alongside his work on optimal currency areas, Mundell developed one of the first models to show how macroeconomic (whole economy) policy interacts with foreign trade and exchange rates. He was awarded the Nobel Prize in economics in 1999 in recognition of his work on macroeconomics.

Key works

1968 *International Economics*
1968 *Man and Economics*
1971 *Monetary Theory*

The "convergence criteria", enshrined in the 1992 Maastricht Treaty, were drawn up to make sure that all those countries wishing to join the euro would share similar economies and be at similar stages in their business cycles (growth or recession). The previous exchange rate mechanism (ERM) had already attempted to fix national currencies against each other within the EU. The euro went a step further, removing all national currencies and, in effect, permanently fixing exchange rates. Important new rules on government debt were introduced. Under the stability and growth pact of 1997, no country was to have a national debt of more than 60 per cent of its gross domestic product (GDP) and the annual deficit was not to exceed 3 per cent of GDP. A new European Central Bank would act for the euro area, replacing the national central banks and setting monetary policy across all the member states.

The eurozone was established in 1999 as the monetary union of the 11 European Union states shown here. By 2012, there were 17 eurozone members, with eight more scheduled to join.

Fatal flaw

However, the provisions for the euro did not contain a mechanism for risk-sharing – crucially, they did not include a means for fiscal (tax revenue) transfers across European countries. The reason for this was simple, and political. Despite the long establishment of some transfer mechanisms, such as the Common Agricultural Policy, there was no desire in any EU country to lose its ability to set its own taxes and spending levels. Fiscal transfers across the continent would have required a strong, central authority, able to take taxes from surplus regions and redistribute to those in deficit – for example, to tax Germany and spend in Greece. But the political will to perform this was lacking. Instead, Europe's leaders hoped that the stability and growth pact would provide enough of a bind on government activities that an explicit fiscal transfer mechanism would not be needed.

Eurozone crisis

For nearly a decade after its launch, the euro functioned well. European trade increased by up to 15 per cent on some estimates. Capital and labour markets became more flexible. Growth, particularly in the poorer countries of Ireland and southern Europe, was impressive. But underneath this picture were profound problems. Differences in labour costs helped exacerbate trade imbalances between different countries. The euro area as a whole was broadly in balance with the rest of the world, exporting roughly as much as it imported. But within the euro area, huge differences appeared. Northern Europe had growing trade surpluses that were matched by rising deficits in the south. Without the mechanisms to provide for fiscal transfers between surplus and deficit countries, these deficits were (in effect) funded by the creation of rising debts in the south. When the financial crisis broke in 2008, the imbalanced system was pushed over the edge.

The euro crisis has raised questions about whether Europe is an optimal currency area. Some countries have seemed ill-matched in trading terms, and the absence of a fiscal transfer mechanism has meant that these imbalances could not be overcome. The stability and growth pact was not robust enough to force distinct national economies to converge.

Euro member countries face difficult choices. If a mechanism to undertake fiscal transfers can be constructed, euro countries may be able to overcome their own unevenness. If the political consensus for such a mechanism can't be reached, the existence of the euro may come under threat. ■

CONTEMPORARY ECONOMIC

1970–PRESENT

In the 25 years following World War II, Keynesian policies, which advocated an active state intervention in the economy, made the Western world prosperous. In the words of British Prime Minister Harold Macmillan, people had "never had it so good". However, in the early 1970s, an oil crisis triggered an economic downturn. Unemployment and inflation both rose rapidly. The Keynesian model no longer seemed to be working.

For some years, conservative economists had been arguing for a return to more free-market policies, and now their arguments were being taken more seriously. US economist Milton Friedman (p.117), was now the foremost economist of the Chicago School, which opposed Keynesian ideas. He suggested that rather than tackling unemployment, inflation should be the focus of economic policy, and the only role of the state should be in controlling the money supply and allowing markets to work – a doctrine known as monetarism.

Rise of the Right

As faith in Keynesian policies waned, the right-wing parties of Ronald Reagan and Margaret Thatcher, both staunch believers in Friedman's monetarist economics, took power in the USA and Britain. The policies they introduced in the 1980s marked a return to the old beliefs in the stability, efficiency, and growth of markets if left to their own devices.

The social policies of so-called Reaganomics and Thatcherism were influenced by the Austrian-born economist Friedrich Hayek (p.105), who put the individual, not the state, at the heart of economic thinking, and by economists who saw tax cuts as a means of increasing tax revenue.

Liberalization became the new watchword. Deregulation of financial institutions not only made it easier for firms to borrow, but also allowed lenders to indulge in the new forms of financial engineering that promised high returns with zero risk. Throughout the 1980s, the economic mood was changing worldwide. Reforms in the Soviet Union were to lead to the eventual break up of the Soviet bloc, reinforcing conservative economists' views that socialist policies did not work. Mainland Europe, however, resisted the Anglo-

American swing from Keynes to Friedman, and only gradually adopted more free-market economic policies.

Rethinking free markets

Although monetarism and the liberalization of markets may have helped to make markets more efficient through the 1980s and 90s, some economists were uneasy about the sustainability of these policies. As early as 1974, US economist Hyman Minsky (p.173) had warned of the inherent instability of financial institutions. An acceleration of the "boom and bust" cycles seemed to confirm his hypothesis. Deregulation encouraged risky borrowing, which led to the collapse of firms and banks. Other economists challenged the efficiency and rationality of the market, arguing that the "scientific" models of the economy were based on the wrong sciences: new ideas in mathematics and physics, such as complexity theory and chaos theory, were perhaps better analogies, and behavioural psychology could better explain the actions of "economic man" than economists' standard notion of rationality.

Meanwhile, younger economies were developing, especially in Asia, where reforms were transforming the Chinese and Indian economies. A new economic bloc emerged to rival the West, in the form of the BRIC nations (Brazil, Russia, India, and China). The prosperity of these new economic powers stimulated a renewed interest in so-called development economics, as other countries remained locked in poverty by crippling debt and political instability. At the same time, the technology that had brought economic prosperity now posed an economic threat in the form of global warming and climate change, which needed to be dealt with at an international level.

In the first decade of the 21st century, a succession of financial crises rocked the Western economies, and it seemed that free-market policies had failed. Once again, economics became concerned with the inequalities and social consequences of free markets. A few economists even wondered whether the failure of free markets was heralding the collapse of capitalism that Karl Marx (p.68) had predicted. Not for the first time, the world seemed to be on the verge of profound economic change. ∎

IT IS POSSIBLE TO INVEST WITHOUT RISK
FINANCIAL ENGINEERING

IN CONTEXT

FOCUS
Banking and finance

KEY THINKERS
Fischer Black (1938–95)
Myron Scholes (1941–)

BEFORE
1900 French mathematician
Louis Bachelier demonstrates that
stock prices follow a consistent but
random process.

1952 US economist Harry Markowitz
proposes a method to build optimal
portfolios based on diversifying risk.

1960s Capital Asset Pricing Model
(CAPM) is developed to determine
the correct rate of return for a
financial asset.

AFTER
1990s Value-at-Risk (VaR) is developed
to measure the risk of loss on a portfolio.

Late 2000s Global financial
markets collapse.

If we assume that financial
markets are efficient, and **prices
will rarely differ widely** from
an average value…

↓

… the probabilities of **future price
variations can be calculated**.

↓

This means a contract to buy
goods at a future price can be
valued accurately and used
to insure against risk.

↓

**It is possible to
invest without risk.**

During the 1960s, the institutional
foundations of the post-war
world were steadily eroded.
The Bretton Woods system (pp.110–11)
of fixed exchange rates, pegged against
a US dollar that was in turn locked into a
fixed price against gold, was starting to
buckle. The USA was running persistent

trade deficits (where imports outstrip
exports), while recurrent balance-of-
payments crises elsewhere provoked
calls for the introduction of freely floating
exchange rates. In 1971, the US president,
Richard Nixon, took definitive action: he
unilaterally ended the dollar to gold peg,
ending the whole Bretton Woods system.

At the same time, domestic economies were experiencing steadily rising rates of inflation. Keynesianism (pp.94–99), the economic thinking that had dominated the post-war years, came under sustained intellectual attack. The financial markets, which had been tightly regulated since the 1930s, pushed for a removal of restrictions on their activities. These restrictions were finally lifted in 1972, when the Chicago Mercantile Exchange was allowed to write the first derivative contract on exchange rates.

Futures contracts

Derivatives have existed for centuries. A derivative is a contract written not directly for a commodity itself, but for some attribute associated with it. For instance, a typical early derivative contract is a "forward", which specifies the price and future date for delivery of a commodity, such as coffee. The advantage of this arrangement is that it allows producers to lock their customers into a price in the future, regardless of how – in agricultural commodities – harvests and production actually turn out. The derivative aimed to reduce risk and insure against the future. This is known as a "hedge". However, the derivative contract can work the other way round. Instead of providing insurance against the future, it can be used to gamble on the future. A forward contract locks in the delivery of goods for a certain price on a certain date. But if the immediate market price (the "spot price") on that date is less than the price in the forward contract, an easy profit could be made. Of course, if the market price is more than the one specified, it results in a loss. Furthermore, as derivative contracts do not involve payment for actual assets or commodities, but only for the right to buy those products in the future, they allow people to deal in huge quantities. Derivatives give traders leverage – more "bang for their buck".

Letting go of the asset

Derivative contracts became standardized, and could then be bought and sold on a market like any other commodity. The first exchange to offer tradeable derivatives

The price of rice may vary with changes in weather. A forward contract, where one party agrees to buy the rice at a certain price on a certain day, allows the grower to manage risk.

in agricultural products was the Chicago Board of Trade, in 1864. However, the possibility for speculation that all derivative contracts contain led to repeated bans on their use. "Cash-settled" contracts provoked particular concern. These were derivative contracts in which the delivery of the underlying asset did not have to take place on the specified day. Cash could be exchanged in its place. At this point, all real connection between the underlying product and the derivative had been lost, and the possibilities for purely speculative behaviour were immense.

Deregulation

Recognition of this speculative potential motivated governments to introduce strict regulations. From the 1930s onwards, cash-settled derivatives in the USA were classified as a form of gambling, rather than investment, and strictly controlled. Exchanges were not allowed to trade them. But with the collapse of the fixed exchange-rate system in 1971, a need rapidly emerged for hedging against potentially volatile floating exchange rates. Restrictions were lifted, and the market for derivatives quickly expanded.

This provided the background to a critical problem. There was no reliable means to accurately price derivatives, since they were, by nature, highly complex contracts. Even a simple "option" (providing the right but not the commitment to trade an underlying »

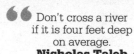

Don't cross a river
if it is four feet deep
on average.
Nicholas Taleb

asset at a certain point in the future) had a price that was determined by several variables, such as the current price of the underlying asset, the time to the option's deadline, and the expected price variation. The problem of providing a mathematical formula for this problem was finally solved in 1973 by US economists Myron Scholes and Fischer Black, and expanded upon by fellow American Robert C Merton the same year.

These economists built on certain assumptions and insights about financial markets to simplify the problem. First, they made use of the "no arbitrage" rule. This means that prices in a properly functioning financial market reflect all the information available. An individual share price would tell you both the value of the company today, and what market traders expect of it in the future. It should be impossible to earn

guaranteed profits by hedging against future risk because prices already incorporate all the information you are basing your hedge on. The second assumption was that it is always possible to put together an option contract that mirrors a portfolio of assets. In other words, every possible portfolio of assets that can be assembled can be perfectly hedged by options. All risk vanishes with this insurance.

Third, they assumed that although asset prices fluctuate randomly over time, they vary in a regular way, known as the "normal distribution". This implies that, in general, prices will not move very far over a short time period.

By using these assumptions, Black, Scholes, and Merton were able to provide a mathematically robust model for pricing a standard option contract on the basis of the underlying asset's price movements. Derivative contracts, once seen as unreliable instruments, could now be processed on a huge scale using computer technology. The path was cleared for a vast expansion of derivatives trading.

The option pricing model Black, Scholes, and Merton devised provided a whole new way to think about financial markets. It could

In the years leading to the 2008 crash, banks assumed that investment risk followed a "normal distribution" pattern (the solid line), where there is a high probability of making a small gain, and a very low probability of making an extreme gain or loss. However, investment risk actually follows a different pattern (the dotted line), in which extreme events are far more common.

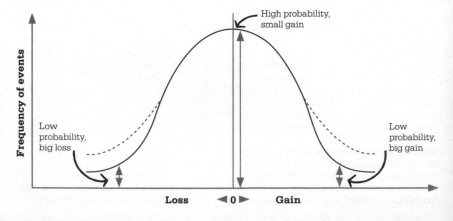

Option contracts are a type of derivative that give someone the option to buy or sell something, such as coffee, at a certain price on a certain date. The option need not be exercised.

even run in reverse. Existing option prices could be fed backwards into the pricing model to generate "implied volatilities". This created a new way to manage risk: instead of trading on the basis of prices or expected prices, portfolios of assets could be put together directly on the basis of their riskiness as implied by the market price. Risk itself, as described by the mathematical models, could be traded and managed.

The 2008 crash

The explosion in financial innovation, aided by sophisticated mathematics and ever-increasing computing power, helped drive the extraordinary expansion of the financial system over several decades. From negligible amounts in the 1970s, the global market for derivatives grew on average by 24 per cent a year, reaching a total of €457 trillion by 2008 – about 20 times the global GDP. Applications multiplied as firms found apparently secure, profitable new ways to manage the risks associated with lending.

By September 2008, when the US investment bank Lehman Brothers filed for bankruptcy, it had become clear that this expansion had fatal weaknesses. Critical among these was the dependence on the assumption of a normal distribution: the idea that most prices cluster around an average, and extreme price movements are very rare. But this had been disputed as early as 1963, when French mathematician Benoît Mandelbrot suggested that extreme price movements were much more common than expected.

Post-crash, these models are being re-examined. Behavioural economists and econophysicists use models and statistical techniques drawn from physics to better understand financial markets and risk. ∎

Low risk, high rewards

US-Lebanese economist Nicholas Taleb claims that by underestimating the risk of extreme price movements, the apparently sophisticated financial models overexposed investors to the real risk. Collateralized debt obligations (CDOs) are a prime example. These are financial instruments that raise money by issuing their own bonds, before investing that money in a mixture of assets such as loans. CDOs took on the risks of very low-quality (subprime) housing debts that had a high chance of defaulting, and mixed them with high-quality debt, such as US Treasury bills. They apparently offered low risk and high rewards. But this relied on an assumption that the combined risk of default followed a normal distribution pattern and was stable. As US subprime mortgages defaulted in increasing numbers, it became clear that this assumption did not hold, and the vast CDO market imploded.

Black swans are rarely sighted but do exist. Nicholas Taleb refers to the highly unexpected, extreme movements of the market as "black swan events".

TAX CUTS CAN INCREASE THE TAX TAKE

TAXATION AND ECONOMIC INCENTIVES

IN CONTEXT

FOCUS
Economic policy

KEY THINKER
Robert Mundell (1932–)
Arthur Laffer (1940–)

BEFORE
1776 Adam Smith suggests that moderate taxes might bring in more revenue than high ones.

1803 French economist Jean-Baptiste Say argues that supply creates its own demand.

AFTER
1981 US President Ronald Reagan cuts top-rate tax and capital gains tax.

2003 US President George W Bush ignores criticism from leading economists and pursues a policy of tax cuts.

2012 In January, the US government deficit hits an unprecedented $15 trillion.

Common sense tells us that if a government wants to raise more money to spend on public services, it must raise taxes, however unpopular that may be. Likewise, cutting taxes seems to imply cutting public services. However, some economists have suggested that this is not always the case, and that cutting taxes can result in governments collecting more, not less, money.

This is a key idea of 1980s "supply-side" economists. The supply side is the part of an economy that makes and sells things, as opposed to the demand side, which is the buying of goods. Supply-side economists argue that the best way to make the economy grow is to improve conditions for the supply side, freeing companies from regulations, and cutting subsidies, and high-rate taxes.

From tax to tax havens

The revenue argument for cutting taxes came from US economist Arthur Laffer. He said that if a government takes no tax, it will get no revenue. If it takes 100 per cent tax, it will get no revenue either, since no one will work. But even below 100 per cent, very high income tax rates discourage people from working. This reduction in hours worked outweighs the high tax rate and the result

The Laffer curve displays the relationship between tax rates and government revenue. It shows that higher taxes do not always result in increased revenues.

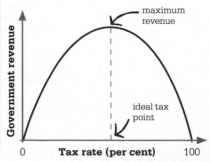

is a fall in tax revenue. When top-rate taxes are very high, revenue can also be lost by the highest income earners leaving the country or putting their money in tax havens – countries charging little or no tax. Laffer drew a bell-shaped curve to show that somewhere between the extremes of no tax and 100 per cent tax, there is a point at which a government will maximize revenue.

The argument then is that from a starting point of high tax rates, tax cuts, along with other policies to strengthen the supply side, can enhance economic efficiency and generate more tax revenues. In the 1970s, when Laffer developed his theories, some countries taxed some people at 70 per cent, and a few taxed the highest earners at 90 per cent. Economists disagreed about where the peak on the Laffer curve lies. Those on the political Right argued that the economy was at a point to the right of the peak of the curve, meaning that tax cuts would increase revenue. Those on the Left disagreed.

A win–win situation

For politicians on the Right, Laffer's theory was attractive. It meant that they could make themselves popular by cutting taxes, yet pledge to maintain public services, too. In the USA in 1981, President Ronald Reagan was able to cut top-rate taxes and still be a hero to many of the USA's poorest. However, there is little evidence that the idea actually works. In the USA and other countries, tax rates are far below the level of the 1970s. However, the supposed tax revenue bonanza has not arrived. Instead, tax cuts have been funded largely by rising borrowing deficits. ∎

If the government **takes no tax**, it receives no revenue.

⬇

If the tax rate is **100 per cent**, the government receives no revenue, because no one will bother to work.

⬇

Somewhere between 0 and 100 per cent lies the point where tax revenues are at a **maximum**.

⬇

If **taxes are set too high**, workers are encouraged to work less and so pay less tax overall, so revenues decline.

⬇

But if **taxes are lowered**, it encourages workers to work more and revenues increase.

⬇

Tax cuts can increase the tax take.

Supply-side economics

The theory of supply-side economics generated a considerable amount of controversy when it was developed in the 1970s. It emerged in response to the apparent failure of Keynesian policies of government intervention (pp.94–99) to deal with a flat economy combined with high inflation – a condition known as stagflation. The term was popularized by US journalist Jude Wanniski, but it was US economist Arthur Laffer's tax curve that caught economists' attention. The Laffer curve was developed under the guidance of Canadian economist Robert Mundell (p.148) who argued that if tax rates were cut, national output would increase, and tax revenues would rise. After a quick dip, revenues did actually rise, but there has been huge debate ever since over whether he was proved right.

PRICES TELL YOU EVERYTHING
EFFICIENT MARKETS

IN CONTEXT

FOCUS
Markets and firms

KEY THINKER
Eugene Fama (1939–)

BEFORE
1863 French broker Jules Regnault publishes *Playing the Odds and the Philosophy of the Stock Exchange*, which states that fluctuations in the stock market cannot be predicted.

1964 US economist Paul Cootner develops Regnault's ideas on fluctuating markets in his *The Random Character of Stock Market Prices*.

AFTER
1980 US economist Richard Thaler publishes the first study of behavioural economics.

2011 Paul Volcker, former chairman of the US Federal Reserve, blames an "unjustified faith in rational expectations and market efficiencies" for the 2008 financial crash.

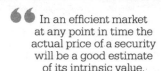 In an efficient market at any point in time the actual price of a security will be a good estimate of its intrinsic value.
Eugene Fama

A commonly held belief among investors is that they can "beat", or outperform, the stock market. The US economist Eugene Fama disagreed. His study, *Efficient Capital Markets* (1970), concluded that it is impossible to beat the market consistently. His theory is now known as the efficient market hypothesis.

Fama claimed that all investors have access to the same publicly available information as their rivals, so the prices of stocks fully reflect all the knowledge available. This is the "efficient market". No one can know what new information will be released, so it should be almost impossible for investors to make a profit without using information unavailable to the competition, or "insider trading", which is illegal.

However, problems with the hypothesis have been highlighted by behavioural economists. They point to the theory's failure to account for investor overconfidence and the "herd" instinct. These problems manifested themselves in the Dotcom bubble of the 1990s, where "irrational exuberance" was blamed for artificially inflating technology stock, and the more recent financial crisis of 2007–08.

After these crises many observers have declared the theory redundant; some have even blamed it for the crashes. Eugene Fama himself has conceded that uninformed investors can lead the market astray and result in prices becoming "somewhat irrational". ∎

OVER TIME, EVEN THE SELFISH COOPERATE WITH OTHERS
COMPETITION AND COOPERATION

IN CONTEXT

FOCUS
Decision-making

KEY THINKER
Robert Axelrod (1953–)

BEFORE
1859 British biologist Charles Darwin publishes *On the Origin of Species*, arguing that the best-adapted species are those most likely to survive.

1971 US biologist Robert Trivers publishes *The Evolution of Reciprocal Altruism*, which shows how altruism and cooperation can benefit individuals.

AFTER
1986 US economists Drew Fudenberg and Eric Maskin explore cooperation strategies for repeated games.

1994 British economist Kenneth Binmore publishes *Playing Fair*, using game theory to explore the development of morality.

I n 1984, US economist Robert Axelrod wrote *The Evolution of Cooperation*. It was based on the results of a series of games, in which the strategies of game theory specialists were pitted against each other via computer programs, to see which was most successful. The game they played was the prisoner's dilemma (p.140), a game involving two thieves captured by the police. Should each thief choose to confess, stay silent, or "sell out" the other thief? The game explores whether it is wiser to cooperate for mutual benefit or to act selfishly.

The best strategy

Axelrod discovered that cooperation can arise through self-interested actions. His series of games tested many strategies. The most successful strategy was simple tit-for-tat, where a player cooperates on the first move and then mirrors his or her opponent, so is never the first to "sell out". The most successful approaches were those that were "nice". Cooperation was found to produce mutually beneficial outcomes. But one must not be too nice – if someone is betrayed it is essential to hit back in the next move. To maintain credibility, players must retaliate immediately if they are "sold out". This approach to the analysis of competition and cooperation has developed into a rich field that examines how social and even moral rules emerge. ∎

When US President Bush and Russian President Putin signed the Treaty of Moscow in 2002, they cooperated to greatly reduce their nuclear arsenals, despite mutual distrust.

THE GOVERNMENT'S PROMISES ARE INCREDIBLE
INDEPENDENT CENTRAL BANKS

IN CONTEXT

FOCUS
Economic policy

KEY THINKERS
Edward Prescott (1940–)
Finn Kydland (1943–)

BEFORE
1961 John Muth publishes *Rational Expectations and the Theory of Price Movements*.

1976 US economist Robert Lucas argues that it is naive to model government policy on solutions that have worked in the past.

AFTER
1983 US economists Robert Barro and David Gordon suggest that high inflation arises from discretionary government policy, and propose central bank independence.

From 1980s Independent central banks are established in many countries worldwide, and commit to simple policy rules.

If governments can act at their **discretion**, they can break their promises, therefore…

⬇

… the government's promises are incredible.

⬇

Rational individuals forecast this breaking of promises, and **change their own behaviour** to suit.

⬇

This prevents **discretionary government policy** from working.

⬇

Governments should credibly commit to following **simple rules**, not use discretionary policy.

F
ollowing World War II, economics was dominated by Keynesian thinking (pp.94–99). This claimed that governments could maintain high employment through two types of discretionary policies, which are introduced to achieve specific goals through a particular set of actions. The two types of policy used for controlling employment were fiscal policy (government spending and taxation) and monetary policy (interest rates and the money supply).

In 1977, two economists – Finn Kydland of Norway and Edward Prescott of the USA – published a paper entitled *Rules Rather than Discretion*, which argued that discretionary policy was in fact self-defeating. Their argument was based on the concept of rational expectations, which was developed by the US economist John Muth. Muth argued that as having incorrect beliefs about prices is costly, rational individuals seek to minimize their errors by planning ahead to avoid this.

Before this, macroeconomic models had operated on the assumption that individuals only look backwards, naively expecting the future to look like the past. The new model predicted that if people collect information and are rational, they can – and will – anticipate government interventions. They then adapt their actions to the government policy they expect, and that policy is in turn rendered less potent. Discretionary policy can only work when individuals are taken by surprise, and it is hard to surprise rational individuals.

To see how this works, imagine a lenient teacher who is trying to make a lazy pupil do his homework. The teacher tells the student that if he doesn't hand his homework in he will be punished. But the pupil knows that the teacher is lenient and does not like to punish. The pupil anticipates that if he doesn't hand in the work, he won't be punished. Knowing this, he does not do the homework. The teacher's aim of getting the pupil to hand in his homework is undermined by the pupil's rational behaviour.

Kydland and Prescott said that government promises of low inflation face the same problem. The government does not like high unemployment. So it will boost the economy to keep unemployment low, but this will push up inflation. Like the teacher, who threatens a punishment he will not inflict, the government has conflicting aims. Individuals know this and so do not believe the government's promise of low inflation. This undoes the aim of increasing demand to lead to higher employment, because people know that higher wages will be offset by higher prices. Accounting for rational expectations, the effect of the boost is simply higher inflation.

An uncompromising rule

The solution for our teacher would be a compulsory school rule for punishing late homework, so he would have to comply. In a similar way, Kydland and Prescott proposed that instead of having a free reign to set economic policy, governments should commit to following clear rules. A more radical solution of the teacher's dilemma would be to delegate punishment-giving to a strict headmaster. In macroeconomic policy, this kind of role can be taken by independent central banks, which place less weight on employment and more weight on low inflation than the government does. Their control of monetary policy allows the government to credibly commit to low inflation. The period of low inflation that arose in the 2000s is often attributed to the rise of independent central banks. ∎

Finn Kydland

Born on a farm in Gjesdal, Norway, in 1943, Finn Kydland was the oldest of six children. After high school, he taught in a junior school for several years, where a fellow teacher suggested he study accountancy, which awakened his interest in business. He started an economics degree at the Norwegian School of Economic and Business Administration (NHH) in 1965. Kydland intended to become a business manager, but after graduation he became an assistant to economics professor Sten Thore, who moved to Carnegie Mellon University, USA, taking Kydland with him. Returning to NHH in 1973, Kydland published his key paper with Edward Prescott. In 1976, Kydland returned to the USA where he has taught ever since. In 2004, he was awarded the Nobel Prize for Economics.

Key works

1977 *Rules Rather than Discretion* (with E Prescott)
1982 *Time to Build and Aggregate Fluctuations*
2002 *Argentina's Lost Decade* (with Carlos E J M Zarazaga)

THE EAST ASIAN STATE GOVERNS THE MARKET
ASIAN TIGER ECONOMIES

After World War II, the economies
of a cluster of East Asian nations
grew dramatically. Led by a new
set of actively interventionist governments,
these countries were transformed from
economic backwaters into dynamic
industrial powers in just a few decades.

The so-called Asian Tigers – South
Korea, Hong Kong, Singapore, and
Taiwan – were followed by Malaysia,
Thailand, and Indonesia, and then by
China. These countries achieved sustained
growth in income per head faster than
in any other region. GDP (gross domestic
product, or total national income from goods
and services) is often used to measure a
nation's wealth. In 1950, South Korea's
GDP-per-person (GDP divided by the size
of the population) was half that of Brazil's;
by 1990, it was double; by 2005, three times
as high. This kind of growth resulted in a
remarkable decline in poverty. By the late
20th century, the original four Asian Tigers
had living standards that rivalled those of
Western Europe, a historically unprecedented
change in fortunes that has been dubbed
the "East Asian miracle".

The environment from which the
Asian Tigers emerged was shaped by
government intervention and dense links
between the state and the economy, an
economic model that came to be known
as the "developmental state". After World
War II, there had been huge expectations
of development in poorer nations, and
the goal of rapid economic advancement
became the driving force behind government
economic policy. Powerful bureaucracies
were involved in directing the economic
activities of the private sector in ways
that seemed to go far beyond anything
attempted in Western Europe. However,
their governments preserved private
enterprise, and their new model had little
in common with the state planning of the

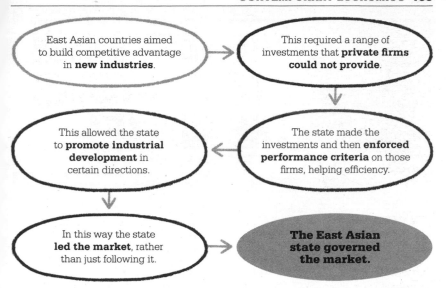

East Asian countries aimed to build competitive advantage in **new industries**.

This required a range of investments that **private firms could not provide**.

This allowed the state to **promote industrial development** in certain directions.

The state made the investments and then **enforced performance criteria** on those firms, helping efficiency.

In this way the state **led the market**, rather than just following it.

The East Asian state governed the market.

communist bloc. Asian Tiger states shaped development by steering investment towards strategic industries and promoting the technological upgrading of producers. This induced a shift of workers from agriculture to the expanding industrial sector. Large investments in education gave workers the skills needed for new industries, and industrial enterprises soon began to export their products, becoming the motors for sustained, trade-driven growth.

A new kind of state

This type of state had never been seen before. It challenged orthodox views about government's role in the economy. Standard economics sees the state's job as correcting market failures – governments provide public goods, such as defence and street lighting, which private markets alone tend not to deliver. They ensure that institutions such as courts function properly, so that contracts can be enforced and property rights protected, but beyond that their role is minimal. Once the basic prerequisites for market activity are in place, classical economics suggests that the state should withdraw and let the price mechanism do its work. It is thought that market-friendly institutions and a limited

state were key to Britain's economic success during industrialization.

Some economists contend that this also occurred in successful East Asian economies: when these states fostered development, they did so by supporting markets, not by interfering with them. Their interventions helped to allocate resources and investment in ways that were in line with markets: in a sense the state "got prices right". To do this, governments cultivated macroeconomic stability, vital for giving certainty to investors. They intervened to correct market failures through the provision of defence and schooling. They also built infrastructure such as ports and railways, whose high set-up costs deterred private firms. The East Asian developmental states were held to be successful because they followed the market.

Leading the market

The New Zealand economist Robert Wade argues that the East Asian development states both led and followed markets. They drove the expansion of favoured industries by providing cheap credit and subsidies. By leading markets, their chosen allocation of resources was markedly different from »

The rapid rise of the Asian Tigers was based on exports. Large facilities to handle container ships, such as these in Singapore, were built by the state to promote growth.

what it would have been, had it been dictated by markets alone.

US economist Alice Amsden has characterized this as the state deliberately "getting prices wrong" in order to build new types of competitive advantage. A crucial part of this was that the new "infant industries", pumped up with subsidies and trade protection, were eventually made to grow up. The state could enforce performance criteria on firms because it was able to withdraw preferential treatment when necessary.

Robert Wade argues that the way these states chose to lead the markets explains the creation of comparative advantages in industries where none previously existed. Initially, the prices of goods from a new industry would normally be internationally uncompetitive. In addition, the production of a new product often requires the simultaneous setting up of other industries and infrastructure. The coordination of this process is difficult if left to private firms, rather than the state.

Moreover, these protected, infant industries became competitive when they were given classical incentives to learn how to become more efficient. In order to achieve the economic education of new firms and the coordination of initial production, governments needed to act in violation of narrow market prices. This occurred in South Korea's steel industry. In the 1960s, the Korean government was advised by the World Bank not to enter the

steel sector because it had no comparative advantage there – others could easily beat its prices. By the 1980s, Posco, a large Korean firm, had become one of the world's most efficient steel producers.

Political interference

Attempts at interventionist policies in regions outside East Asia were unsuccessful, which tarnished the reputation of the developmental state. In Latin America and Africa, the preferential treatment of firms and sectors generated poor incentives: firms were shielded from competition, but the state did not enforce performance criteria. Infant industries never grew into successful exporters.

In Latin America especially, preferential treatment became linked to politics with little economic pay-off: well-connected firms received subsidies and tariff protection but did not become more productive. Over time, these firms became a drain on their governments' budgets, absorbing rather than generating resources. "Getting prices wrong" did not help to build comparative advantages in new industries. It led instead to inefficient production and economic stagnation.

In East Asia, successful states seemed better able to resist pressures from private interests. After setting up its new steel firm in the 1960s, the South Korean government ensured that the firm was meeting efficiency targets. If political interests had emerged that had prevented the state from disciplining the firm, the state would have become the servant of narrow interests, not of the overall economic efficiency of the economy. The state had to remain autonomous and resist pressures for favouritism from particular groups. At the same time, the state

 The state… has set relative prices deliberately 'wrong' in order to create profitable investment opportunities.
Alice Amsden

provided firms with credit and technical assistance – to do this and to monitor firms' performance, it was necessary for the tentacles of the state to reach into the smallest cogs of the economy. The economic bureaucracy needed to hold detailed information about all potential investments, and to maintain effective relationships with industrial managers.

US economist Peter Evans has called these markers of successful developmental states "embedded autonomy". Only when this is in place is there a chance for a state to "get prices wrong" without being co-opted by vested interests. Embedded autonomy is not easy to create and its absence may be a factor behind the poor outcomes of state intervention in other developing regions.

The rise of China
With the East Asian financial crisis of the 1990s, the developmental state model was again called into question. Many sensed that the institutions that had fostered rapid industrial growth after World War II had lost their potency by the late 20th century. On the other hand, the spectacular rise of China has resurrected the idea of the developmental state, or at the very least of policies and institutions that produce rapid economic transformation while deviating from the prescriptions of standard, classical economics.

China began a series of reforms of its communist system in the late 1970s. It created its own brand of developmental state, which resembled the Asian Tigers, and had an authoritarian government that was responsible for promoting the private sector and exports. Agriculture was de-collectivized, and state-owned industries were given more autonomy and subjected to greater competition. These reforms helped unleash a vast expansion of private economic activity, without the introduction of Western-style property rights.

Alternative incentives emerged from China's unique institutions: for example, from the "Household Responsibility System", whereby local managers are held responsible for an enterprise's profits and losses, without the need for private property ownership. The results have been dramatic. While China remains poor relative to Western Europe, its rapid growth took 170 million people out of poverty during the 1990s, accounting for three-quarters of the poverty reduction in developing regions.

The histories of China and the Asian Tigers show that there is no unique path to development. The way that their states intervened in the economy was very different from anything that took place in Europe when it was developing. However, it seems that all development models, even successful ones, eventually run into constraints. The benefits of the development state petered out in the Asian Tigers in the 1990s – institutions that had worked in one decade began to fail in the next. One day the Chinese state, too, may lose its potency. It may have to reinvent itself, if its spectacular rise is to continue. ■

Industrial policy and incentives

The East Asian developmental states gave preferential treatment to firms in favoured sectors, while creating incentives for performance. They did this by requiring enterprises to meet performance criteria, partly through contests in which firms competed for prizes.

Typically, the criterion for winning was successful exports. The prize was credit lines or access to foreign exchange. In South Korea and Taiwan, for instance, firms had to show proof that they had won an export order. Only then did they receive their prize. South Korea launched competitions in which private firms bid for large projects in new industries such as shipbuilding. Successful firms received protection from the international market for a time. Performance criteria involved firms becoming internationally competitive by a certain deadline. Failing firms were punished.

BELIEFS CAN TRIGGER CURRENCY CRISES
SPECULATION AND CURRENCY DEVALUATION

IN CONTEXT

FOCUS
Global economy

KEY THINKER
Paul Krugman (1953–)

BEFORE
1944 Greece experiences the largest currency crash in history.

1978 US economic historian Charles Kindleberger stresses the role of irrational behaviour in crises.

AFTER
2009 US economists Carmen Reinhart and Kenneth Rogoff publish *This Time is Different: Eight Centuries of Financial Folly*, in which they draw similarities between crises over the centuries.

2010–12 Divergent national priorities, serious policy errors, and huge speculative pressures threaten the break-up of the euro.

A currency crisis is a large and sudden collapse in the value of one nation's currency relative to other currencies. For about 30 years after World War II, the world's main currencies were governed by the Bretton Woods system (pp.110–11), which was based on fixed, but adjustable, exchange rates.

When this system ended in 1971, currency crises became more common.

In general, a currency crisis is triggered by people selling a country's currency in large amounts. This behaviour seems to stem from the interaction of people's expectations and certain underlying economic weaknesses (known as "fundamentals") – in other words, people's reactions to perceived problems. Economists have tried to model this interaction mathematically, but every time they think they have found a model that fits the data, a new type of crisis seems to emerge.

Currency crises in context
Like hurricanes, financial crises happen surprisingly often but are hard to predict. Centuries ago, when money was based on precious metals, a currency usually lost its value through currency debasement, which occurred when a ruler reduced the precious metal content of the coinage. After money began to be printed on paper by central banks, high inflation would cause a country's currency to collapse. This happened in Germany in 1923, where at one point prices were doubling every two days. However, a country does not need hyperinflation to have a currency crisis. For example, during the Great Depression of 1929–33, prices of commodities such as minerals and food collapsed, and the currencies of Latin American countries, which were reliant on this export trade, fell with them.

Inconsistent policies
Writing in 1979, US economist Paul Krugman showed that for a currency crisis to happen, all that is needed is

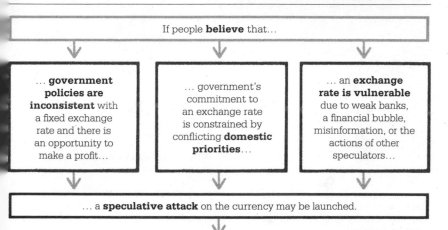

If people **believe** that…		
… **government policies are inconsistent** with a fixed exchange rate and there is an opportunity to make a profit…	… government's commitment to an exchange rate is constrained by conflicting **domestic priorities**…	… an **exchange rate is vulnerable** due to weak banks, a financial bubble, misinformation, or the actions of other speculators…

… a **speculative attack** on the currency may be launched.

Beliefs can trigger currency crises.

for a government to carry out policies that are inconsistent with the exchange rate.

Krugman's argument is the foundation for a first generation of currency crisis models. These models start by assuming that there is a fixed exchange rate between the home currency and an external currency, and that the home government is running a budget deficit (it is spending more than it is collecting in tax), which it is financing by printing money. By increasing the supply of the currency, this policy creates an inconsistency with the value of the currency set by the fixed exchange rate. Other things being equal, the policy will cause the "real" value of the home currency to fall.

Next, the models assume that the central bank sells its own reserves of foreign currency in order to support the currency. However, it is assumed that people can see that eventually the foreign currency reserves of the central bank will be exhausted. The exchange rate will then have to "float" (be traded freely) and decline. The model proposes that there is a "shadow exchange rate", which is what the exchange rate would be if the central bank were not defending the fixed exchange rate. People know what this shadow exchange rate is (and will be) at any given time by looking at the government deficit. The moment

they see that it is better to sell the home currency at the fixed exchange rate than at the shadow exchange rate, they will launch a speculative attack, and buy all the foreign currency reserves at the central bank. The home currency will then be forced to float and the depreciating shadow exchange rate will become the actual exchange rate. »

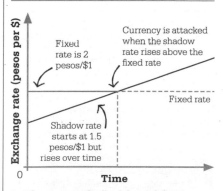

In "first generation" crisis models, when one currency is fixed to another, its "real" value, or shadow rate, may fall below the value at which it is fixed. In this case, this is the point at which the shadow exchange rate rises above 2 pesos/$1. When this happens, the currency is vulnerable to attack, as speculators buy the country's foreign currency reserves in anticipation of a devaluation.

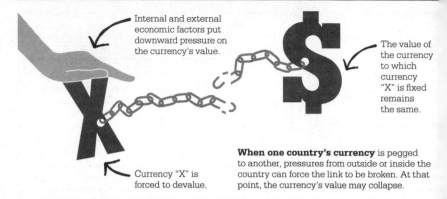

Internal and external economic factors put downward pressure on the currency's value.

The value of the currency to which currency "X" is fixed remains the same.

Currency "X" is forced to devalue.

When one country's currency is pegged to another, pressures from outside or inside the country can force the link to be broken. At that point, the currency's value may collapse.

The speculative attack occurs at the point where the steadily depreciating shadow exchange rate equals the fixed exchange rate.

This model seemed relevant to the currency crises in Latin America in the 1970s and 1980s, such as the crisis in Mexico in 1982. However, in 1992–93, a currency crisis erupted in the European Monetary System (EMS), which appeared to contradict this model. Under this system's Exchange Rate Mechanism (ERM), European countries effectively fixed, or pegged, their currencies to the German Deutsche Mark (DM). Several currencies came under pressure from speculators, notably the financier George Soros. It would be difficult to argue that countries such as the UK were running policies inconsistent with the targeted exchange rate. The UK had a very small budget deficit, and had previously been running at a surplus, yet in 1992, the country was forced to withdraw from the ERM, to the great political embarrassment of Chancellor of the Exchequer (finance minister) Norman Lamont. A new model was needed to explain these events.

Self-fulfilling crises

In the first generation models, government policy is "fixed": the authorities mechanically use up their foreign reserves to defend the currency. A second generation of models allowed the government to have a choice. It may be committed to a fixed exchange rate, but this "rule" has an escape clause. If unemployment becomes very high, the

government may abandon its commitment to the fixed exchange rate, because the social costs of defending the currency (for instance, through high interest rates) are too great. We can see these hard choices in the plight of Greece in 2012. However, without a speculative attack, these extra social costs would not arise. These models imply that more than one outcome is possible, what economists call "multiple equilibria". A speculative attack might occur if enough people believe that other people are going to attack the currency. They will then attack it and a crisis will unfold. But if people don't hold these beliefs, the crisis may not happen. In these models, crises are "self-fulfilling". At an extreme, they suggest that a crisis could happen irrespective of the economic fundamentals of a country. These new models, based on the work of economists such as the American Maurice Obstfeld, seemed more realistic than the earlier ones, as they allowed for governments' use of instruments, such as interest rates, to defend the currency, raising interest rates to prevent devaluation. They also seemed to chime with the experience of the ERM crisis, where government policies were constrained by high levels of unemployment.

Financial fragility

The East Asian crisis of 1997 (see opposite) seemed not to fit the first two types of model. Unemployment was not a concern, yet East Asian currencies came under

The only absolutely sure-fire way not to have one's currency speculated against... is not to have an independent currency.
Paul Krugman

sudden, massive speculative attack. In the second generation models, the escape clause of devaluation was supposed to relieve the economy from social costs, but the sharp collapse of their currencies was followed by a severe – though short-lived – downturn. Financial fragility, caused by a banking boom and bust, played an important role. In light of this, economists began to focus on the interaction of weaknesses in the economy and speculators' self-fulfilling expectations. This third generation of model now took into account new kinds of financial fragilities, such as those that arise when firms and banks borrow in foreign currency and lend in local currency. Banks would be unable to pay their debts in the event of currency devaluation. These kinds of weaknesses could spark speculative attacks and crises.

As well as developing theories, economists have looked at the evidence for possible warning signs of currency crises. In a 1996 article, Jeffrey Frankel and Andrew Rose reviewed currency crashes in 105 developing countries from 1971 to 1992.

They found that devaluations occur when foreign capital inflows dry up, when the central bank's foreign currency reserves are low, when domestic credit growth is high, when major external (especially US dollar) interest rates rise, and when the real exchange rate (prices of traded goods from home relative to those abroad) is high, which means that a country's goods become uncompetitive in foreign markets. Economists argue that by monitoring such warning signs, crises may be predictable up to one or two years in advance.

Avoiding crises
Studies suggest that between 5 and 25 per cent of recent history has been spent in one crisis or another. New crises will continue to surprise us, but there are signals – such as the real exchange rate, exports and the current account, and the amount of money in the economy relative to the central bank's international reserves – that may help to warn us when currency hurricanes are approaching. The experiences of the last few decades have exposed the financial roots of crises. Economists now talk of "twin crises" – vicious spirals of currency and banking crises. Rapid financial deregulation and liberalization of international capital markets are thought to have led to crises in countries with weak financial and regulatory institutions. As well as paying attention to the macroeconomic signs of future crises, governments also need to attend to these institutional vulnerabilities. ∎

The East Asian financial crisis

The 1997 East Asian crisis seemed to come from nowhere, overwhelming countries with strong growth records and government surpluses. Before the crisis, most countries in the region had pegged their exchange rates to the US dollar. The first signs of trouble were businesses failing in Thailand and South Korea. On 2 July 1997, after months of battle to save its pegged rate, Thailand devalued. The Philippines was then forced to float on 11 July, Malaysia on 14 July, Indonesia on 14 August. In less than a year, the currencies of Indonesia, Thailand, South Korea, Malaysia, and the Philippines fell by between 40 and 85 per cent. Only Hong Kong held out against the speculators.

The crisis has been blamed on a severe banking crisis. Borrowing was often short-term, and when foreign lenders withdrew their capital, contagion ensued and currencies collapsed.

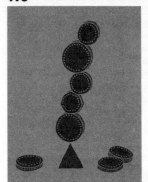

STABLE ECONOMIES CONTAIN THE SEEDS OF INSTABILITY
FINANCIAL CRISES

IN CONTEXT

FOCUS
Banking and finance

KEY THINKER
Hyman Minsky (1919–96)

BEFORE
1933 US economist Irving Fisher shows how debt can cause depression.

1936 British economist John Maynard Keynes claims the financial markets have a larger role in the functioning of the economy than was previously thought.

AFTER
2007 Lebanese-American risk theorist Nassim Nicholas Taleb publishes *The Black Swan*, which criticizes the risk-management procedures of financial markets.

2009 Paul McCulley, former managing director of a large US investment fund, coins the term "Minsky moment" for the point at which booms bust.

The instability of economic systems has been debated throughout the history of economic thought. The view of classical economists, following in the tradition started by Adam Smith, is that an economy is always driven towards a stable equilibrium. There will always be disturbances that create booms and slumps – a pattern that is sometimes called the business cycle – but ultimately the tendency is towards stability, with a fully employed economy.

The Great Depression of 1929 led some economists to examine business cycles in more detail. In 1933, US economist Irving Fisher described how a boom can turn to bust through instabilities caused by excessive debts and falling prices. Three years later, John Maynard Keynes (p.99) questioned the idea that the economy is self-righting. In his *General Theory*, he developed the theory that an economy could settle into a depression from which it had little hope of escaping.

These works were staging posts in understanding the unstable nature of modern economies. In 1992, Hyman Minsky looked at the problem again in his paper "The Financial Instability Hypothesis". The paper suggested that the modern capitalist economy contains the seeds of its own destruction.

In Keynes's view, the modern capitalist economy was different from the economy that had existed in the 18th century. The major difference was the role played by money and financial institutions. In 1803, the French economist Jean-Baptiste Say (p.51) gave a classical interpretation of the economy as essentially a refined barter system, in which people produce goods that they exchange for money, which is used to exchange for the goods they want. The real exchange is good for good: money is just a lubricant. Keynes argued that money does more than this: it allows transactions to occur over time. A firm could borrow money today to build a factory, which it hopes will generate profit that can be used to pay back the loan and the interest in the future. Minsky pointed out that it is not only firms that are part of this process. Governments finance their national debts, and consumers borrow large sums to buy cars and houses. They too are part of the complex financial market that funds transactions across time.

Merchants of debt

Minsky argued that there was a second big difference between modern and pre-capitalist economies. He pointed out that the banking system does not merely match lenders with borrowers. It also strives to innovate in the way it sells and borrows funds. Recent examples of this include financial instruments called collateralized debt obligations (CDOs), which were developed in the 1970s. CDOs were made by pooling different financial assets (loans) together, some high-risk, others low-risk. These new assets were then cut up into smaller sections to be sold. Each section contained a mix of debts. In 1994, credit default swaps were introduced to protect these assets by insuring them against the risk of default. Both of these innovations encouraged the supply of loans into the financial system, which increased the supply of liquidity, or money, into the system. Minsky concluded that these innovations meant that it was no longer possible for a government to control the amount of money in its economy. If the demand for loans was there, the financial markets could find a way to meet it.

According to Minsky, after World War II, capitalist economies had moved away from being dominated by either big government or big business. Rather, they were subject to the influence of big money markets. The influence of the financial markets on the behaviour of people created a system that held within it the seeds of its own destruction. He argued that the longer the period of stable economic growth, the more people believed that the prosperity would continue. As confidence rose, so did the desire to take risks. Paradoxically, longer periods of stability resulted in an economy that was more likely to become fatally unstable.

Minsky explained the pathway from stability to instability by looking at three different types of investment choices that people can make. These can be simply illustrated by looking at the way houses are bought. The safest decision is to borrow an amount that allows the person's income to repay the interest on the loan and also the original value of the loan, over a period of time. Minsky called these hedge units, and they create little risk for the lender or borrower. If people felt more confident about the future, they might buy a larger interest-only mortgage, where their income could pay back the interest on the loan but not the loan itself. The hope would be that a stable period of positive economic growth »

The longer an economy remains stable, the greater **people's confidence** in the future…

…the greater people's confidence in the future, the **riskier their borrowing**.

Over time in a stable economy, **debt grows**, asset prices rise and risky borrowing comes to dominate.

Eventually, asset prices peak and then fall, and borrowers start to default. **Lending collapses** and the economy goes into recession.

Stable economies contain the seeds of instability.

would increase demand, so that the value of the house would be greater at the end of the period than at the start. Minsky called these people speculative borrowers.

As time passed, if stability and confidence continued to last, the desire to take greater risks would encourage people to buy a house for which their income could not even pay the interest, so that the total level of debt would increase, at least in the short run. The expectation would be that house prices would rise fast enough to cover the shortfall in the interest repayments. This third type of investment would create the greatest amount of instability in the future. Minsky named this third type of investor Ponzi borrowers, after Charles Ponzi, the Italian immigrant to America who was one of the first to be caught running the financial scam that now bears his name. "Ponzi schemes" attract funds by offering very high returns. Initially, the con men use new investors' money to pay the dividends. In this way, they can maintain the illusion that investment is profitable and attract new customers. However, soon the scheme collapses due to the failure to meet the high level of returns that were promised. Investors in such schemes are likely to lose a large proportion of their money.

Housing bubble

The recent history of the US housing market is an example of how an economy that has had a long period of stability creates within itself the conditions for instability. In the 1970s and 80s, the standard mortgage was sold in a way that made sure that the interest and the capital could be paid off, in what Minsky viewed as hedge units. However, by the end of the 1990s, a sustained period of growth had pushed house prices up, persuading an increasing number of people to buy interest-only mortgages as they speculated that prices would continue to rise. The financial system then began to supply a whole array of "Ponzi"-style mortgage deals to borrowers who had incomes so low that they could not afford to pay even the interest on the loan – these were the "subprime" mortgages. The monthly shortfall was to be added to their total debt. As long as house prices continued to rise, the value of the property would be worth more than the debt. As long as new people kept entering the market, prices kept rising. At the same time, the finance industry that sold the mortgages bundled them up and sold them on to other banks as assets that would deliver a stream of income for 30 years.

The end of the game arrived in 2006. As the US economy stalled, incomes fell, and the demand for new houses weakened. As house price increases began to slow, the first of an increasing number of defaults was triggered, as borrowers saw their debts grow rather than shrink. Rising numbers of repossessed houses came onto the market, and prices tumbled.

In 2007, the US economy reached what has become known as the "Minsky moment". This is the point at which the unsustainable speculation turns into crisis. The collapse of the housing market left banks with

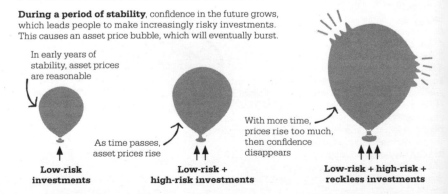

During a period of stability, confidence in the future grows, which leads people to make increasingly risky investments. This causes an asset price bubble, which will eventually burst.

In early years of stability, asset prices are reasonable

As time passes, asset prices rise

With more time, prices rise too much, then confidence disappears

Low-risk investments

Low-risk + high-risk investments

Low-risk + high-risk + reckless investments

House prices in the USA climbed steeply from the late 1990s until 2007, as banks increasingly granted mortgages to people without the income to pay the money back.

enormous debts and, since no one knew who had bought the toxic mortgage debt, institutions stopped lending to each other. As a result, banks began to fail, most famously Lehman Brothers in 2008. As Minsky had foretold, a near-catastrophic collapse of the financial system beckoned because a period of stability had generated enormous levels of debt that created the conditions for enormous instability.

The three possible actions taken to halt the fatal instability, and the problems associated with making these corrections, had also been predicted by Minsky.

First, the central bank could act as the lender of last resort, bailing out the failing banking system. Minsky saw that this might further increase instability in the system in the future, as it would encourage banking firms to take greater risks, safe in the knowledge that they would be saved.

Second, the government could increase its debt to stimulate demand in the economy. However, even governments have problems financing debts in times of crisis. Third, the financial markets could be subject to stricter regulation. Minsky strongly believed that, in the long run, this was necessary. However, the speed at which innovation takes place in the money markets would make increased regulation very difficult.

For Minsky, financial instability is key to explaining modern capitalism. Money is no longer a veil that hides the real workings of the economy; it has become the economy. His ideas are now drawing increasing attention. ∎

Hyman Minsky

An economist of the political Left, Hyman Minsky was born in Chicago to Russian-Jewish immigrant parents who had met at a rally to honour Karl Marx (p.68). He studied mathematics at the University of Chicago before switching to economics. Minsky had a vision of a better world and yet was equally fascinated by the practical world of commerce. He worked as an adviser and director of an American bank for 30 years. After a period overseas with the US army during World War II, he returned to spend most of his working life as a professor of economics at Washington University.

An original thinker and natural communicator, Minsky made friends easily. Academically, he was more interested in the idea than mathematical rigour. The notion that pervades all his work is the flow of money. During his lifetime, partly by choice, he remained on the margins of mainstream economic thought, but since his death, and particularly since the crash of 2007–08 that he predicted, his ideas have become increasingly influential. Married with two children, he died of cancer in 1996, aged 77.

Key works

1965 *Labor and the War Against Poverty*
1975 *John Maynard Keynes*
1986 *Stabilizing an Unstable Economy*

THE BIGGEST CHALLENGE FOR COLLECTIVE ACTION IS CLIMATE CHANGE
ECONOMICS AND THE ENVIRONMENT

IN CONTEXT

FOCUS
Economic policy

KEY THINKERS
William Nordhaus (1941–)
Nicholas Stern (1946–)

BEFORE
1896 Swedish scientist Svante Arrhenius predicts a doubling of atmospheric carbon dioxide will produce a 5–6°C rise in global surface temperature.

1920 British economist Arthur Pigou proposes levying taxes on pollution.

1992 The United Nations Framework Convention on Climate Change is signed.

1997 The Kyoto Protocol is ratified; by 2011 more than 190 countries sign up to it.

AFTER
2011 Canada retracts from the Kyoto Protocol.

The Industrial Revolution that began about 150 years ago has led to countries burning huge amounts of fossil fuels. These emissions create a "greenhouse effect" in the atmosphere.

conomic development and prosperity since the Industrial Revolution have come about through technology, largely driven by fuels such as coal, oil, and gas. It is increasingly clear, however, that this prosperity comes at a cost – not only are we fast depleting these natural resources, but burning fossil fuels pollutes the atmosphere. A growing body of evidence points to emissions of greenhouse gases, in particular carbon dioxide (CO_2), as a cause of global warming, and the consensus now among scientists worldwide is that we risk devastating climate change unless emissions are cut quickly and drastically.

The implications are as much economic as environmental, but both economists and governments are divided on the measures that should be taken. Until recently, many have argued that the costs of combating climate change are more damaging to economic prosperity than the potential benefits. Some continue to dispute the evidence that climate change is human-made, while others argue that global warming could even be beneficial. A growing number now accept that the issue is one that must be addressed, and economic solutions have to be found.

The economic facts

In 1982, US economist William Nordhaus published *How Fast Should We Graze the Global Commons?*, looking in detail at the economic impact of climate change, and possible solutions. He pointed out that certain features of the climate problem make it unique in terms of finding economic solutions: the long time scale, the uncertainties involved, the international scope of the problem, and the uneven distribution of benefits and costs across the globe.

In 2006, the UK government commissioned a report by British economist Nicholas Stern on the economics of climate change. The Stern Review was unequivocal in its findings; it presented sound economic arguments in favour of immediate action to reduce greenhouse gas emissions. Stern estimated that the eventual cost of climate change could be as much as 20 per cent of GDP (gross domestic product, or total national income), compared with a cost of around 1 per cent of GDP to tackle the problem if action was taken promptly. In 2009, Nordhaus estimated that without intervention, economic damages from climate change would be around 2.5 per cent of world output per year by 2099. The highest damages would be sustained by low-income tropical regions, such as tropical Africa and India.

The question was no longer whether we could afford to cut emissions, but whether we could afford not to, and how this could best be achieved. There are strong arguments for government intervention: the atmosphere can be considered in economic terms as a public good (pp.30–31), which tends to be under-supplied by markets; pollution can be seen as an externality where the social costs of an action are not reflected in prices and so are not fully borne by the person taking it. For these reasons Stern described climate change as the greatest market failure ever experienced.

Unequal nations

The first hurdle for economists such as Nordhaus and Stern was to convince governments to introduce measures that would be harmful to their economies in the short run, but would mitigate more damaging consequences in the long run. The second was to find the most efficient way of enforcing an emissions policy. Not all governments were easily persuaded. The more developed economies, which are mainly in temperate areas, are not likely to suffer the worst consequences of a rise in global temperatures. The likely changes in climate will hit poorer countries much harder. This means that, in many cases, »

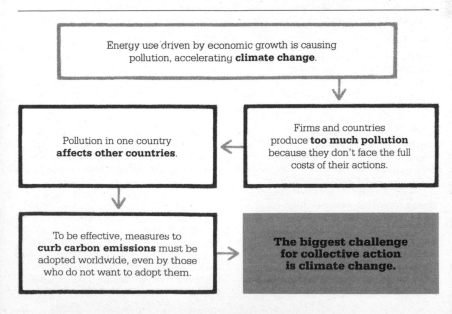

Energy use driven by economic growth is causing pollution, accelerating **climate change**.

Firms and countries produce **too much pollution** because they don't face the full costs of their actions.

Pollution in one country **affects other countries**.

To be effective, measures to **curb carbon emissions** must be adopted worldwide, even by those who do not want to adopt them.

The biggest challenge for collective action is climate change.

William Nordhaus devised a computer program called DICE to show how the elements of climate change interact, and where the ecological and financial costs lie. This financial modelling system allows governments to factor in their current consumption, resources, and needs, and weigh up the costs and benefits – to them and the Earth – of the choices available.

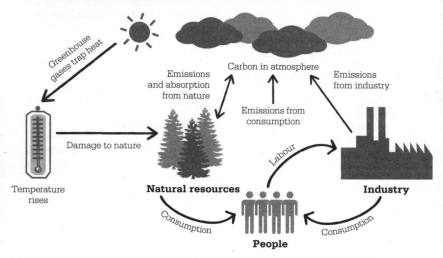

the countries with the greatest incentive to mitigate the effects of climate change are those that are producing the least pollution.

The worst polluters, such as the USA, Europe, and Australia, have been reluctant to accept that governments should impose expensive policies. Even if they did, the pollution is not restricted to their land masses. The problem is global and demands collective action on a global scale.

The need for collective action was first recognized at a UN "Earth Summit" in 1992, which called for all its members to curb their emissions of greenhouse gases. Many governments have developed environmental policies and strategies for implementing those policies. Regulation in the form of punishments, such as fines for excessive production of pollutants, is one solution, but it is difficult to set emissions quotas that are fair to all businesses concerned. The fines are also difficult to enforce.

Another option, which was first suggested by British economist Arthur Pigou in 1920, is the imposition of taxes on pollution. Levying taxes on firms that emit greenhouse gases, and on energy suppliers and producers for the amount of carbon they release into the atmosphere, would act as a disincentive to pollute. Taxes on fossil fuels would discourage their excessive consumption. Pigou's idea is to make individuals face the full social costs of their actions, to "internalize" the externality.

Carbon-trading schemes

Pollution can be viewed as a market failure because normally there is no market for it. Economists suggest that if there was, the socially optimal amount of pollution would be emitted because polluters would face the full costs of their actions. Therefore, another proposed solution to the climate problem is to create a market for pollution through emissions trading. This involves a government (or, in some cases, a number of governments working together) determining an acceptable level of, for example, CO_2 emissions, and then auctioning permits to firms whose business involves the discharge of carbon dioxide. The permits are tradable, so if a firm needs to increase its emissions, it can buy permits from another that has not used its quota. This kind of scheme has the advantage of rewarding the firms who cut their emissions and can then sell their

Price-type approaches like harmonized taxes on carbon are powerful tools for coordinating policies and slowing global warming.
William Nordhaus

surplus permits. It can discourage firms from exceeding their quotas and having to buy extra permits. However, the total amount of emissions remains the same and is controlled by a central authority.

The Kyoto Protocol

While emissions trading schemes are certainly a step in the right direction, the problem needs to be tackled globally to avert the risk of climate change. However, international agreements such as the Kyoto Protocol have failed to achieve universal ratification. In 1997, 141 countries took part in discussions, but by 2012 only 37 countries had agreed to implement its targets for greenhouse gas emissions. The USA has consistently rejected the terms of the agreement, and Canada pulled out in 2011. Even those countries that pledged to curb

their emissions have often failed to meet their reduction targets. Developed countries such as the USA and Australia argue that it would be too harmful to their economies; developing economies such as China, India, and Brazil argue that they should not have to pay for the pollution caused by the West (even though they themselves are fast becoming major polluters). On the other hand, more eco-advanced nations, such as Germany and Denmark, agreed to reduction targets of more than 20 per cent.

Economic modelling

Economists have devised various models for studying the economic impact of climate change, such as Nordhaus's Dynamic Integrated model of Climate and the Economy (DICE), first presented in 1992 (see opposite). This links together CO_2 emissions, the carbon cycles, climate change, climatic damages, and factors affecting growth.

Most economists now agree that climate change is a complex problem with the potential to cause serious long-term damage. The solution is far from obvious, but in 2007, Nordhaus said that he believed the secret to success lies not in large, ambitious projects, such as Kyoto, but in "universal, predictable, and boring" ideas, such as harmonized carbon taxes. ∎

India's growing needs

India's growth rate for 2019 was predicted to be 7 per cent for the year. The country's business leaders are aware that if this rate of growth continues, there will be a huge energy shortage. The fear is that the shortfall will be met by the use of low-cost "dirty" coal and diesel fuel, so efforts are being made to increase efficiency while also encouraging the use of renewable energy products, using solar, wind, and geothermal technologies.

Economists hope that renewable energy forms, together with nuclear energy (judged to be a "clean" energy provider) can combine to meet all of India's growing needs. However, as yet the renewable energy forms, such as solar, are not commercially viable industries on a large scale. This means that they will need a short-term boost from state subsidies to expand. This was provided for in India's ambitious National Action Plan on Climate Change, introduced in June 2008.

Solar panels capture sunlight in the Himalayas in northern India. Solar power may be an efficient source of renewable energy in India, where sunshine is intense.

WE CAN KICK-START POOR ECONOMIES BY WRITING OFF DEBT

INTERNATIONAL DEBT RELIEF

IN CONTEXT

FOCUS
Growth and development

KEY THINKER
Jeffrey Sachs (1954–)

BEFORE
1956 The Paris Club, a grouping of creditor nations, was established to facilitate debt relief between individual countries.

AFTER
1996 The IMF and World Bank launch the Heavily Indebted Poor Countries (HIPC) initiative, to give debt relief and initiate policy reform in poor countries.

2002 Seema Jayachandran and Michael Kremer argue that countries may not be legally liable for "odious" debts incurred by corrupt regimes.

2005 G8 countries agree to write off $40 billion of debt under the MDRI Multilateral Debt Relief Initiative as part of the Gleneagles summit.

Debt in poor countries has grown so large that they **cannot afford** to service the debt and invest in growth.

↓

Many of the loans were made by rich countries to **corrupt governments**.

↓

The loans should **not have been made** in the first place.

↓

Cancelling the loans will enable poor countries to invest in growth.

↓

We can kick-start poor economies by writing off debt.

I n the last few decades of the 20th century, the world's poorest countries piled up a staggering amount of debt, which grew from $25 billion in 1970 to $523 billion in 2002.

By the 1990s, it was clear that there was a debt crisis. No heavily indebted African nation had ever prospered. Indeed, most were in such dire economic straits that they could not even service their debts without terrible suffering, let alone make the investments needed to climb out of the vicious circle of economic decline. Campaigns for debt cancellation intensified.

Many campaigners took a moral stance, criticising the negligent or self-interested role of the rich countries and institutions such as the World Bank and International Monetary Fund (IMF), which had made many of the loans. Campaigners argued that since rich countries had made these loans either to buy support in the Cold War or to secure contracts for their own companies, they had an obligation to lift the debt. US economist Michael Kremer took a legal line. He said that since many debts were incurred by corrupt regimes to feather their own nests, they could be considered "odious". This would mean that countries have no legal obligation to repay them. The World Bank, for instance, continued to lend to former dictator Mobutu Sese Seko in Zaire (now the Democratic Republic of Congo), even after an IMF representative pointed out that he was stealing the money. Many of South Africa's debts were borrowed by the apartheid regime, considered by many not to have been a legitimate government.

Others, such as Jeffrey Sachs, gave an economic argument. Sachs argued that cancelling debt and increasing aid could kick-start growth in poor countries. Such was the appeal of these arguments that the G8 countries (the eight largest economies in the world) agreed to write off over $40 billion in 2005. Another American, William Easterly, argues that debt relief rewards poor policies and corruption by recipient countries. Many criticize the free-market reform programmes that are a made a condition for relief, which may damage the economic prospects of the countries receiving the relief.

Interestingly, the debt crisis has now shifted from the less developed world to the once-flourishing countries of Europe. Here, similar free-market austerity measures are being pushed through – but, crucially, without the debts being cancelled. ∎

In South Africa, high debts were incurred by the apartheid regime. Many argue that the debts from the apartheid era should be cancelled as the government was not legitimate.

Jeffrey Sachs

One of the world's most controversial economists, Jeffrey Sachs was born in Detroit, USA, in 1954. He first came into the public eye in 1985, with a plan to help Bolivia deal with hyperinflation. The plan came to be called "shock therapy", and centred on making the country easily accessible to foreign business. This meant opening up the Bolivian market, ending government subsidies, eliminating import quotas, and linking the Bolivian currency to the US dollar. Inflation was indeed brought under control, and Sachs became known as a global economic troubleshooter. He was on-hand in 1990 to shift Poland out of communism with breakneck privatization and did the same in Russia in the early 1990s. In the 2000s, Sachs turned his attention to global development issues, arguing that, with the right interventions – including aid and microloans – extreme poverty could be eradicated in 20 years.

Key works

2005 *The End of Poverty*

PESSIMISM CAN DESTROY HEALTHY BANKS

BANK RUNS

IN CONTEXT

FOCUS
Banking and finance

KEY THINKERS
Douglas Diamond (1953–)
Philip Dybvig (1955–)

BEFORE
1930–33 One third of all US banks fail, leading to the creation of the Federal Deposit Insurance Corporation (FDIC) to insure depositors' money.

1978 US economic historian Charles Kindleberger publishes a landmark study of bank runs, *Manias, Panics and Crashes: A History of Financial Crises*.

AFTER
1987–89 At the peak of the decade-long US savings and loan crisis, US bank failures rise to a level of 200 per year.

2007–09 Thirteen countries across the world experience systemic banking crises.

D uring the Great Depression of the early 1930s, some 9,000 US banks failed – a third of the total. However, it was not until the 1980s that economic theory came to grips with basic questions such as why banks exist, and what causes a bank run – where depositors panic and rush to withdraw their money from banks they think are at risk of failing. The article that started the debate was *Bank Runs, Deposit Insurance, and Liquidity*, written in 1983 by US economists Douglas Diamond and Philip Dybvig. They showed that even healthy banks can suffer from a bank run and go bust.

Liquid investments

Diamond and Dybvig made a mathematical model of an economy to demonstrate how bank runs occur. Their model has three points in time – such as Monday, Tuesday, and Wednesday – and assumes that there is only one good or product available to people, which they can consume or invest.

Each person starts off with a certain amount of the good. On Monday, people can do two things with their good: they can store it, in which case they get back the same amount on Tuesday to consume; or they can invest it. If they choose to invest the good, which is only possible on Monday, they will receive much more of it back on Wednesday. However, if they cash in the investment early on Tuesday, they will receive less than they invested. These investments, which are made for a set period, are what is known as "illiquid" investments. This means that they cannot easily be transformed into ready cash, as liquid assets can.

Patient and impatient

Diamond and Dybvig assume there are two types of people: patient people, who want to wait until Wednesday, when they can consume more, and impatient people, who want to consume on Tuesday. However, people do not discover which type of person they are until Tuesday. The decision that people face on Monday is how much to store and how much to invest. The only uncertainty in this model, is whether these people are patient or impatient. Banks might have a good idea about probabilities: in general, 30 per cent of people might prove to be impatient and 70 per cent patient. So it is possible that people will store and invest amounts that reflect these proportions. But whatever people choose, it will never be the most efficient outcome overall, because impatient people should never invest, and patient people should not store anything. A bank can solve this problem. We can think of a bank in this model as a place where people all agree to pool their goods and share risks. The bank gives people a deposit contract and then itself invests and stores the goods in bulk.

The deposit contract offers a higher return than storage and a lower return than investment, and allows people to withdraw their goods from the bank on either Tuesday or Wednesday with no penalty. Having pooled people's goods, the bank, knowing the share of patient and impatient people, can then store enough of the good to cover the needs of impatient people, and invest enough to cover the wants of patient people. In the Diamond–Dybvig model, this is a more efficient solution than people could reach independently, because with large

> A bank run in our model is caused by a shift in expectations, which could depend on almost anything.
> **Douglas Diamond Philip Dybvig**

numbers, the bank can do this in a way that the individual cannot.

On Tuesday, the bank has illiquid assets – the patient people's investment that will reap a return on Wednesday. At the same time, it has to pay the impatient people their deposits straight away. Its ability to do this is the reason for its existence.

Diamond and Dybvig showed that this property also makes the bank vulnerable to a run. A run occurs when, on Tuesday, patient people become pessimistic about what they will receive from the bank on Wednesday, and so withdraw their deposits on Tuesday. Their actions mean that the bank must sell investments at a loss; it will not have the resources to pay all of its patient and impatient customers, and those later in the queue will not receive anything. Knowing this, customers become eager to be at the front of the queue.

Pessimism can arise out of concerns about investments, other people's withdrawals, or the bank's survival. »

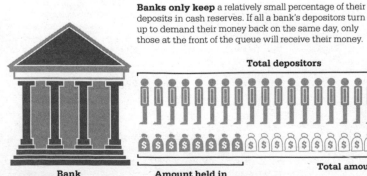

Banks only keep a relatively small percentage of their deposits in cash reserves. If all a bank's depositors turn up to demand their money back on the same day, only those at the front of the queue will receive their money.

Total depositors

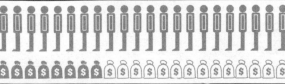

Bank

Amount held in cash deposit

Total amount on deposit

A panicking crowd is held back by police outside a German bank in 1914. The declaration of war had caused pessimism among savers, leading to a number of bank runs.

Crucially, this allows for the possibility of a self-fulfilling bank run even if the bank is sound. For instance, suppose that on Tuesday I believe that other people are going to withdraw their deposits – I then decide to do so as well, because I fear that the bank may fail. Then suppose that many other people think in the same way that I have. This itself can cause a run on the bank, even if the bank would otherwise be able to meet its obligations today and tomorrow. This is an example of what economists call "multiple equilibria" – more than one outcome. Here there are two outcomes: a "good" one in which the bank survives and a "bad" one in which it is sunk by a run. Where we end up may depend on the people's beliefs and expectations rather than the true health of the bank.

Preventing bank runs
Diamond and Dybvig showed how governments could alleviate the problem of bank runs. Their model was partly a defence of the USA's system of federal deposit insurance, under which the state guarantees the value of all bank deposits up to a specified amount. Introduced in 1933, this system reduced bank failures. In March 1933, President Franklin D Roosevelt also declared a national bank holiday to prevent people from withdrawing their savings. Alternatively, the central bank can act as the "lender of last resort" to banks. However, there is often uncertainty about what the central bank will do. Deposit insurance is ideal, as it ensures that patient people will not participate in a bank run.

Alternative views
There are alternative explanations for the existence of banks. Some focus on banks' investment role. The bank can gather and keep private information about investments, choosing between good and

---

A modern bank run

In September 2007, the first serious British bank run since 1866 took place. Northern Rock, Britain's eighth-largest bank, was a fast-growing mortgage lender. To expand its business, it had become over-reliant on "wholesale" funding – funding provided by other institutions – rather than personal deposits. When wholesale financial markets froze on 9 August 2007, a gradual, unseen wholesale run began, and rescue plans were explored. At 20.30 on Thursday 13 September, BBC Television News reported that the UK central bank, the Bank of England, would announce emergency liquidity support the next day.

It emerged later that Mervyn King, the Governor of the Bank of England, had opposed a rescue offer by Lloyds, another British bank. King had suggested that central bank support might reassure depositors. However, there was no such reassurance, and a run on personal deposits began over the internet that evening. Under Britain's deposit insurance scheme, deposits above £2,000 were not fully insured, and the next day, long queues formed outside Northern Rock branches. The run ended the following Monday evening after the government announced a guarantee for all deposits.

bad investments, and reflect this private information efficiently through the returns it offers to savers. It can offer a return to depositors that is only possible if it carries out its monitoring role well.

In 1991, US economists Charles Calomiris and Charles Kahn published an article that took issue with the Diamond–Dybvig view. They argued that bank runs are good for banks. In the absence of deposit insurance, depositors have an incentive to keep a close eye on how well their bank performs. The threat of a run also provides an incentive to the bank to make safe investments. This is one side of so-called "moral hazard". The other side is that managers will take riskier decisions than they would if there were no deposit insurance. The problem of moral hazard became apparent in the 1980s US savings and loan crisis, when mortgage lenders were allowed to make riskier loans and deposit insurance was enhanced. US bank failures rose.

Recent crises

It is hard to prove which of these two views about bank runs is correct, as in practice neither explanation can be isolated. There are many forms of moral hazard in a bank. A bank shareholder may encourage risk-taking because all he can lose is his investment. A bank employee, offered bonus incentives, may take risks because all that is at stake is a job. One commonly proposed solution to moral hazard is tougher regulation.

Recent bank crises have usually begun with investment losses. Banks are forced to sell assets to reduce their borrowing. This leads to further falls in asset prices and further losses. A run on deposits follows, which can spread to other banks to become a panic. If the whole banking system is affected, it is called a systemic banking crisis. In the 2007–08 crisis, runs occurred despite the system of deposit insurance. A large part of the recent crisis took place in institutions that are not regulated as banks, such as hedge funds, but were doing much the same as a bank: borrowing for short terms and lending for long terms.

Many countries strengthened their deposit insurance schemes during the

A bank makes **long-term investments** but keeps some cash on deposit for depositors who wish to withdraw.

⬇

If customers become **fearful** about the future…

⬇

… they will want to **withdraw** ahead of others, leading to a run on the bank.

⬇

To **honour their withdrawals**, the bank must sell investments at a loss…

⬇

… and so will **default** on its last remaining depositors.

⬇

Pessimism can destroy healthy banks.

financial crisis that began in 2007–08. This is understandable, as bank failures can have a devastating effect on the real economy, breaking the connection between people with savings and people who need money to invest. The moral hazard argument is like fire prevention, in that it is concerned with protecting the economy from a future crisis. However, the midst of a crisis may not be the time to be talking about preventative actions. ∎

SAVINGS GLUTS ABROAD FUEL SPECULATION AT HOME
GLOBAL SAVINGS IMBALANCES

IN CONTEXT

FOCUS
Global economy

KEY THINKER
Ben Bernanke (1953–)

BEFORE
2000 US economists Maurice Obstfeld and Kenneth Rogoff raise concerns about the large US trade deficit.

2008 British historian Niall Ferguson describes a world of crisis because of overuse of credit.

AFTER
2009 US economist John B Taylor argues against the existence of a savings glut.

2011 Economists Claudio Borio of Italy and Piti Disyatat of Thailand argue that it is wrong to think that global imbalances in savings triggered the financial crisis.

I n February 2012, 111 million Americans watched the Super Bowl on television. At halftime, an advertisement for Chrysler cars was shown. It was to become a national talking point. "It's halftime in America, too," said the advert. "People are out of work and they're hurting... Detroit's showing us it can be done. This country can't be knocked down with one punch."

Since the closure of plants such as this Chrysler factory in Detroit, the USA has been running trade deficits, meaning that it has been importing more than it has been exporting.

The unashamedly patriotic implication of the advert – to buy Chrysler because it would save American jobs – was in tune with the feeling among many Americans that the USA had let economic power slip into foreign, especially Chinese, hands. It was this type of feeling that made the explanations of the 2008 global financial crisis offered by former US Federal Reserve chairman Ben Bernanke so widely appealing. He had developed his argument from 2005 onwards, before the crisis really hit, and his thesis focused on global imbalances in savings and spending.

Central to Bernanke's idea is America's balance of payments (BOP). A country's BOP is the account of all money transactions between that country and the rest of the world. If a country imports more than it exports, its trade balance is in deficit, but the books must still balance. The shortfall is made up in some other way – for example, by funds from foreign investments, or by running down central bank reserves. Bernanke pointed out that the US deficit rose sharply in the late 1990s, reaching $640 billion, or 5.5 per cent of GDP, in 2004. Domestic investment remained fairly steady at this time, but domestic saving dropped from 16.5 per cent of GDP to 14 per cent between 1996 and 2004. If domestic savings fell, yet investment remained steady, the deficit can only have been financed using foreign money.

The savings glut

Bernanke argued that the deficit was being funded by a "global savings glut" – an accumulation of savings in countries other than the USA. For instance, the Chinese, who have a huge positive trade surplus with the USA, were neither putting all their American export earnings into investment at home nor buying things; they were simply squirrelling it away in

savings and currency reserves. Bernanke highlights a number of reasons for the global savings glut besides Chinese frugality, including the rising oil prices, and the building up of "war-chests" to guard against future financial shocks.

Saving seems, at first sight, a prudent thing to do, a safeguarding of the future. However, savings in the global capitalist world are a mixed blessing. Any money that goes into savings is money lost to direct investment or consumer spending, but it doesn't just vanish. Bernanke's argument is that money from the savings glut overseas ended up flooding the financial markets of the USA.

An abundance of money

All this money damped down interest rates and reduced the incentive for Americans and Europeans to save. With loans markets apparently awash with easy money, lenders bent over backwards to offer deals. To meet the demand for outlets for the foreign cash, America's financial engineers came up with products such as collateralized debt obligations (CDOs), which packaged high-risk mortgages with lower-risk debts to make bonds that were given AAA credit ratings, meaning that they were rated very low-risk. Meanwhile, »

In the 1990s, a new financial instrument called a collateralized debt obligation (CDO) was invented. High-risk mortgages were combined with low-risk bonds to create the illusion of low-risk debt. These debt obligations were central to the failure of the credit system in 2007–08.

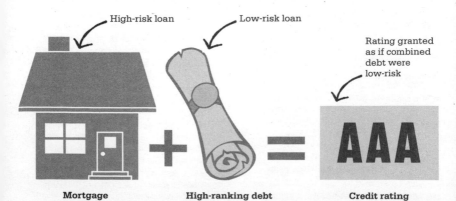

High-risk loan

Low-risk loan

Rating granted as if combined debt were low-risk

+

=

AAA

Mortgage

High-ranking debt

Credit rating

house prices boomed in two dozen countries, as even those on lower incomes were able to find a foot on the property ladder. Some of the mortgages granted to fund this boom – the so-called "subprime" mortgages in the USA – were given to people who could not pay them back.

The crisis

In 2008, a cluster of subprime mortgage failures exposed how massively many financial institutions had invested many times more than the value of their capital. The Lehman Brothers investment bank collapsed in 2008, and many other financial institutions seemed in such great danger of going into meltdown that they had to be rescued by government bailout packages in most of the world's rich countries.

The simple thrust of Bernanke's message seemed to be that the financial crisis was all down to Chinese saving and American overspending. This was also the message in Niall Ferguson's *Ascent of Money* (2008), in which he analysed the credit crunch and focused on the fated "Chimerica" – the symbiotic (or, as some saw it, parasitic) link between China and the USA. The notion appealed to many people in American financial circles as it seemed to imply that it was the frugal Chinese who were to blame for the financial crisis.

Bernanke is adamant that it was Chinese cash that stoked American fires, though he argues that only a small proportion went into high-risk assets. In 2011, he said, "China's current account surpluses were used almost wholly to

> 66 In the longer term, the industrial countries as a group should be running current account surpluses and lending... to the developing world, not the other way around.
> **Ben Bernanke** 99

If one country is **importing more** than it is exporting (in trade deficit), another country must be exporting more than it is importing (in surplus).

⬇

The country in deficit must fund its imbalance, while the country in surplus can build up a **savings glut**.

⬇

The savings in the country in surplus are **borrowed in the country in deficit**, and this can fuel financial speculation.

⬇

Savings gluts abroad fuel speculation at home.

acquire assets in the United States, more than 80 per cent of which consisted of very safe Treasuries and Agencies."

The vanishing glut

Many economists have challenged Bernanke's theory. In the financial blog "Naked Capitalism", Yves Smith has suggested that the global savings glut is a myth, noting that global savings have stayed almost rock steady since the mid-1980s. US economist John B Taylor argues that although there was increased saving outside the USA, the decline in saving within the USA meant that there was no global gap between saving and investment – so the idea of a world awash with cheap cash is false.

Other economists point out that the current account deficits in the USA and other countries amounted to much less than 2 per cent of the money flow, so surely would have only a marginal affect. The savings glut theory also becomes harder to sustain when applied to Europe. Germany, for instance, in the years leading up to the 2008 crisis, was savings-rich. The savings glut theory would imply that German savers took up speculative financial arrangements in Ireland and Spain rather than put their money in institutions at home in Germany, which seems highly unlikely.

A "banking glut"?

Princeton University economics professor Hyun Song Shin has argued that the floods of speculative money chasing after mortgage securities came not from a savings glut but the "shadow" banking system – the complex variety of financial entities that fall outside the normal banking system, including hedge funds, money markets, and structured investment vehicles. European and American shadow banks were eager to find these securities, and found them in Ireland and Spain as well as the USA.

The markets played in by these shadow banks are dominated by derivatives. These are "financial instruments" – bets upon bets as to which way markets will go, underpinned by ingenious mathematical formulas. The charge here is that derivatives trading can encourage excessive risk-taking. It also creates a market in which financial institutions can make massive profits by betting on failures, including the failure of mortgage-backed securities.

The extra reserves of a savings glut might be irrelevant in this virtual casino. Indeed, the problem seems to have been that the banks were trading without sufficient cash back-up. Bernanke points out that while Chinese and Middle Eastern buyers bought into American securities with funds from trade surpluses and oil exports, the European banks had to borrow money to buy in, leaving them exposed when the crisis hit.

Economists differ in their views about the trade imbalances that underlie the savings glut. Some have argued that the US trade deficit can be sustained, and that it would always be funded easily by foreign savings. Others worry about a hard landing for the US economy if capital flows were to dry up. Much of this has become a political issue between the USA and China, as US politicians have charged China with keeping its currency unfairly low in order to support its trade surplus. ∎

Ben Bernanke

Ben Shalom Bernanke was born and raised in South Carolina, USA. In the early 1970s, Bernanke went to Harvard University and then to the Massachusetts Institute of Technology, where he did a PhD in economics under the supervision of Stanley Fischer, future governor of the Bank of Israel.

Bernanke joined the US Federal Reserve in 2002. In 2004, he proposed the idea of the Great Moderation, which suggested that modern monetary policies had virtually eliminated the volatility of the business cycle. In 2006, Bernanke was made chairman of the Federal Reserve. His two-term tenure as chairman of the Reserve was not smooth, and he has been criticized for failing to foresee the financial crisis and for bailing out Wall Street finance houses.

Key works

2002 *Deflation: Making Sure It Doesn't Happen Here*
2005 *The Global Saving Glut and the US Current Account Deficit*
2007 *Global Imbalances*

MORE EQUAL SOCIETIES GROW FASTER

INEQUALITY AND GROWTH

IN CONTEXT

FOCUS
Growth and development

KEY THINKERS
Alberto Alesina (1957–)
Dani Rodrik (1957–)

BEFORE
1955 US economist Simon Kuznets publishes *Economic Growth and Income Inequality*, which concludes that inequality is a side effect of growth.

1989 US economists Kevin Murphy, Andrei Shleifer, and Robert Vishny claim income distribution affects demand.

AFTER
1996 Italian economist Roberto Perrotti claims that there is no link between lower taxes and higher growth.

2007 Spanish economist Xavier Sala-i-Martin argues that growing economies have reduced inequality.

F or much of the 20th century, economists asked themselves how economic growth affects people's incomes. Does growth increase or decrease income inequality? In 1994, Italian economist Alberto Alesina and Turkish economist Dani Rodrik turned the question on its

 The greater the inequality of wealth and income, the higher the rate of taxation, and the lower growth.
**Alberto Alesina
Dani Rodrik**

head. They wondered how income distribution affects economic growth.

Alesina and Rodrik examined two factors in their model: labour and capital (accumulated wealth). They argued that economic growth is fuelled by growth in total capital, but government services are funded by a tax on capital. This means the higher the taxes on accumulated wealth, the less incentive will there be to accumulate capital and the lower the growth rate of the economy will be.

Those whose income derives mostly from accumulated capital prefer a lower tax rate. On the other hand, an individual who has no accumulated wealth and whose income derives entirely from his labour, tends to prefer a higher tax rate. This will provide him with public services and allows for a better redistribution of accumulated wealth.

The tax rate is set by governments, which react to popular concerns. Even a dictatorship cannot ignore the popular will, due to the fear of being overthrown. For this reason the tax rate is set with the aim of pleasing as many people as possible – that is, the rate preferred by the median voter (the person at the exact middle of the spectrum of voters' views). According to Alesina and Rodrik's logic, if the distribution of capital and accumulated wealth is shared equally through society, the median voter will be relatively rich in capital and will therefore demand a modest tax rate, which will not impede growth. If, however, there are large inequalities in wealth, with much of the accumulated capital being concentrated in a small elite, the majority will be poor and will demand a higher tax rate, which would stifle growth. Alesina and Rodrik argue that the more economic equality there is in any society, the higher the growth rate of its economy will be.

Growth and equality

Alesina and Rodrik's explanation is not the whole story. Some people think that the two economists have misidentified cause and effect. Spanish economist Xavier Sala-i-Martin (1962–), for instance, claims that economic growth has fuelled a diminishing rate of income inequality across the globe. The World Bank has argued that the reduction of poverty worldwide – which can help to lessen inequality – is due mainly to economic growth. On the other hand, slower-developing countries, such as many in Africa, have suffered from decades of little or no growth. This has hurt living standards and impeded poverty reduction; the poorest lag behind, and inequality persists. ∎

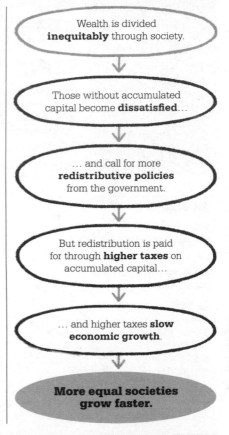

Wealth is divided **inequitably** through society.

↓

Those without accumulated capital become **dissatisfied**…

↓

… and call for more **redistributive policies** from the government.

↓

But redistribution is paid for through **higher taxes** on accumulated capital…

↓

… and higher taxes **slow economic growth**.

↓

More equal societies grow faster.

Alberto Alesina

Alberto Alesina was born in 1957, in the northern Italian town of Broni. He studied economics and society at Boccini University in Milan, graduating with distinction in 1981. He went on to complete his MA and PhD in the economics department at Harvard, USA. After completing his studies in 1986, he became a full professor at Harvard in 1993 and was chairman of the economics department from 2003 to 2006.

Alesina has published five books. His work straddles politics and economics and focuses especially on the economic and political systems of the USA and Europe. He has achieved wide recognition for drawing attention to the influence of politics over economic matters.

Key works

1994 *Distributive Politics and Economic Growth* (with Dani Rodrik)
2003 *The Size of Nations* (with Enrico Spolaore)
2004 *Fighting Poverty in the US and Europe: A World of Difference* (with Edward Glaeser)

EVEN BENEFICIAL ECONOMIC REFORMS CAN FAIL
RESISTING ECONOMIC CHANGE

IN CONTEXT

FOCUS
Economic policy

KEY THINKERS
Dani Rodrik (1957–)
Daron Acemoğlu (1967–)

BEFORE
1989 British economist John Williamson uses the term "Washington Consensus" for the first time (see box, opposite).

2000 South African economist Nicolas van de Walle documents the failure of IMF-backed "structural adjustment" reforms in Africa.

AFTER
2009 US economists Douglass North, John Wallis, and Barry Weingast propose a new approach to reform based on societies' responses to the problem of violence.

2011 Reform packages in Europe following the 2008 financial crisis run into opposition.

Reforms are proposed which would **benefit the economy**.

⬇

Powerful elites may resist these changes…

⬇

… because they wish to preserve their **control of resources**.

⬇

They **distort the reforms**, which become ineffective or achieve the opposite of their intended aims.

⬇

Even beneficial economic reforms can fail.

Reform is designed to kick-start an economy and benefit a whole population through the transformation of institutions. One might think that reforms that benefit the economy would be welcomed and carried through. However, sometimes there is substantial resistance to reform, even from those who might eventually benefit. In order to "fix" an economy and return it to growth, it is necessary to remove the inefficiencies within the economic system. This can be difficult if the country is run by an

Sani Abacha seized power in Nigeria in 1994. His corrupt dictatorship was above the jurisdiction of the courts, which allowed his family to appropriate £5 billion from state funds.

unaccountable political class for its own benefit, as is often the case in the developing world.

Reform and influence

Turkish economists Dani Rodrik and Daron Acemoğlu have pointed out that when powerful groups expect to see their privilege disappear as a result of economic reform, they may use their influence to introduce economic policies that redistribute income or power to themselves. Alternatively, they may distort policies so that measures are not implemented effectively. Acemoğlu has argued that this often happens when political elites are highly unaccountable, so there are limited checks and balances on their actions. Reforms typically fail in these cases because they tend not to address these deeper political constraints. However, in countries with highly accountable leaders, the benefits of reforms may already have been reaped. For these reasons, reforms are most effective in "intermediate countries", where reforms are likely to have significant and positive results, and at the same time, the political elites are not dominant enough to derail them.

Winners and losers

However, there are also problems when introducing reform into intermediate societies. When economic reform is proposed, it is often not clear who the winners and losers of the reform will be. This discourages people from accepting the measures, even where there would ultimately be more winners than losers. There may be a bias towards maintaining the status quo; individuals like to protect what they already have and minimize the risk of losing out. If a beneficial economic reform is proposed but shelved due to lack of popular support, politicians and economists may later propose it again, in the belief that it will benefit the economy and society. However, without new, supportive information, a society may well reject the measure again. On the other hand, if beneficial reform is implemented despite a lack of popular support, and goes on to create more winners than losers, it often goes on to gain popular support and is not repealed.

Most attempts at reform focus on measures designed to change "formal" institutions such as courts and voting systems. Their success depends on whether underlying "informal" institutions and surrounding politics support them. Without this, reforms of laws and constitutions are unlikely to change much. ∎

The Washington Consensus

The term Washington Consensus was first coined in 1989 by British economist John Williamson to refer to the package of free-market economic reforms prescribed to developing countries in crisis during the 1980s.

These policies aimed to move the state-run economies of Latin America and post-socialist Eastern Europe towards the privatized free market. They focused on privatization of state enterprises, liberalization of domestic and international trade, the introduction of competitive exchange rates, and balanced fiscal (tax) policies.

The Washington Consensus was discredited in the 1990s. Reforms were said to have been implemented with little sensitivity to the differing political constraints evident in such a diverse group of countries. In Africa, in particular, dynamic markets raise the poorest out of poverty.

THE HOUSING MARKET MIRRORS BOOM AND BUST
HOUSING AND THE ECONOMIC CYCLE

IN CONTEXT

FOCUS
The macroeconomy

KEY THINKER
Charles Goodheart (1936–)

BEFORE
1965 US economist Sherman Maisel is the first to explore the effects of residential investment on the economy.

2003 US economists Morris Davis and Jonathan Heathcote conclude that housing prices are related to the overall state of the economy.

AFTER
2007 US economist Edward Leamer argues that housing construction trends are an early warning of recession.

2010 US mortgage-lenders Fannie Mae and Freddie Mac are de-listed on the New York Stock Exchange, after lowering underwriting standards during the subprime crisis (offering mortgages to those unable to repay).

Movements in the housing market are a reflection of "boom and bust" cycles in the wider economy. These are the periods where an economy's real output reaches its highest and lowest levels during the business cycle, which moves through periods of contraction and expansion, usually over periods of between three and seven years.

There are many reasons why residential investment is high in periods of economic growth. There are more jobs available and a booming economy leads a greater number of people to think about buying their own home. At the same time, mortgage lenders begin to relax their lending requirements, making buying easier, so more houses are sold. As this happens, the rising demand means that house prices rise. Those who sell are able to pay off large mortgages in full. House builders continue to invest in further housing stock to profit from the higher prices.

House prices are often relatively resilient, meaning that they do not change quickly in response to factors that could influence them. This is one of the reasons housing is seen as such a good investment, and rather than prices adjusting downwards, they can remain stable even when the volume of sales falls.

Signs of a recession

Although house prices are usually resilient, they have been known to stagnate; the accompanying decline in residential investment is often the first indicator that a recession is about to occur. In more developed countries, the housing market has begun to decline before each major recession of the last 50 years. The housing market recovers only when consumers are confident that the value of their houses will

As the economy grows, more people feel **confident enough to purchase** a house.

↓

This increased demand leads to a **rise in house prices**. House builders invest in further building.

↓

Prices reach an **unsustainable level** and demand stagnates.

↓

Residential investment is halted and jobs in associated industries are lost. **House prices stagnate** and the wider economy falters.

↓

The housing market mirrors boom and bust.

Irresponsible lending in the housing market

The economic crash of 2008 owed much to the liberalization of the mortgage market and irresponsible lending by banks. At first, lenders enforced strict requirements on borrowers, lending only to those who could cover both the interest and repayments on the base amount that had been lent. However, as the economy improved, mortgages were offered to those who could afford to pay only the interest payments. These people were relying on an increase in their income or in the price of their home to pay off the balance of their loan.

In the USA, lenders then began to offer mortgages to people who did not earn enough even to cover the interest payments – these loans could only be serviced with strong growth in house prices and income. When the economy faltered and borrowers began to fail to pay back their loans, the whole economy collapsed.

During the wave of bank foreclosures that followed the 2008 financial crisis, boarded up homes such as this one in New Jersey, USA, became a common sight.

rise. This confidence rises in step with an improving economy. As residential sales begin to return to a normal level, residential investment increases, providing jobs and further fuelling a return to economic growth.

Economists have analysed the relationship between the housing market and the overall economy, and believe that by studying the levels of investment in housing, it is possible to accurately forecast recessions and recoveries. In their 2006 book *Housing Prices and the Macroeconomy*, British economists Charles Goodheart and Boris Hofmann showed that there is a correlation between economic performance and housing prices. They claim that by following appropriate policies in the future, it should be possible to strongly mitigate, or even avoid, the worst effects of a recession.

Unfortunately, this was not the case with the housing "bubble" that burst in the USA in 2008. Here, rapid financial innovations created instability in mortgage financing that led to unwarranted consumer confidence, and an unsustainable boom. The housing market was the cause of the eventual bust. ∎

GLOSSARY

Absolute advantage The ability of a country to produce a product more efficiently than another.

Aggregate The total amount; for instance, aggregate demand is the total demand for goods and services in an economy.

Asymmetric information An imbalance of information; for instance, buyers and sellers may have more or less information about the product than each other.

Austrian School A school of economics founded by Carl Menger in the late 19th century. It attributes all economic activity to the actions and free choice of individuals, and opposes all forms of government intervention in an economy.

Balance of trade The difference in value of a country's imports and exports over a given time period.

Bankruptcy A legal declaration that an individual or a firm cannot repay their debts.

Barter system A system of exchange in which goods or services are exchanged for one another directly, without the use of a medium of exchange, such as money.

Bear market A period of decline in the value of shares or other commodities.

Behavioural economics A branch of economics that studies the effects of psychological and social factors on decision-making.

Bond An interest-bearing form of loan used to raise capital. Bonds are issued as certificates by the bond issuer (such as a government or firm) in return for a sum of money; the bond issuer agrees to repay the borrowed sum plus interest at a fixed date in the future.

Bretton Woods system A system of exchange rates agreed between the world's major industrial nations in 1945. It tied the value of the US dollar to gold, and the value of other currencies to the US dollar.

Budget A financial plan that lists all planned expenses and incomes.

Budget constraint The limit on the goods and services that a person can afford.

Bull market A period during which the value of shares or other commodities increases.

Business cycle An economy-wide fluctuation in growth that is characterized by periods of expansion (boom) and periods of contraction (bust).

Capital The money and physical assets (such as machines and infrastructure) used to produce an income. A key ingredient of economic activity, along with land, labour, and enterprise.

Capitalism An economic system in which the means of production are privately owned, firms compete to sell goods for a profit, and workers exchange their labour for a wage.

Cartel A group of firms that agree to cooperate in such a way that the output of a particular good is restricted and prices are driven up.

Central bank An institution that manages a country's currency, alters money supply, and sets interest rates. It may also act as a lender of last resort to banks.

Central planning A system of centralized government control of an economy, where decisions regarding production and allocation of goods are made by government committees.

Chaos theory A branch of mathematics that shows how small changes in initial conditions can cause larger effects later on.

Chicago School An avidly free-market group of economists – linked to the University of Chicago, USA – whose ideals of market liberalization and deregulation became mainstream in the 1980s.

Classical economics An early approach to economics developed by Adam Smith and David Ricardo, focusing on the growth of nations and free markets.

Collusion An agreement between two or more firms not to compete, so they can fix prices.

Command economy An economy in which all aspects of economic activity are controlled by a central authority, such as the state. Also called a planned economy.

Commodity A general term for any product or service that can be traded. Often used in economics to refer to raw materials that are always of approximately the same quality and can be bought in bulk.

Communism A Marxist economic system in which property and the means of production are collectively owned.

Comparative advantage The ability of a country to produce a product relatively more efficiently than another country, even if the other country is more efficient overall.

Competition Competition arises when two or more producers attempt to win the custom of a buyer by offering the best terms.

Consumption The value of goods or services purchased. Individual buying acts are aggregated by governments to calculate a figure for national consumption.

Credit crunch A sudden reduction in the availability of credit in a banking system. A credit crunch often occurs after a period in which credit is widely available.

Debt A promise made by one party (the debtor) to another (the creditor), to pay back a loan.

Default The failure to repay a loan under the terms agreed.

Deficit An imbalance. A trade deficit is an excess of imports over exports; a government budget deficit is an excess of spending over tax revenues.

Deflation A fall in the price of goods and services over time. Deflation is associated with periods of economic stagnation.

Demand The amount of goods and services that a person or group of people are willing and able to buy.

Demand curve A graph showing the amount of a product or service that will be bought at different prices.

Dependency theory The idea that resources and wealth flow from poor countries to rich countries in such a way that the poor countries are unable to develop.

Depreciation A decrease in the value of an asset over time, caused by wear and tear, or obsolescence.

Depression A severe, long-term decline in economic activity, in which output slumps, unemployment rises, and credit is scarce.

Diminishing marginal returns A situation in which each extra unit of something produces successively smaller benefits.

Duopoly A situation in which two firms have control over a market.

Economic liberalism An ideology claiming that the greatest good is achieved when people are given the maximum personal freedom to make choices over consumption. Economic liberalism advocates a free-market economy.

Economy The total system of economic activity in a particular country or area, comprising all the production, labour, trade, and consumption that take place.

Elasticity The sensitivity of one economic variable (such as demand) to another (such as price). Prices of products may be elastic or inelastic.

Entrepreneur A person who undertakes commercial risk in the hope of making a profit.

Equilibrium A state of balance within a system. In economics, markets are in equilibrium when supply equals demand.

Eurozone Countries within the European Union that have formed a monetary union. They all use the same currency, the euro, and monetary policy is controlled by the European Central Bank.

Exchange rate The ratio at which one currency can be exchanged for another. An exchange rate is the price of a currency in terms of other currencies.

Externality A cost or benefit from any economic activity that is felt by a person not directly involved in that activity and is not reflected in price.

Factors of production The inputs used to make products or services: land, labour, capital, and enterprise.

Fiat money A form of money that is not backed by a physical commodity such as gold, but gains its value from the confidence people have in it. The world's main currencies are fiat money.

Fiscal policy A government's plans for taxes and spending.

Free-market economy An economy in which decisions about production are made by private individuals and companies on the basis of supply and demand, and prices are determined by the market.

Free trade The import and export of goods and services without tariffs or quotas being imposed.

Game theory The study of strategic decision-making by interacting individuals or firms.

GDP See *gross domestic product*.

Globalization The free flow of money, goods, or people across international borders; increased economic interdependence between countries through the integration of goods, labour, and capital markets.

GNP See *gross national product*.

Gold standard A monetary system in which a currency is backed by a reserve of gold and can theoretically be exchanged on demand for a quantity of gold. No country currently uses the gold standard.

Good Something that satisfies the desire or requirement of a consumer; normally used to refer to a product or raw material.

Great Depression A period of worldwide economic recession from 1929 to the mid-1930s. It started in the USA with the Wall Street Crash.

Gross domestic product (GDP) A measure of national income over the course of a year. GDP is calculated by adding up a country's entire annual output and it is often used to measure a country's economic activity and wealth.

Gross national product (GNP) The total value of all goods and services produced in one year by domestic-owned businesses, whether those businesses operate within the country or abroad.

Hyperinflation A very high rate of inflation.

Inflation A situation in which the prices of goods and services in an economy are rising.

Interest rate The price of borrowing money. The interest rate on a loan is generally stated as a percentage of the amount per year that must be repaid in addition to the sum borrowed.

International Monetary Fund (IMF)
An international organization set up in 1944 to supervise the post-war exchange rate system, later moving into the provision of finance to poor countries.

Inverse relationship A situation in which one variable decreases as another increases.

Investment An injection of capital aimed at increasing future production, such as a new machine or training for the workforce.

Invisible hand Adam Smith's idea that as individuals pursue their own interests in the market, it leads inevitably to the collective benefit of society, as if there were some guiding "invisible hand".

Keynesian Multiplier The theory that an increase in government spending in an economy produces an even greater increase in income.

Keynesianism A school of economic thought based on the ideas of John Maynard Keynes, advocating government spending to pull economies out of recession.

Laissez-faire A French term meaning "let it do", which is used to describe markets free from government intervention.

Liquidity The ease with which an asset can be used to buy something, without this causing a reduction in the asset's value. Cash is the most liquid asset as it can be used immediately to buy goods or services, with no effect on its value.

Macroeconomics The study of the economy as a whole, looking at economy-wide factors such as interest rates, inflation, growth, and unemployment.

Marginal cost The increase in total costs caused by producing one more unit of output.

Marginal utility The change in total utility, or satisfaction, that results from the consumption of one more unit of a product or service.

Market failure Where a market fails to deliver socially optimal outcomes. Market failure may be due to lack of competition (such as a monopoly), incomplete information, unaccounted costs and benefits (externalities), or lack of potential private profit (as with public goods).

Mercantilism A doctrine that dominated Western European economics during the 16th and 18th centuries. It stressed the importance of government control over foreign trade to maintain a positive balance of trade.

Microeconomics The study of the economic behaviour of individuals and firms.

Mixed economy An economy in which part of the means of production is owned by the state and part of it is owned privately, combining aspects of planned economies and market economies. Strictly speaking, nearly all economies are mixed economies, but the balance can vary widely.

Monetarism A school of economic thought that believes that the primary role of government is to control the money supply. It is associated with US economist Milton Friedman and conservative governments of the 1970s and 80s.

Monetary policy Government policies aimed at changing the money supply or interest rates, in order to stimulate or slow down the economy.

Monopoly A market in which there is only one firm. Monopoly firms generally produce a low output, which they then sell at a high price.

Neoclassical economics The dominant approach to economics today. It is based around supply and demand and rational individuals, and is often couched in mathematical terms.

New classical macroeconomics
A school of thought within macroeconomics that uses forms of analyses that are based entirely on a neoclassical framework.

Nominal value The cash value of something, expressed in the money of the day. Nominal prices or wages change due to inflation, so cannot be usefully compared across different time periods (a wage of £50 would not buy the same amount of goods in 1980 and 2000).

Oligopoly An industry with only a few firms. In an oligopoly, there is a danger that firms may form cartels to fix prices.

Pareto efficiency A situation in which no change can be made in the allocation of goods to make someone better off without making somebody else worse off. Named after Vilfredo Pareto.

Perfect competition An idealized situation in which buyers and sellers have complete information and there are so many different firms producing the same product that no individual seller can influence the price.

Phillips curve A mathematical graph illustrating the supposed inverse relationship between inflation and unemployment.

Planned economy See *command economy*.

Price The quantity of payment, in money or goods, given by a buyer to a seller in return for a good or service.

Protectionism An economic policy aimed at restricting international trade, in which a country imposes tariffs or quotas on imports.

Public good Goods or services, such as street lighting, that will not be provided by private firms.

Quantitative easing The injection of new money into an economy by a central bank.

Real value The value of something measured in terms of the amount of goods or services they can buy.

Recession A period during which an economy's total output decreases.

Shares Units of ownership in a company; also known as equities.

Social market The economic model developed in West Germany following World War II, characterized by a mixed economy in which private enterprise is encouraged, but government intervenes in the economy to ensure social justice.

Stagflation A period of high inflation, high unemployment, and low growth.

Sticky wages Wages that are slow to change in response to market conditions.

Supply The amount of a product that is available to buy.

Supply curve A graph showing the amount of a product or service that sellers will produce at different prices.

Surplus An imbalance. A trade surplus is an excess of exports over imports; a government budget surplus is an excess of tax revenues over spending.

Tariff A tax imposed on imports, often to protect domestic producers from foreign competition.

Tax A charge imposed on firms and individuals by governments. Its payment is enforced by law.

Utilitarianism A philosophy that claims that choices should be made so as to increase happiness for the greatest number of people.

Utility A unit used to measure the satisfaction, or happiness, gained from consuming a product or service.

INDEX

Numbers in **bold** refer
to a person's main entry.

N

O

PQ

T

ACKNOWLEDGMENTS

Dorling Kindersley would like to thank Niyati Gosain, Shipra Jain, Payal Rosalind Malik, Mahua Mandal, Anjana Nair, Pooja Pawwar, Anuj Sharma, Vidit Vashisht, and Shreya Anand Virmani for design assistance; Lili Bryant for editorial assistance; Suhita Dharamjit for jacket design; Harish Aggarwal for DTP design assistance, Priyanka Sharma for jackets editorial coordination; and Saloni Singh, Managing Jackets Editor.

PICTURE CREDITS

The publisher would like to thank the following for their kind permission to reproduce their photographs:

(Key: a-above; b-below/bottom; c-centre; f-far; l-left; r-right; t-top)

12 Getty Images: AFP (cr). **13 Getty Images:** Nativestock / Marilyn Angel Wynn (br). **14 Corbis:** Bettmann (cr). **16 Dorling Kindersley:** Judith Miller / The Blue Pump (tr). Getty Images: John Moore (bl). **17 Getty Images:** Jason Hawkes (br). **19 Library Of Congress, Washington, D.C.:** (tr). **21 Getty Images:** Universal Images Group / Leemage (tl). **25 Alamy Images:** The Art Archive (bl). **Getty Images:** Hulton Archive (tr). **26 Corbis:** The Gallery Collection (br). **28 Alamy Images:** The Art Gallery Collection (bl). **29 Getty Images:** Hulton Archive (bl). **31 Corbis:** Bettmann (tr); Hemis / Camille Moirenc (bl). **33 Corbis:** John Henley (tl). **34 The Art Archive:** London Museum / Sally Chappell (cr). **35 Corbis:** Johnér Images / Jonn (bl). **36 Getty Images:** The Bridgeman Art Library (bl). **38 Corbis:** Robert Harding World Imagery / Neil Emmerson (br). **39 Corbis:** Justin Guariglia (tl). **Library Of Congress, Washington, D.C.:** (tr). **41 Dreamstime.com:** Georgios Kollidas (bl). **42 Corbis:** Tim Pannell (cr). **43 Getty Images:** AFP (br). **45 Corbis:** Bettmann (tr). **47 Getty Images:** Bloomberg (bl). **49 Library Of Congress, Washington, D.C.:** (br). **51 Library Of Congress, Washington, D.C.:** (tr). **54 Getty Images:** Archive Photos / Lewis H. Hine (cr). **57 Corbis:** Getty Images: Hulton Archive (tr). **59 Corbis:** Cameron Davidson (tr). **63 Getty Images:** Hulton Archive / London Stereoscopic Company (tr). **64 Corbis:** Bettmann (bl). **68 Corbis:** Bettmann (bl). **69 Getty Images:** CBS Photo Archive (tr). **74 Getty Images:** AFP (tr).

75 Alamy Images: INTERFOTO (bl). **77 Alamy Images:** INTERFOTO (tr). **78 Getty Images:** Jeff J. Mitchell (bl). **81 Library Of Congress, Washington, D.C.:** (bl). **82 Getty Images:** Photographer's Choice / Hans-Peter Merten (cr). **84 Getty Images:** Bloomberg (cr). **83 Hulton Archive** (bl). **89 Corbis:** Bettmann (tr); **Courtesy of the Ludwig von Mises Institute, Auburn, Alabama, USA** (bl). **91 Corbis:** Bettmann (tr). **96 Getty Images:** Gamma-Keystone (tr). **98 Getty Images:** Ethan Miller (tr). **99 Corbis:** Bettmann (tr); Ocean (bl). **103 Corbis:** Reuters / Korea News Service (br). **105 Corbis:** Hulton-Deutsch Collection (tr). **107 Corbis:** Heritage Images (tr). **Getty Images:** AFP (bl). **111 Corbis:** Reuters (br). **115 Corbis:** Reuters / Carlos Hugo Vaca (bl). **116 Library Of Congress, Washington, D.C.:** U.S. Farm Security Administration / Office of War Information / Dorothea Lange (cr). **117 Corbis:** Bettmann (tr). **123 Getty Images:** AFP (tr). **125 Getty Images:** Chris Hondros (br). **127 Getty Images:** The Bridgeman Art Library (tr). **130 Getty Images:** AFP / Frederic J. Brown (cr). **131 Corbis:** Sygma / Ira Wyman (tr). **134 Getty Images:** Science & Society Picture Library (tl). **137 Courtesy Professor János Kornai** (bl). **139 Dreamstime.com:** Artemisphoto (tl). **140 Digital Vision:** (br). **141 Corbis:** Reuters (tr). **142 Corbis:** Lawrence Manning (bl). **143 Corbis:** Tim Graham (t). **144 Corbis:** EPA / George Esiri (cr). **148 Corbis:** Sygma / Regis Bossu (tl). **153 Corbis:** Robert Essel NYC (tr). **155 Getty Images:** Glow Images, Inc. (tl); **Dreamstime.com:** Zagor (br). **159 Getty Images:** Konstantin Zavrazhin (br). **164 Corbis:** Justin Guariglia (tl). **174 Getty Images:** UpperCut Images / Ferguson & Katzman Photography (cr). **177 Corbis:** Eye Ubiquitous / David Cumming (br). **179 Corbis:** EPA / Kim Ludbrook (br). **Getty Images:** WireImage / Steven A. Henry (tr). **320 Library Of Congress, Washington, D.C.:** George Grantham Bain Collection (tr). **184 Getty Images:** Archive Photos / Arthur Siegel (cr). **187 Getty Images:** Mark Wilson (tr). **189 Getty Images:** Bloomberg (bl). **191 Getty Images:** AFP / Issouf Sanogo (tl). **193 Corbis:** Star Ledger / Mark Dye (br).

All other images © Dorling Kindersley.

For more information see:
www.dkimages.co.uk